Praise for *Job Hunting For Dummies*

"Comprehensive and easy-to-understand, this street-smart reference is a *must* read! *Job Hunting For Dummies* helps you take control of the process in finding the best job possible, regardless of your chosen field or level of experience. It's like navigating through your search with a knowledgeable partner."

> — Tony Lee, Editor in Chief of *The Wall Street Journal*'s interactive career site, `Careers.wsj.com`

"Max Messmer is a renowned authority on finding the right job. His cutting-edge job hunting guide taps the expertise of his company, which places thousands of job seekers every year."

> — George T. Shaheen, Managing Partner/CEO, Andersen Consulting

"It would be hard to find a better advisor for your job search. Max Messmer has authored articles and books covering virtually every aspect of getting the job you want. His advice is put together here on an in-depth level for the first time — you can't miss if you read this!"

> — Daniel P. Tully, Chairman Emeritus, Merrill Lynch & Co., Inc.

"Max talks today, not yesterday. His advice can make the difference in putting you on top."

> — Joyce Lain Kennedy, Syndicated Career Columnist

Praise for Max Messmer and *50 Ways to Get Hired*

"Useful, practical insights and how-to advice on one of life's most anxious and oft-frustrating tasks — getting a good job."

> — Steve Forbes, Editor in Chief, *Forbes Magazine*

"From outlining goals and chasing down leads to marketing yourself like a pro, *50 Ways to Get Hired* gives you proven tips and techniques for landing the right job."

> — Lawrence A. Weinbach, Managing Partner-Chief Executive, 1989–1997, Arthur Andersen & Co, SC

"America is the land of opportunity. This book provides job candidates with the road map needed to make the most of it."

— Hugh L. McColl, Jr., Chief Executive Officer, NationsBank Corporation

What readers say about ...For Dummies Business and General Reference Books

"The minute I read the table of contents, I knew this was a book I should have had 30 years ago. I strongly believe that all young people just starting out in their first job should have this book."

— Ellinor Juarez, Alameda, CA

"Excellent! Informative! I liked the simple layman's terms and humor. I like this book very, very, very, very, very, very, very, very much!"

— Laura Goosby, Poughkeepsie, NY

"Covers important information clearly and concisely — it will be my reference guide as I start my 'adult life' with my first post-college salaried job."

— Andrew Potter, Washington, D.C.

"Clear, concise, informative, and humorous. I read it cover to cover."

— M. Byrne, Etobicoke, Ont.

"Appreciated answers to all 'dumb' questions. . . "

— Lorraine Gosselin, Montreal, Que.

"Light approach to important information."

— David Bartle, Salt Spring Island, B.C.

BUSINESS AND GENERAL REFERENCE BOOK SERIES FROM IDG

^{TM}

BUSINESS AND GENERAL REFERENCE BOOK SERIES FROM IDG

References for the Rest of Us!™

Do you find that traditional reference books are overloaded with technical details and advice you'll never use? Do you postpone important life decisions because you just don't want to deal with them? Then our *...For Dummies*™ business and general reference book series is for you.

...For Dummies business and general reference books are written for those frustrated and hard-working souls who know they aren't dumb, but find that the myriad of personal and business issues and the accompanying horror stories make them feel helpless. *...For Dummies* books use a lighthearted approach, a down-to-earth style, and even cartoons and humorous icons to diffuse fears and build confidence. Lighthearted but not lightweight, these books are perfect survival guides to solve your everyday personal and business problems.

> **"More than a publishing phenomenon, 'Dummies' is a sign of the times."**
> — *The New York Times*

> **"A world of detailed and authoritative information is packed into them..."**
> — *U.S. News and World Report*

> **"...you won't go wrong buying them."**
> — *Walter Mossberg, Wall Street Journal, on IDG's ...For Dummies*™ *books*

Already, millions of satisfied readers agree. They have made *...For Dummies* the #1 introductory level computer book series and a best-selling business book series. They have written asking for more. So, if you're looking for the best and easiest way to learn about business and other general reference topics, look to *...For Dummies* to give you a helping hand.

^{TM}

IDG BOOKS WORLDWIDE

5/97

JOB HUNTING FOR DUMMIES®

JOB HUNTING FOR DUMMIES

by Max Messmer,
Chairman & CEO,
Robert Half International Inc.

Foreword by
Robert Half
Founder of Robert Half International Inc.

IDG Books Worldwide, Inc.
An International Data Group Company

Foster City, CA ♦ Chicago, IL ♦ Indianapolis, IN ♦ Southlake, TX

Job Hunting For Dummies®

Published by
IDG Books Worldwide, Inc.
An International Data Group Company
919 E. Hillsdale Blvd.
Suite 400
Foster City, CA 94404
www.dummies.com (Dummies Press Web site)
www.idgbooks.com (IDG Books Worldwide Web site)

Library of Congress Catalog Card No.: 95-78774

ISBN: 1-56884-388-7

Printed in the United States of America

10 9 8 7 6 5 4

1E/SX/RQ/ZX/IN

Distributed in the United States by IDG Books Worldwide, Inc.

Distributed by Macmillan Canada for Canada; by Transworld Publishers Limited in the United Kingdom; by IDG Norge Books for Norway; by IDG Sweden Books for Sweden; by Woodslane Pty. Ltd. for Australia; by Woodslane Enterprises Ltd. for New Zealand; by Longman Singapore Publishers Ltd. for Singapore, Malaysia, Thailand, and Indonesia; by Simron Pty. Ltd. for South Africa; by Toppan Company Ltd. for Japan; by Distribuidora Cuspide for Argentina; by Livraria Cultura for Brazil; by Ediciencia S.A. for Ecuador; by Addison-Wesley Publishing Company for Korea; by Ediciones ZETA S.C.R. Ltda. for Peru; by WS Computer Publishing Corporation, Inc., for the Philippines; by Unalis Corporation for Taiwan; by Contemporanea de Ediciones for Venezuela; by Computer Book & Magazine Store for Puerto Rico; by Express Computer Distributors for the Caribbean and West Indies. Authorized Sales Agent: Anthony Rudkin Associates for the Middle East and North Africa.

For general information on IDG Books Worldwide's books in the U.S., please call our Consumer Customer Service department at 800-762-2974. For reseller information, including discounts and premium sales, please call our Reseller Customer Service department at 800-434-3422.

For information on where to purchase IDG Books Worldwide's books outside the U.S., please contact our International Sales department at 415-655-3200 or fax 415-655-3295.

For information on foreign language translations, please contact our Foreign & Subsidiary Rights department at 415-655-3021 or fax 415-655-3281.

For sales inquiries and special prices for bulk quantities, please contact our Sales department at 415-655-3200 or write to the address above.

For information on using IDG Books Worldwide's books in the classroom or for ordering examination copies, please contact our Educational Sales department at 800-434-2086 or fax 817-251-8174.

For press review copies, author interviews, or other publicity information, please contact our Public Relations department at 415-655-3000 or fax 415-655-3299.

For authorization to photocopy items for corporate, personal, or educational use, please contact Copyright Clearance Center, 222 Rosewood Drive, Danvers, MA 01923, or fax 508-750-4470.

is a trademark under exclusive license to IDG Books Worldwide, Inc., from International Data Group, Inc.

About the Author

Max Messmer's mother once told him to start pulling his own weight and get a job. So at age 11, he began making ladies' hand-crafted bracelets. He sold scores of them to her friends, neighbors, students, and even teachers. He enjoyed selling them so much it created a stir at school and took him away from his studies. His mom then put him out of business, forcing him back to basic homework.

He learned something, though. Nothing happens until you make a sale. The job hunting process is no exception. No one will know your capabilities until you become an expert at selling them. (And if you saw these bracelets today, you'd know what a sales job it was, he says.) Inability to sell one's skills is one of the most frequent failings of job candidates, according to Messmer.

Today, Max Messmer is Chairman and CEO of Robert Half International Inc. (RHI), the world's largest specialized staffing firm. He is a widely recognized expert on careers and hiring, and the author of two other critically acclaimed books, *50 Ways to Get Hired* (William Morrow & Co., Inc., 1994) and *Staffing Europe: An Indispensable Guide to Hiring and Being Hired in the New Europe* (Acropolis Books Ltd., 1992).

Messmer's job search expertise has been featured in major business publications, such as *Fortune, Forbes, Time,* and *The Wall Street Journal,* as well as on CNN and network morning shows. His bylined articles and columns on job seeking, hiring, and management topics also are extensive.

Robert Half International (NYSE symbol: RHI), a *Fortune* Top 100 fastest-growing firm, was one of only 38 companies listed on *The Wall Street Journal's* "Honor Roll" for its stock-market returns to investors for the past one-, three-, five-, and ten-year periods. Founded in 1948 by Robert Half, the company's specialized staffing services and the fields they serve include: Accountemps® and Robert Half®, for accounting and finance; RHI Consulting®, for contract information technology; OfficeTeam®, for highly skilled office support; and The Affiliates®, for legal staffing support.

Messmer has served on the boards of directors of several major companies, including NationsBank Corporation and Pacific Enterprises. He currently serves on the boards of Airborne Freight Corporation, Health Care Property Investors, Inc., and Spieker Properties, Inc. During the Reagan administration, he served on the President's Advisory Committee on Trade Negotiations. A *summa cum laude* graduate and valedictorian at Loyola University, Messmer also graduated *cum laude* from the New York University School of Law.

ABOUT IDG BOOKS WORLDWIDE

Welcome to the world of IDG Books Worldwide.

IDG Books Worldwide, Inc., is a subsidiary of International Data Group, the world's largest publisher of computer-related information and the leading global provider of information services on information technology. IDG was founded more than 25 years ago and now employs more than 8,500 people worldwide. IDG publishes more than 275 computer publications in over 75 countries (see listing below). More than 60 million people read one or more IDG publications each month.

Launched in 1990, IDG Books Worldwide is today the #1 publisher of best-selling computer books in the United States. We are proud to have received eight awards from the Computer Press Association in recognition of editorial excellence and three from *Computer Currents'* First Annual Readers' Choice Awards. Our best-selling *...For Dummies*® series has more than 30 million copies in print with translations in 30 languages. IDG Books Worldwide, through a joint venture with IDG's Hi-Tech Beijing, became the first U.S. publisher to publish a computer book in the People's Republic of China. In record time, IDG Books Worldwide has become the first choice for millions of readers around the world who want to learn how to better manage their businesses.

Our mission is simple: Every one of our books is designed to bring extra value and skill-building instructions to the reader. Our books are written by experts who understand and care about our readers. The knowledge base of our editorial staff comes from years of experience in publishing, education, and journalism — experience we use to produce books for the '90s. In short, we care about books, so we attract the best people. We devote special attention to details such as audience, interior design, use of icons, and illustrations. And because we use an efficient process of authoring, editing, and desktop publishing our books electronically, we can spend more time ensuring superior content and spend less time on the technicalities of making books.

You can count on our commitment to deliver high-quality books at competitive prices on topics you want to read about. At IDG Books Worldwide, we continue in the IDG tradition of delivering quality for more than 25 years. You'll find no better book on a subject than one from IDG Books Worldwide.

John Kilcullen
CEO
IDG Books Worldwide, Inc.

Steven Berkowitz
President and Publisher
IDG Books Worldwide, Inc.

Eighth Annual Computer Press Awards ≥ 1992

Ninth Annual Computer Press Awards ≥ 1993

Tenth Annual Computer Press Awards ≥ 1994

Eleventh Annual Computer Press Awards ≥ 1995

Dedication

To my wife, Marcia, who has provided endless support throughout my career —
even when I told her I wanted to leave the security of corporate management
for entrepreneurship (she didn't even call me a Dummy — to my face, anyway).
And to my two sons, Michael and Matthew, for whom I am so grateful.

Publisher's Acknowledgments

We're proud of this book; please register your comments through our IDG Books Worldwide Online Registration Form located at http://my2cents.dummies.com.

Some of the people who helped bring this book to market include the following:

Acquisitions, Development, and Editorial

Project Editor: Pamela Mourouzis

Copy Editor: Diane L. Giangrossi

Technical Editor: David Helfand

Editorial Assistants: Constance Carlisle, Chris H. Collins, Ann Miller, Kevin Spencer

Production

Associate Project Coordinator: Sherry Gomoll

Layout and Graphics: Cameron Booker, Elizabeth Cárdenas-Nelson, Angela F. Hunckler, Carla C. Radzikinas, Gina Scott

Proofreaders: Phil Worthington, Melissa D. Buddendeck, Kelli Botta, Joel K. Draper, Dwight Ramsey, Robert Springer

Indexer: Alexandra Nickerson

General and Administrative

IDG Books Worldwide, Inc.: John Kilcullen, CEO; Steven Berkowitz, President and Publisher

IDG Books Technology Publishing: Brenda McLaughlin, Senior Vice President and Group Publisher

Dummies Technology Press and Dummies Editorial: Diane Graves Steele, Vice President and Associate Publisher; Mary Bednarek, Acquisitions and Product Development Director; Kristin A. Cocks, Editorial Director

Dummies Trade Press: Kathleen A. Welton, Vice President and Publisher; Kevin Thornton, Acquisitions Manager

IDG Books Production for Dummies Press: Beth Jenkins, Production Director; Cindy L. Phipps, Manager of Project Coordination, Production Proofreading, and Indexing; Kathie S. Schutte, Supervisor of Page Layout; Shelley Lea, Supervisor of Graphics and Design; Debbie J. Gates, Production Systems Specialist; Robert Springer, Supervisor of Proofreading; Debbie Stailey, Special Projects Coordinator; Tony Augsburger, Supervisor of Reprints and Bluelines; Leslie Popplewell, Media Archive Coordinator

Dummies Packaging and Book Design: Patti Crane, Packaging Specialist; Lance Kayser, Packaging Assistant; Kavish + Kavish, Cover Design

♦

The publisher would like to give special thanks to Patrick J. McGovern, without whom this book would not have been possible.

♦

Acknowledgments

A number of very talented and dedicated people have helped make *Job Hunting For Dummies* a reality. Special thanks go to Barry Tarshis, who provided invaluable research, insight, and assistance; Lynn Taylor, vice president of corporate communications and director of research at Robert Half International, for her excellent advice throughout; members of Lynn's staff, including Reesa McCoy Staten, Leslie Chamberlain, Kate Reynolds, and Laurel Goddard; Kathy Welton, vice president and publisher at IDG Books Worldwide, who saw the need for this book; and my very capable editors and reviewers, including Pam Mourouzis, Diane Giangrossi, and David Helfand.

I would also like to acknowledge Mr. Robert Half, a great friend and colleague, who, for many years has distinguished himself as a world-class career authority. He became a pioneer in specialized personnel services in 1948, when he founded our company — and his name has become synonymous with ethics and professionalism in the staffing field ever since. Mr. Half has my utmost gratitude for his continuing support and encouragement.

If you've lost your job, remember that you are not alone. Most people have been let go more than once in their career. It no longer carries the stigma it once did, especially with the series of downsizings and mergers that have transformed today's workplace. In the grand scheme of things, this time will be relatively short.

Best of luck in your search!

— Max Messmer

P. S. As for the reference to Dummies, I think we all know that the only dumb question is the one that's never asked. So *you* deserve a round of applause for taking charge of your career and seeking answers!

Contents at a Glance

Cartoons at a Glance
By R.J. Matson

Table of Contents

Foreword

Looking for a new job probably wasn't on your list of fun things to do this year.

And job hunting is probably one skill that most people don't care to get real good at. With one exception. I once received a resume from an innovative job candidate who had virtually no work history. His entire resume was based on his job search experience, including product development (identifying his strengths); communications (resume writing); telemarketing (calls to employers); sales presentations (interviewing); budgeting (tracking job search expenses); and so on.

While I wouldn't recommend this approach, you can't help but give this job seeker some credit for trying to put his best foot forward. Job hunting takes courage, persistence, and faith.

My first "job" was a paid internship as a junior accountant at a small CPA firm in the early 1940s. The income was, well, embarrassing — $4 a week (that's not a typo, so please keep it between us). However, I needed the experience to eventually qualify as a CPA and realized that many internships offered no pay at all. So I viewed the money as a token. After the internship, my boss proudly announced that he was offering me "real" pay . . . *$8* a week! Based on my reaction, he replied straight-faced, "What's wrong, why would you want to leave? You're doubling your salary in six months!" I left. I was even able to find a higher paying job, and six years later, I founded Robert Half International.

As you conduct your search, keep in mind that with every call you make and letter you send, you're getting closer to the finish line. And the more knowledge you gain, the faster you'll get there.

Job Hunting For Dummies is an up-to-date, easy-to-follow reference book that you shouldn't be without. You'll probably find more material jam-packed in here than you will in any other single job hunting source. It's also entertaining, which is both refreshing and necessary at times like this. Max Messmer has an insider's view of what works and what doesn't for job candidates — he heads what has become the world's largest and fastest growing specialized staffing firm.

When Max approached me about selling my company in 1986, it was the farthest thing from my mind. But 17 days later, I sold the business to him. His sensitivity to people and business savvy were extraordinary. I knew he was someone to whom I could entrust my business of 40 years.

Similarly, I know you can trust him for invaluable job hunting advice — you're already one step closer to career success.

Robert Half
Founder, Robert Half International Inc.

Introduction

Welcome to *Job Hunting For Dummies,* a book written with one overriding purpose in mind: to give you an edge in today's knock-down, drag-out job market.

Since there isn't exactly a shortage of job and career books on the market today, you may wonder whether this book has anything to say about this subject that you haven't already read or heard hundreds of times before.

The answer is *yes.* The ammunition that this book gives you comes in the form of advice and guidance about job hunting that is insightful, detailed, comprehensive, up-to-date, and *real world* — all of it presented in a clear, no-nonsense, easily accessible manner.

This is a book to take into the trenches. It's practical and hands-on and tells you what you need to know to help ensure a successful job search — including how to get yourself in gear so that you can gain an edge. And because this book looks at the job hunting process from start to finish, you can get a lot out of it, regardless of your current situation.

Who This Book Is For

You may be a recent high school or college graduate looking for your first ever full-time job. Or you may be a retiree who wants to ease into the job market on a part-time basis. (If you're in this situation, by the way, here's some good news: The job market has never been better for retirees looking for part-time work.)

You may already have a job — either full-time or part-time — and you may not be happy there. Or you may have reason to suspect that if you don't make the jump to another job fairly soon, you are going to be pushed.

There is a better-than-even chance that you are unemployed — and not by your own choosing. If you are unemployed, you may have been looking for a job for months now. Or maybe you learned only yesterday that your company has announced a series of layoffs and that your name happens to be on the list.

Regardless of your circumstances — what you're looking for, how long you have been looking, and *why* you're looking — one thing is certain. To get what you want, you have to work your way through a process. And the more methodical and efficient you are in this process, the better your results will be.

What You'll Gain from This Book

Take a look now at the main benefits you can expect from this book, regardless of your situation or goals:

✔ A clearer idea of how to *target* your job search: how to establish a logical relationship between the kind of job you ideally want and the kind of job you have a reasonable chance of getting, given current market conditions and the skills and experience you bring to the party.

✔ More insight into the specific skills you need to develop to make yourself a more marketable job candidate — and how to get up to speed on those skills as quickly as possible.

✔ Detailed advice on getting yourself launched: how to organize a job search game plan that's well focused and realistic, and which tools you need to help you stay on track and achieve the objectives of that plan.

✔ Step-by-step advice for organizing and writing a winning resume — without having to spend money on outside help. And while you're at it, you'll discover how to write a cover letter that will induce someone to read your resume.

✔ New ideas and proven approaches to becoming more resourceful and proficient in the various ways to generate job leads: being more creative when digging up leads, broadening the scope of your network, getting the most from recruiters, arranging face-to-face meetings with people you've never met (and may have been embarrassed to approach) but who can help you, and turning leads into interviews.

✔ Proven techniques for being at the top of your game when the time comes to shake hands with the person who could decide whether you get the offer: how to really prepare for the interview, how to take control when you're actually being interviewed, and how to handle all those tricky situations that frequently crop up during interviews.

Now about that word, *Dummy.* Of course you're not a dummy! (The last thing in the world a true dummy looking for a job would be doing is reading a book about how to find a job.) But it's no secret that a great many people looking for jobs — particularly people who, after years of working for the same company, suddenly find themselves unemployed — are initially overwhelmed by the prospect of job hunting. They feel intimidated simply because they have never had to think about or go through the process you must go through to find a satisfying job.

Just about everyone who has ever looked for a job has experienced this feeling. If you use this book properly, however, you won't feel intimidated for long.

What You Won't Gain from This Book

What you're *not* going to find in this book is a "sure-fire" formula for getting hired, and for good reason: There *is* no such thing. This book is not going to introduce you to any specific "system," because no one system works for everyone.

The focus of this book is on the *process* of finding a job. That process is broken down for you so that you can get a clearer sense of the various aspects of the job search. More importantly, this book alerts you to the specific tasks that go into each phase and tells you how to go about these tasks efficiently.

How This Book Is Organized

This book is organized in a logical, step-by-step manner, beginning with the things you ought to be doing initially to get yourself organized and to put yourself in the proper frame of mind, and ending with the best way to get off on the right foot (fingers crossed!) when you're hired and start your new job.

Part I focuses on the foundation you need to create. It gives you a general picture of today's job market (which is not as dismal as you might think) and helps you separate what's *really* happening out there from the many myths and misconceptions that send so many job hunters off in mistaken directions. These chapters also help you to organize your job search — and establish a base that you can work from efficiently and (why not?) enjoyably.

The focus in Part II is on *you*. These chapters should help you strike a happy medium between what you ideally want to be doing in your next job and the job you can reasonably expect to get, given your background and qualifications.

Part III takes you through a step-by-step process keyed to two fundamental tools in your job search — your resume and the cover letter that accompanies it. The chief goal of these chapters is to keep the resume you send to would-be employers out of the pile marked "Rejects" and get it into the pile marked "Interview Possibilities."

After you put together a solid resume and know how to write compelling cover letters for a variety of situations, you are ready for the trench warfare aspect of job hunting: drumming up job leads. That's the focus of Part IV. These chapters take you through all the possibilities — networking in particular — and offer dozens of proven, practical ideas for getting more mileage out of all the various job leads that are waiting to be tapped.

The Internet and job-related databases are the focal points of Part V. Here, too, the emphasis is on generating job leads. Because using a computer as a lead-generating tool is such a new and exciting aspect of job hunting (it simply wasn't done by anyone except computer experts until a few years ago), it deserves a section of its own.

Part VI deals almost exclusively with what you need to do when the job leads you have been pursuing and cultivating begin to bear fruit and you get a chance to go on actual interviews. Key topics in these chapters include preparing for interviews, controlling your nerves, making the best first impression, fielding difficult questions, and winding things up on a positive note. These chapters also deliver solid advice on how to respond when you get an offer.

Finally, Part VII, the Part of Tens, offers a potpourri of useful information presented in a list format. And the Appendix will serve you well as a resource reference.

How to Get the Most from This Book

You can use this book in any number of different ways, depending on your situation, your goals, and how familiar you already are with the various aspects of job hunting.

One approach is to read the book through from cover to cover, taking notes, pulling out specific ideas or pieces of advice that seem interesting and relevant to you, and incorporating these ideas into what you're already doing.

Another approach is to use this book as a reference tool. It can work in this way because each topic is fairly self-contained — you can find what you need quickly. Plus, it includes a number of forms and samples designed to be user friendly and to help you tailor proven strategies to your own situation.

Icons Used in This Book

You may be wondering what all the little pictures in the margins of this book mean. These icons point out really important information, warning you not to do some things and tipping you off to others that may give you an advantage in your job hunt. Following is a list of the icons and a brief description of what each one does:

This icon flags little tidbits of information that you'll want to take note of.

This icon marks the main things that you should keep in mind as you go about your job search. Use these key points to make your search as efficient and effective as possible.

This icon points out the things that might trip you up if you're not careful.

These are things that you should definitely avoid at all costs. Some of them are humorous, but most of them have been the downfall of at least one job seeker before you. Beware!

As an industry leader, Robert Half International Inc. has access to a lot of information that you and I wouldn't normally be privy to. This icon points out the fun facts, important statistics, and other insider information that RHI has compiled.

Some resumes deliver a message that — well, the job hunter may not have intended to send. This icon points to resume "bloopers" in the form of typos, misuse of words, and other bizarre verbiage that job candidates have written. You'll also find similar bloopers that relate to interviews.

Don't make these mistakes!

Part I
Getting a Handle on the Process

"YOUR FATHER AND I ARE AFRAID YOU'VE TAKEN THIS HOME OFFICE CONCEPT ONE STEP TOO FAR, DEAR..."

In this part...

Before you begin looking for a job, you need to get yourself on track; you need to know what you're up against and organize your efforts. This part briefs you on today's job market (really, it's not as bad as you think!) and guides you through setting up your job hunt headquarters.

Chapter 1

Getting Off on the Right Foot

· ·

In This Chapter

▶ Understanding what the job market numbers really mean to you

▶ Debunking the most common myths of job hunting

▶ Keeping the pressures of job hunting in perspective

· ·

*I*t would be easy to devote the next 25 pages of this book to facts, figures, graphs, and pie charts that document what has been happening in the U.S. and international job markets over the past ten years or so.

But I'm afraid the facts and figures would require a separate *...For Dummies* book for deciphering purposes. So instead of dazzling — or dazing — you with numbers, this chapter zeros in on those broad trends in the job market that are likely to have the most impact on you and on the strategies you need to adopt to be successful in your job search.

Three trends are particularly worth thinking about, as the following sections explain.

Has Anybody Around Here Seen a Traditional Job?

So-called traditional jobs — that is, highly departmentalized, reasonably secure, 9 to 5, function-driven corporate jobs with clearly defined job descriptions and well-defined career paths — are rapidly disappearing from the job market, and for two basic reasons.

One is that the key source of these traditional jobs, major corporations, are restructuring and redefining themselves in response to new realities of the global economy. Major corporations are still a significant source of jobs throughout the world today, but the growth rate of new, in-house positions in major corporations, according to U.S. Department of Labor surveys, is clearly on the decline. More and more large companies are *outsourcing* — that is, hiring outside consultants or smaller companies to handle functions that used to be handled in-house. And in an effort to keep their fixed personnel costs down, companies of all sizes are relying more and more on temporary and part-time workers.

The second reason that traditional jobs are disappearing so rapidly is that the major source of new hires throughout the world today is smaller, more entrepreneurial companies. These companies cannot afford the luxury of having employees who specialize in one very narrow area. Small companies need people who can contribute to the bottom line in many different ways. If you're looking for a job as a service technician for a high-tech office equipment company, for example, the companies you approach are going to be looking not only at your technical expertise but at your people skills. That's because your job will probably go beyond fixing machines and involve customer service as well.

What it means to you: Forget about the way things used to be in the good ol' days. Begin to think of yourself not in terms of a specific job title or function, but in much broader terms: as being able to bring to a potential employer a mix of skills and expertise that can contribute to the company's success in a variety of ways. In other words, be prepared in your next job to wear a lot of hats. And be flexible. Accept the possibility that your next "job" might be two or even three part-time jobs.

Sometimes They Even Give Us Sundays Off

The downsizing trend that swept through the corporate world in the late 1980s has eased somewhat in the 1990s, but most companies, despite the fact that the world economy has improved, are taking their time restocking their employment ranks. The result: Most people in the workforce today — especially people with management responsibilities — are stressed out, handling jobs that at one time may have been handled by two or three people. People in general are working longer and harder (overtime in the U.S. is at an all-time high), and competitive pressures on businesses are more intense than ever.

What it means to you: Two things. One, you need to position yourself in today's job market as someone who is versatile, tough-minded, and adaptable — someone who can meet the rigors of these new pressures. Two, you need to be sensitive to the time constraints and other pressures that workers are under today. Don't take it personally when people don't respond to your calls as promptly as you would like.

INSIDE SCOOP

Hard data

How much does your willingness to put in an honest day's work influence the hiring decisions in major companies today? More than you might think. Hiring managers in major companies were recently asked in an independent study commissioned by Robert Half International to name the one quality, apart from basic skills, that takes precedence in their hiring decisions. Nearly 60 percent answered, "Work ethic." Here's a look at all the numbers:	**Work ethic**	**59%**
	Intelligence	23%
	Enthusiasm	12%
	Education	4%
	Other/Don't know	2%
	Source: Robert Half International Inc.	

Nerds 'R' Us

Not too long ago, the last thing managers had to be concerned about was how letters got typed, how the various machines in the office worked, or how information got accessed from databases. But things have changed. Being computer literate and technologically savvy is no longer a luxury for job seekers. It has rapidly become a necessity.

REMEMBER

What it means to you: Make yourself as technologically self-sufficient as possible. One factor that carries enormous weight in today's hiring decisions is how much training and administrative support will be required to bring a newly hired employee up to speed. The better equipped you are to hit the ground running, the better your chances are of getting hired.

Common Job Hunting Myths

It's tough to make intelligent decisions when the assumptions that underlie those decisions are based on myths or misconceptions. What follow are some of the more common — and most self-defeating — misconceptions about job hunting.

"Being unemployed puts you at a tremendous disadvantage when you're looking for a job"

This misconception has roots in the outdated notion that because you're unemployed, the companies you approach will assume that you have a major character flaw. Otherwise, why aren't you working? Some people may have been skeptical years ago, but in light of everything that has happened in the economy over the past ten years, being unemployed no longer carries the stigma it once did. Most people recognize that a high percentage of unemployed job seekers are out of work not because they weren't good at their jobs but because their jobs were simply eliminated.

"You should give 100 percent effort to every job lead you uncover"

This truism has a nice, inspirational ring to it — sort of like having Vince Lombardi as your career counselor — but if you follow it to the letter, you're going to burn yourself out very quickly. Yes, you should be willing to investigate and pursue every job lead that comes your way, but you need to set priorities — that is, focus the bulk of your time and efforts on those leads that are most likely to result in an offer that you would be willing to accept.

The number of leads you uncover in your job search isn't the only factor that will ultimately determine whether you'll find the kind of job you're looking for. It's the *quality* of those leads and the quality of your efforts that count.

"Finding a job is harder than any job you will ever have"

Looking for a job is hard work, but the really hard part isn't so much the specific things you have to do throughout the course of a job search — the calls you make, the research you do, the interviews you go on, and so forth. The hard part is dealing with all the pressures — psychological, familial, and financial —

that often arise during the course of a job search. The truth is, you don't need innate talent or highly specialized skills to conduct a successful job search. You simply need to be able to do a lot of the things you already know how to do in a focused, disciplined, and systematic way.

"When you're unemployed, you can't afford to turn down a job offer"

Depending upon any number of factors — how long you've been looking for a job, the kind of financial shape you're in, your level of insomnia — you may very well have to accept a job offer that you're not really thrilled about accepting. Unless it's absolutely necessary, however, it's wrong to assume that you *have* to accept the first job you're offered. Other strategies available today — temporary work, for example — can help keep the wolf away from your door and at the same time allow you to keep your job search going until you get an offer that makes sense.

"The only way to get a good job in many industries is to have the right connections"

Having the right connections is an enormous advantage in any business endeavor — not just job hunting. And in certain so-called "glamour industries" (publishing, show business, professional sports, and so on), it definitely helps to know people in high places. But a major part of conducting a successful job hunt is making the connections you need as your search progresses.

Steady temp work is comparable to a full-time position

Temporaries have become such an integral part of the workforce that 78 percent of executives believe that consistent temporary employment is comparable to full-time work. These findings help to take the pressure off job seekers who feel that they must accept any full-time job to avoid having gaps in their resumes.

Source: Independent study commissioned by Robert Half International Inc.

"Being good at interviews is the most important job hunting skill"

The ability to make a strong, positive impression when you're being interviewed for a job opening is certainly one of the most valuable skills you can possess as a job hunter. Bear in mind, though, that before you can put those interviewing skills to practical use, you have to know how to generate job leads and then convert those leads into interview opportunities. Don't make the mistake of underestimating the time, effort, and skill it takes to become good at the less obvious — but no less important — aspects of job hunting.

"The only person you can really depend on in a job search is yourself"

Job hunting may seem like a solitary activity to you, but the process works much better and will take you much further if you view it as a team activity. It is extremely difficult — make that next to impossible — to do it all yourself. You need plenty of help from friends, family members, network contacts, and, in some cases, recruiters and professional career counselors. Early on in your job search, you need to figure out what help you need, how to access that help, and how to show your gratitude when you get that help.

Keeping Things in Perspective

It's no secret that looking for a job can be one of life's most stressful experiences, ranking immediately behind moving cross-country and losing the remote control to your television. Everyone knows it. There's no point in pretending otherwise, and it doesn't help matters when people try to tell you how lucky you are to be "exploring new horizons."

It is fair to suggest, though, that you have more power to keep the pressures of job hunting under reasonable control than you may think. The key is what you're focusing on at any given moment in your job search. One of the curious things about the human brain is that it focuses on only one thing at a time. So the more time you spend focusing on the specific things you need to be doing to find a good job — and there is plenty to focus on — the less time you will have to worry and brood. It sounds simplistic, admittedly, but it's true.

In the meantime, here are some observations designed to give you the perspective you need in order to develop — and maintain — a positive, success-oriented mindset.

- ✔ You're not alone. As someone currently looking for a job, you are part of a group that includes not only the millions of people throughout the world who are currently unemployed but also the estimated 75 percent of executives and managers who, according to a recent Cornell University study, are employed but interested in finding a different job. Included in this vast constituency of job seekers are people from every walk of life: blue-collar workers and white-collar workers, high school dropouts and PhDs, engineers and scientists, and people of all ages, races, and religions.

- ✔ Brooding about what was or what could have been is a waste of time and energy. Whatever sequence of events, whatever twists of fate, whatever unfortunate choices or strings of bad luck or internal politics may have landed you in your current situation — all that is history. Keep looking ahead, not behind you.

- ✔ Virtually everything you do in the course of your job search — every phone call you make, every person you meet, every meeting you attend, and every article you read — has the potential to produce the one lead that will eventually result in your being hired for a job that you can get truly excited about.

- ✔ The easiest way to get the help you need is to ask for it. And the worst thing that can happen is that someone might say no.

Small world

Percentage of human resources managers in the nation's largest companies who believe that the best career opportunities over the next five years lie with small companies: 46

Percentage of human resources managers in the nation's largest companies who believe that the best career opportunities over the next five years lie with medium-sized companies: 47

Percentage of human resources managers in the nation's largest companies who believe that the best career opportunities over the next five years lie with large companies: 6

Source: Robert Half International Inc.

"I WANT TO BE A PROJECT COORDINATOR FOR A TEAM-ORIENTED REGIONAL MARKET MANAGEMENT CONSULTING FIRM WITH FLEX TIME WHEN I GROW UP. HOW ABOUT YOU?"

Chapter 2
Getting Organized

In This Chapter

▶ Setting up your job hunt headquarters

▶ Tooling up: A guide to basic job search gear

▶ Eight keys to enhancing your job search productivity

*M*ost books about job hunting cut right to the chase. They plunge you immediately into the basic tasks of job hunting: setting objectives, getting your resume ready, building up your list of contacts, preparing for interviews, and so on.

There is nothing wrong with jumping right into the swim this way. Sooner or later in your job search, you are going to have to roll up your sleeves, dig in, and focus on these basics. But the assumptions behind this jump-right-into-the-pool advice are that you have established a structure and a routine for yourself and that you're in a position to run your job search smoothly and efficiently.

Many people who are looking for jobs — perhaps because they figure that their situation is only "temporary" — never really get themselves properly organized. Consequently, once they get started, they never really work as productively as they should be working, given what's at stake. They don't manage their time properly. They're not proactive. They frequently fail to spot and capitalize on opportunities.

Not a good idea.

To keep you from falling victim to this pitfall, this chapter is devoted entirely to the productivity and time management aspects of job hunting, even though you may have taken courses in time management and personal productivity.

One final point: Some of the things suggested in this chapter require a financial investment. And spending money that you really don't have to spend may not strike you as the most intelligent thing to do if you're out of work.

Fair enough. The last thing you need when you're looking for a job — especially if you are unemployed — is additional financial pressure. The main thing, though, is to keep an open mind (if not an open wallet or purse). A relatively small investment can make a huge difference not only in how productive you are on a day-to-day basis, but also in your frame of mind. Looking for a job is no one's idea of fun, and anything you can do to help you meet the challenge more efficiently with less stress is worth thinking about.

Setting Up Your Job Hunt Headquarters

Every job search needs a base or operations center — a single place where you can manage your job search efficiently.

Yes, it's possible that you could be hired for a new job in only a few weeks, in which case it would be ridiculous to go to the bother and expense of setting up and outfitting a full-fledged home office. The reality, though, is that your job search — especially if you have a specific target in mind and are not willing to settle for anything else — is likely to last for several *months,* not several weeks. If you're not well organized, the wait will probably seem even longer.

In a perfect world, your job search headquarters would be a spacious, palatial office with wall-to-wall windows and a panoramic view of the ocean. More than likely, though, your job search "office" will be a cubbyhole in an outplacement firm, a section of your kitchen table, or maybe a small desk in the corner of your bedroom.

Wherever it is, do whatever you can to make things more pleasant. Make sure that there's enough light. Get a chair that's really comfortable. Surround yourself with photographs of the people you love or admire. Paste up some inspirational slogans or cartoons that bring a smile to your face. Keep a radio, tape recorder, or CD player nearby and play your favorite music — that is, the music that makes you feel the most relaxed. Remember, this is not a prison sentence — avoid the jail cell decor.

Tooling Up: A Guide to Basic Job Search Gear

Common sense and an eye toward productivity should be your guides when you're trying to decide which items (if any) you need to buy to outfit your job search "office." Certain items — a computer, for example — deliver benefits that have a clear-cut bearing on your job search activities; they make you more productive, unless, of course, you use the computer to play Solitaire and never actually get around to using it in your search for employment. Other items — say, an electronic labeler that enables you to create your own laminated adhesive labels — give you benefits (there's nothing wrong with having file folders with professional-looking labels), but you have to ask yourself whether those benefits are going to enhance your chances of getting hired. (In this case, I doubt it.)

So weigh your purchases carefully. Make a distinction between luxury and necessity. And, again, don't close your mind to certain items simply because of the cost. Consider value. If an item measurably improves your productivity and isn't going to force you to give up lunches for the next two months, give serious thought to the investment.

Listed in the following sections are some of the items and pieces of equipment that are pretty basic to a well-organized job hunt. Some, as you can see, are more essential than others. You'll have to be the judge, basing your decisions on your own needs.

Telephone options

A telephone should never be more than an arm's reach from where you intend to sit and do the bulk of your job search work. You have two choices: One is to set up your temporary office where the phone is already installed. The other (assuming that you don't want to go through the expense and bother of relocating your existing phone) is to get an additional, maybe a cordless, phone or to see whether the phone system you have lends itself to the new adapters that plug into regular electrical sockets.

Be careful in selecting a cordless phone, particularly if you're bent on buying a cheap model. See if you can try it out at home so that you can check the quality of the reception. The last thing you want when talking to would-be employers is to sound as though you're in the middle of a wind tunnel.

At the beep: Composing a professional answering machine message

Since answering machines have become so commonplace today, there's a good chance that you already have an answering machine or some other means (voice mail, for example) of receiving and retrieving messages.

You need to think about that message of yours, though — the one where the dog barks, ukulele music plays, and then comes a comic message that all your friends find hilarious.

Here's a diplomatic suggestion with respect to that message: Bury it. At least until you find the job you want. Replace it with a simple, professional-sounding message, something like this:

> "Hi, this is Ellen Jones. Sorry I missed your call. Please leave a message after the beep, and I will get back to you as soon as I can. Thanks."

Take your time when you're recording your message. Try not to leave too long a gap between the end of your recorded message and the beep that signals the other person to start talking. And make sure that the instructions you give are consistent with what the caller actually hears. Some answering machines, for example, make sounds other than beeps or give more than a single beep.

And after you finish recording, listen to your outgoing message. Make sure that you sound upbeat and professional — like the sort of person a prospective employer would be interested in getting to know better.

Other phone options to consider:

- ✔ **A calling card:** If you don't have one already, send away for a calling card number — a special number that you can use to charge phone calls. It won't cost you anything, and having such a number will simplify your life, especially when you have to use a pay phone to make your calls and you don't have $5 in change. Instead of having to access an operator and charge calls to your home number, you simply punch in the digits of your calling card when you're on the road.

- ✔ **Memory and speed-dialing:** Most newer TouchTone phones have a memory or speed-dialing feature. You know how it works: You program a certain number into the phone, give it a one- or two-digit code, and then, to call the person at that number, you simply press the code. Just make sure that you label them correctly; accidentally calling your reference librarian when you *think* you're dialing Grandma can be so disconcerting!

Will speed-dialing make a major difference in your job search efficiency? Obviously not. But if the speed-dialing feature comes with the phone anyway, take it. You can program the phone numbers you dial most frequently, such as job hotlines and professional associations.

One quick buying tip: If you're buying a phone and want the speed-dial feature, make sure that the phone has a scrolling capability that scans through names until the one you're looking for pops up. If your phone has this feature, you don't need to compile and maintain a special directory of the speed-dial codes of your frequently dialed numbers.

✔ **Speakerphone:** A speakerphone can be convenient to use in terms of hands-free conversation. But using one is not a good idea when you're speaking with prospective employers or job contacts! You'll probably offend them.

The only time you might use a speakerphone is when you're going to be on hold for a while. While you're waiting, you may be able to fit in some simple paperwork.

Big-ticket items that may (or may not) be worth the investment

A computer

Recommendation: Definitely worth the investment

The only argument that would justify *not* making a computer a key part of your job search weaponry is that buying one might force you or your loved ones to walk shoeless in the winter. Even then, you could argue that the money you spend on the computer is well worth the investment.

You can buy a highly serviceable computer these days for less money than some top restaurants charge for dinner, and you can also rent computers by the hour, by the day, or longer.

If you don't have a computer and are sitting on the fence on the question of getting one — and everyone knows how painful that can be, to quote David Letterman — here are just a few of the benefits to consider:

✔ Instead of having to type (or having someone else type) a letter every time you want to send a cover letter, you can keep a master cover letter on file, bring it up on-screen, customize it to your particular situation, and then print it out.

✔ With a simple database program, you not only can store names, addresses, and phone numbers of key contacts, but you also can sort that list of contacts in dozens of different ways: by state, by industry, by size, or by the name of the person who gave you the contact name, for example.

✔ Without a computer, you have no way of tapping into the information superhighway — you'll never even make it to the entrance ramp. You have no way to access all the online information that Part V tells you about.

✔ Not knowing your way around a computer is now considered a major liability in many industries, especially at the entry and middle levels and in smaller companies where you're pretty much expected to be your own secretary.

✔ A computer, accompanied by a printer that gives you letter-quality output, enables you to produce professional-looking correspondence without having to go to the expense of having the correspondence typed elsewhere or reprinted at a commercial printer or copying service.

Obviously, I can't tell you in one short paragraph which computer is right for you, but the best advice you can follow about buying a computer is to *keep things simple.* Contrary to what the salesperson at your computer store may tell you, you do *not* need a supercharged, state-of-the-art machine for most of the things that you need to do in a basic job search. What you need, in short, is a computer that lets you run simple word processing and database programs.

So which machine should you buy? The simple fact is that it's pretty hard to go wrong with most models in stores today, as long as you buy from a reputable dealer and don't waste money on features that you don't really need. The one feature you don't want to skimp on is speed. You'll need a fast processor and at least 16MB of RAM if you plan to use your computer for Internet research (see Chapter 17).

A facsimile machine or fax-modem

Recommendation: May be worth the investment

Assuming that your budget allows it, give thought to buying a telephone facsimile (fax) machine or including one as a built-in or external component of the computer you purchase or rent. You'll have to spend at least $300 (more if you want bells and whistles) for a stand-alone fax and at least $150 for a fax-modem and software. But apart from your phone and a computer, no other piece of equipment is more valuable to someone looking for a job. Even if you get lucky and find yourself with an attractive job offer just two or three days after you shell out the cash, you'll still find plenty of uses for a fax machine.

The best part about having a fax machine at your disposal is that it gives you the ability to respond quickly when an opportunity arises. More and more resumes and cover letters these days are coming into offices by fax. Because they arrive via a route that's different from the way standard correspondence arrives, they stand a slightly better chance of being read.

There's an image element to consider here as well. Being able to communicate via fax to a would-be employer enhances your image as a professional.

As to which option — a stand-alone fax machine or one that is built into your computer — is better for you, it's really a matter of cost and preference. Assuming that you already have a computer, it's less expensive to add a fax-modem than it is to buy a stand-alone fax machine. Plus, you have the added luxury of being able to send faxes through your modem without having to print out the document. You simply fax it directly from your computer to the fax machine at the other end of the line.

The downside to fax-modems is that in order to *receive* faxes, you have to leave your computer on. The incoming message, depending on how powerful a computer you have, can interfere with your ability to get work done. Yet another advantage of stand-alone fax machines is that they also double as bare-bones copiers.

A portable cellular phone

Recommendation: Nice to have if you can afford it

Given how important a phone is in a typical job search, there are obvious advantages to having a portable cellular phone. You can make phone calls from just about anywhere — your car, a commuter train, or the street. If you're running late for an important appointment and you're stuck in a traffic jam, you don't have to make that stomach-wrenching decision: "Do I get off the road to make a phone call and make myself even later?"

The big tradeoff, though, is price. The phones themselves don't cost much, but monthly fees — even if you're careful — are going to be at least $30. And if you're *not* careful (bearing in mind that a daytime call lasting ten minutes can cost you as much as $10), you can easily be looking at monthly phone bills in the hundreds of dollars.

 If you shop around, you can probably find a cellular phone plan that sets a low limit on the number of hours per month that you can use the phone but that doesn't cost you an arm and a leg each month. Look around for a plan that meets your needs.

Other items worth thinking about

- **Personalized stationery:** Not a necessity if you are looking for an entry-level job, but more important as your job target becomes more ambitious. The stationery on which you send a letter is the first thing readers notice, even before they begin to read what you have written. While you're at it, you might think about getting personalized 5 × 8 note pads, which work nicely for informal correspondence.

    Most word processing programs today allow you to create personalized stationery yourself. The key, though, is the quality of the printing device you use.

- **Business cards:** It's also a good idea to have personalized business cards printed with your name, address, and telephone number. You can also include you area of expertise, such as computer programmer or marketing specialist.

- **A decent-looking briefcase:** A quality briefcase is a small — but often important — component of the first impression you make when you go into someone's office.

- **A pocket-sized tape recorder:** You can pick up a portable, pocket-sized tape recorder these days for as little as $30 or $40. It comes in handy when you're doing research in a library or when ideas come to you but you can't get your hands on a pen and piece of paper. They tend to work best, of course, when they have working batteries and a tape in them.

- **Miscellaneous office stuff:** Have on hand plenty of file folders (they help you keep your desktop clear), stamps, sticky notes (they work well as bookmarks in directories), message pads (to be stationed anywhere in your house or apartment where there's a phone), a stapler, plenty of paper clips, and a wastebasket.

Eight Keys to Job Search Productivity

Productivity and *time management* are concepts normally associated with people who are working full-time and have difficulty juggling everything they have to do throughout the course of their 15-hour workdays.

But you need to think about being productive and managing your time efficiently in your job search all the more. The unstructured nature of job hunting — the lack of a boss, a set schedule, and a clearly defined set of tasks — makes this imperative.

Here are some helpful tips for keeping yourself on track.

Buy a personal organizer

If you don't already have one, buy and begin to rely on a personal organizer (that's a *thing*, not a person). It can be one of those notebook-style organizers — the kind with the different sections and the nifty doodads like a plastic compartment for business cards and other miscellaneous papers. Or it can be one of those harmonica-sized electronic organizers, most of which have become so sophisticated that they operate, in effect, as miniature computers. A third option that you should consider if you are going to be using a computer in your job search is to buy one of the growing number of Personal Information Management (PIM) software packages available.

There is something to be said for each system. Notebook-style organizers are versatile, but you have to do all the work of compiling and listing information by hand. Electronic organizers give you a way of tying into your personal computer but do not offer the flexibility of the notebook-style organizers. PIM software is a wonderful tool; even the simplest of these programs automatically updates your to-do list on a daily basis and gives you a place to store names and addresses.

Which kind of personal organizer works best for a job search? Any system designed for salespeople would be ideal for launching a full-scale job search campaign. There are, after all, striking parallels between selling a product to customers and selling your credentials to would-be employers.

Whichever system you choose, make sure that you do one thing above all: Maintain a duplicate (or in the case of a computer, a backup copy) of *all* important information you gather as you move forward in your search — particularly your list of network contacts. You don't even want to *think* about the consequences of losing your personal organizer when you are two or three months into your search.

Plan and prioritize every day

Be prepared to spend at least a half-hour at the beginning of each week and ten minutes at the beginning of each day writing down a to-do list and setting priorities. Going through this routine should be habitual, like brushing your teeth.

True, this is very basic advice. But that quiet half-hour you spend each Sunday mapping out your week and the ten minutes or so you spend each morning (or the preceding evening) writing down priorities are critical.

Prioritize your tasks

Prioritizing the items on your to-do list is probably the single most important principle to follow as part of any time-management system. It's also one of the trickiest principles to follow in a typical job search.

Problem number one is figuring out what your priorities should be: Given a choice, should you spend your time digging up new leads and expanding your network or cultivating leads that you've already uncovered? And assuming that you have an interview scheduled, do you drop everything and concentrate only on preparing for that interview? Decisions, decisions.

The key to setting priorities in a job search is *balance*. That is, on a typical day you should be working on all phases of your job search: generating new leads, following up on leads you've uncovered, and preparing for interviews.

If there's a great deal at stake in one particular interview that you're scheduled to go to sometime next week, it's okay to temporarily shove everything aside and devote 100 percent of your time to getting ready for that interview and learning as much as you can about the company and the person interviewing you, which is covered in detail in Chapter 20.

Generally speaking, most priority-setting systems recommended by time-management professionals are built along the same principle. You start by setting long-range priorities (a minimum of a month down the road). Then you set priorities for each to-do item in your schedule, and finally you set priorities each day.

In a typical system, you assign number values (one to four, for example) based on two general factors: how important a particular task is to your overall goal and how important it is that you complete this particular task that month, that week, or that day. Crunch time comes when you find yourself with so many priorities that you can't decide which one to deal with first. Even then, the priority discipline has to hold. Think of it as time-management triage. If there simply isn't enough time to deal with all your top priorities, you have to sacrifice some of them — at least until tomorrow.

Set up a routine

Try to plan your weeks and days in as structured a manner as possible — making sure, of course, that you leave some room for the unexpected, such as winning $50 million in the state lottery. Set aside (within reason) certain days of the week or certain hours of the day for job search activities, doing your best to base your scheduling decisions on which specific slot in the day or week makes the most sense.

If you need to spend time researching companies in the library, for example, try to schedule your sessions during a time when the library isn't likely to be busy, such as weekday mornings, when schools are in session. If accessing on-line databases is part of your strategy, set aside one or two evenings a week (dialing up on-line services is frequently less expensive at night). If you're trying to expand your networking list and have to make a lot of phone calls, schedule your calls at those times of the day — before 8 a.m., for example — when you may be able to reach you contact directly.

Generally, too, try to plan your day so that you complete the most difficult and mentally challenging tasks — such as getting out of bed and writing highly customized cover letters — in the morning, when your energy level is reasonably high and your mind is fresh.

As you plan your day, also try to minimize the number of times that you have to shift gears — that is, bounce back and forth from one activity to another. That kind of bouncing can wear you down.

Set goals

Setting goals should be part of your daily and weekly routine, but the goals you set don't have to involve huge stretches. A daily goal could be simply, "Establish contact with a minimum of four new networking sources," or, "Get names of two companies that might have openings," or perhaps, "Set VCR to record *Star Trek* at 11:00."

The real payoff is that achieving goals on a day-to-day basis keeps you in a success mode, never mind that your ultimate goal — getting hired — is still to be achieved.

Avoid the busywork trap

One job seeker I know recently spent nearly two weeks filling a database with the names and key data of nearly 300 companies. There's only one problem: He has yet to get in touch with any of them.

This is a familiar pitfall: You get involved in a task that may be repetitive and boring, but it keeps you busy and, more important, doesn't subject you to the risk of being rejected. Your job search objective is *not* simply to keep busy. It's to make sure that the things you're doing to keep busy are producing meaningful results.

Pay attention to your productivity

Be sensitive to how much time it takes you to complete the various tasks that you undertake each day. Always be on the lookout for ways to improve your efficiency.

The best way to do so is to keep a *log* — a daily record of how you actually spend your time in a typical day. Analyzing the log will tell you whether what you're actually *doing* throughout the course of a day is strategically keyed to your priorities.

You don't have to maintain a log every day, but you should keep it fairly regularly during the early days of your search and then, just to keep yourself on track, cut back to once a week. The key things to look for are time bandits — all the little things (calls that last too long, interruptions, and so on) that go unnoticed while in progress but that combine with other time-wasters to take a major chunk out of your day.

Meet procrastination head-on

If you like, you can postpone this productivity principle until tomorrow (just kidding). Everyone tends to put off or postpone to some extent tasks that are difficult, frustrating, or possibly embarrassing. But if you let this tendency get out of hand during your job search, it can cost you dearly in the way of lost opportunities.

Not that procrastination is an easy pattern to break. Some people constantly put off or postpone tasks because they haven't clarified their goals and are running into resistance at a subconscious level. Still others procrastinate out of fear: fear of rejection, fear of failure, or fear of change.

If procrastination is simply a bad habit you've gotten into, then try some of the following anti-procrastination tips from the experts (yes, there are such people!).

The one-a-day strategy

A frequently effective way to avoid the problems that procrastination creates is to establish as one of your daily to-dos the completion of at least one task that you have been consistently putting off. This strategy may not be easy for you, so you should begin on a small scale, choosing a task that doesn't seem either overwhelmingly difficult or objectionable. The idea behind this strategy is to allow the sense of accomplishment (and relief) that comes from completing a task you've been avoiding to be its own motivator. The simple fact that you've completed the task that has been preying on your mind can inspire you to directly address other tasks you've been avoiding.

The paint-yourself-in-a-corner strategy

This more ambitious strategy doesn't work well for people whose procrastination problems go beyond poor work habits. What you do is make a commitment — that is, promise someone (other than yourself) that you will do something at a certain time. Note that this technique works best — for obvious reasons — when the failure to deliver on the commitment can have consequences that you'd rather not deal with.

The now-for-the-lollipop approach

This is a simple and obvious technique, but you would be amazed at how effective it can be. What you do, simply, is build in some kind of reward for tackling a task that you have been putting off. The trick here is to make the "reward" something that you wouldn't normally do for yourself.

Part II
Setting Your Targets

"I'M THINKING OF BECOMING A COMMODITIES BROKER, BUT, FIRST, I THOUGHT I SHOULD TALK TO SOME PEOPLE IN THE FIELD..."

In this part...

Knowing what you're looking for makes it much easier to find what you want. This part helps you to assess your needs and objectives, and then it helps you to set job targets that match those needs and objectives.

Chapter 3

What Are You Looking for, Anyway?

You may remember an old joke about a guy who works for the circus but has a really ghastly job. He follows around the elephants with a bucket and broom so that he can clean up whenever the elephants make a mess (which elephants tend to do quite a bit). One day a friend says to the guy, "How can you do a job like that? Why don't you quit?" The guy looks shocked and says, "I couldn't quit. I love show business too much."

You have every right as an individual in a free society to work at a job you love, regardless of what other people think. And you owe it to yourself to focus your search on jobs that you can get excited about — jobs that you'll find interesting, challenging, and enjoyable.

Now for the fine print. You may not be as "fortunate" as the man in the joke, which is to say that your "dream" job — the job you would *ideally* love to have — may well be just that: a dream, and for any number of reasons. For one thing, the job may not exist — not anymore, at any rate. (When was the last time you saw a help-wanted ad for a stagecoach dispatcher?) Or if the job does exist, it may be clearly beyond your talents or physical capabilities. (If you want to be a tenor at the Metropolitan Opera, you'd better be able to sing a high C. If you want to be a statistician, you can expect to have trouble finding work if you don't have a head for figures. And when was the last time you saw a professional football player who weighed less than 125 pounds?)

Even if your dream job does exist and you are qualified to fill it, you may still face obstacles that you aren't able to overcome — not unless you're willing to make major changes in your life. If you need, say, $30,000 a year to meet your monthly expenses, you can't very well afford to take a job that pays, say, $12,000, unless you can figure out a way to cut down on your monthly expenses or compensate in some other way for the $18,000 shortfall. No employer (apart from your parents, perhaps) who has been paying $12,000 a year for a particular job is going to say to you, "Oh, you need an additional $18,000? No problem."

The point is that the goals you set for yourself in your job search need to strike a productive balance between what you would ideally like to have and what you have a reasonable chance of being hired for, all things considered.

The purpose of the next two chapters is to help you find this balance. These chapters focus on an aspect of job hunting generally referred to as "setting job targets," and depending on the sort of person you are, you will find these next two chapters either the easiest chapters or the most difficult chapters in this book. In this chapter, you will be looking inward — at your values, your aspirations, and your dreams. In the next chapter, you'll be looking outward — at the hard-boiled realities of the job market.

If you're looking for your first job or considering a career change, take your time when you go through these chapters. And bear in mind that you're not going to be able to complete this process in a matter of hours or days or even weeks. Finding a balance between what you would truly love to do and what you do to earn your living is really a lifetime challenge, and the decisions you make with respect to that balance may not be the same today as they would have been a few years ago — or are likely to be in the future.

Don't be afraid to aim high — especially in the early stages of your job search. Yes, the job market may be tight, and the prospects of your breaking into a particular industry may be intimidating. But you can always lower your sights if you aim too high.

Remember, too, that the more excited you are about the job targets you set, the more enthusiasm and energy you're going to pour into your job search. And while finding a job in today's market takes more than enthusiasm and energy, without enthusiasm and energy, you're unlikely to find what you're looking for — even if you're aiming low.

Taking Stock: Figuring Out What You Like to Do

When you were younger, you were probably asked — more often than you wanted to be — "What do you want to be when you grow up?" Now that you're grown up, the question becomes, "What exactly do you want your day-to-day job experience to be like?"

In other words, if you could choose your ideal job (within reason, of course), what would you actually be *doing* on a day-to-day basis and under what conditions would you be doing it — forgetting for the moment how qualified you may be? Would you be working in a big company or a small company, by yourself or as part of a team, in an office or on the road, in front of a computer or in the middle of a mountain range, with animals or with people, with kids or with older folks? Would your chief motivation be making enough money to afford a fleet of Rolls Royces, or would it be doing something meaningful for your fellow human beings? (Doing both is not impossible.)

Don't concern yourself for the time being with how *practical* these desires are. You'll have time in the next chapter to worry about the practical, job market-related aspects of these aspirations. For now, the focus should be on you and what gets you excited.

To help you answer the question of what, ideally, you would like to be doing in your next job, do the following exercise. It shouldn't take you too long to complete it. The following sections show you the steps.

Develop a list of activities

Write down as many activities as you can think of (job-related and otherwise) that you *have actually* engaged in over the past 5, 10, 15, or even 20 years or more.

Try to be as specific as possible. Instead of writing **Asst. manager of restaurant**, write down the *specific tasks* you had to perform in the course of carrying out that job. Check out this example:

- ✔ **Recruited and hired new waiters and waitresses**

- ✔ **Conducted training programs**

- ✔ **Greeted and seated guests**

- ✔ **Developed and wrote training manuals**

It doesn't matter whether you *enjoyed* the activity. You'll have time later in the exercise to make those judgments. And if you have had only limited professional work experience, don't worry. Write down leisure activities or specific tasks that you performed on your own or in an organization you belonged to.

- ✔ **Sold raffle tickets door to door**
- ✔ **Managed Little League baseball team**

> ✔ **Served food in homeless shelter**
>
> ✔ **Collected stamps**
>
> ✔ **Worked as a stage manager for an amateur theater group**
>
> ✔ **Did volunteer work in a hospital**
>
> ✔ **Headed PTA fundraising drive**

The importance of putting down on paper as *many* of these tasks as possible cannot be emphasized enough. The more activities in which you have *first-hand* experience, the better this exercise works.

Measure your likes and dislikes

After you complete your list, your next job is to assign a satisfaction/dissatisfaction rating to each item on the list. Don't overintellectualize. Don't overthink. Simply ask yourself the following question: "How much personal satisfaction (or dissatisfaction) did this activity bring me?"

Use a scale of -10 to +10. If you enjoyed the activity or task a great deal, give it a 9 or 10. If you found the job extremely distasteful, give it a -9 or -10.

Analyze your list

The next step is a little more difficult. You need to isolate those tasks that come out on the high side of the satisfaction scale (7 or above) as well as those tasks that come out on the high end of the dissatisfaction scale (-7 to -10). You may want to transfer the items in each category onto a separate sheet of paper.

After you do so, think about each item and ask yourself, "What about this activity did I enjoy or find distasteful?"

Look for patterns

Now for the tricky part. Read over and analyze your answers to the preceding questions. See if you can uncover certain patterns and common threads.

If you find, for example, that a common thread among the activities that brought you satisfaction is *people,* it's a safe bet that you're an extrovert. Hence, you are not going to be happy in any job that obliges you to be isolated from other people for any length of time. If one of the common threads is *helping* other people, your tendencies are clearly service-oriented.

But don't stop there. Narrow the "people" pattern down. Do you like *working with* people as part of a team, *managing* people, *training* people?

And look for other patterns as well. Do the activities you find satisfying (or highly unsatisfying) call for problem-solving skills or creativity? Is there a competitive aspect to those activities, or are they cooperative?

The important thing about this exercise is not to judge yourself. Don't think in terms of whether you *should* or *shouldn't* find an activity satisfying. All you're looking for here is some insight — affirmation of what you may already know but have never really taken the time to think about.

If you list enough activities — 25 is not an excessive amount to work with — you should be able to find some patterns. Again, don't rush this exercise. The more insights you gain from this stage of job targeting, the easier it will be for you to complete the other stages.

Finding Out What You're Good At

This exercise is similar to the preceding one, except for one thing. The purpose here is to help you get a reasonably objective idea of how *good* you are — or were — at the various activities you listed in the previous exercise.

Granted, it's tough to be objective when you're evaluating how good you are at things, but this exercise takes this difficulty into account, as you will see.

Go back to the list you just filled out. This time, though, do two things when you look at each item: First, give yourself a skill rating (1 to 10, with 10 being the highest) that represents how well you think you performed that task. Second, ask yourself, "What did I *accomplish*?"

About this accomplishment business: Regardless of how good you think you might be at any activity, it's helpful to find some reasonably objective criteria that can verify your perceptions. How *many* raffle tickets did you sell compared to other people, for example? How much money did the fundraising drive you headed actually raise? How well did the team you manage actually do, relative to the talent you had to work with? Again, try to be as honest with yourself as you can. Nobody is keeping score here but you. If you didn't accomplish anything, let it go at that.

The main thing to be alert to in this phase of the exercise is any discrepancy between the "how-good-am-I-at-this" rating you give yourself and the specific accomplishments you are able to enumerate. If you give yourself a high rating but aren't able to specify any accomplishments, you may want to rethink your rating. If, on the other hand, you give yourself a low rating on a particular item and yet are able to write down several accomplishments, chances are that you are underrating yourself. You're probably a lot more skilled than you think.

Narrowing Your Focus

If you take sufficient time with these exercises, you should have a general idea of your likes and dislikes and a general idea of what you're good at. Now it's time to focus on the specific features that the various jobs you might consider are likely to offer you.

What follows is a list of "what-I'm-looking-for-in-a-job" statements. Go through the list and respond to each statement as follows:

If the feature is *very important* to you, write **VI**.

If the feature is *important* to you, write **I**.

If the feature is *unimportant,* write **U**.

If, by some chance, the feature listed is absolutely repugnant to you, write **X**.

Financial rewards and other benefits:

_____1. A salary that will enable you to *measurably* improve your current lifestyle.

_____2. Generous benefit package and plenty of perks (expense account lunches, trips, and so on).

_____3. The potential to make a lot of money in the future.

_____4. The potential to make a lot of money in the future — but in a short period of time.

The organization you work for:

_____5. A chance to be part of a big and prestigious company or organization.

_____6. A chance to be part of a small, entrepreneurial company with new and exciting ideas.

_____7. A chance to work for a company that is involved in a product or service that interests you personally.

_____8. A chance to work for an organization offering a product or service that helps to make the world a better place.

Work environment and coworkers:

____9. A lively, social working environment where there's real team spirit.

___10. A low-key, predictable working environment that enables you to leave your job at the office and not have to think about it 24 hours a day.

___11. A supportive, nurturing atmosphere where people look out for one another.

___12. A challenging, pressured environment where you're never bored but where you pretty much sink or swim on your own.

___13. The opportunity to work for or interact with a dynamic person (or people) from whom you feel you can learn a great deal.

___14. A chance to spend a lot of time outdoors, rather than in an office.

Personal job satisfaction and career considerations:

___15. The opportunity to spend the bulk of your time doing the things you were trained to do and enjoy doing.

___16. A chance to do things you've never done before.

___17. An opportunity to work on your own, without supervision.

___18. A chance to demonstrate your creativity.

___19. A chance to work with high-tech equipment.

___20. An opportunity to learn or develop a skill or gain experience that could lead to a better job down the road.

___21. An opportunity to establish a foothold in a career in which you can advance fairly quickly.

Lifestyle considerations:

___22. A flexible schedule that will enable you to stay in control of other aspects of your personal life (your obligations as a parent, for example).

___23. A convenient location that doesn't require a long commute and doesn't oblige you to spend an excessive amount of time traveling.

Take note of those features you rated VI (very important). Obviously, these features should figure prominently as you begin formulating job targets. If you find, for example, that most of your VIs are in the section that talks about job satisfaction and career considerations, those factors should play an important part in the job targets you select. And don't ignore the Xs. Use them to rule out those job possibilities that are clearly going to make you unhappy.

Bear in mind, finally, that the procedure you've gone through is not a *science* or a *formula*. Its sole purpose is to give you some added insight into yourself. Don't hesitate to modify the procedure or add to this list as many considerations as you want.

Career Counselors: Can They Help You?

Career counselors specialize in helping people get a better fix on which specific career options they should be pursuing. They don't *find* you jobs in the way that recruiters do (see Chapter 15 for more information about recruiters). Rather, they help you figure out for yourself, through a variety of methods, which career paths and jobs make the most sense, given all the various factors — skills, aptitude, aspirations, and so on — that you need to consider. Many counselors coach their clients through all phases of the job search, including how to negotiate the offer.

Most career counselors hold degrees in psychology, social work, guidance, or counseling. Many have their own practices. Others work for government and nonprofit organizations. Some offer career counseling as part of a range of services. Others specialize almost solely in career counseling. Fees can run anywhere from $40 to $100 an hour, depending on the region and the reputation of the counselor.

Tools of the trade

Most career counselors rely on a combination of testing and interviewing to clarify for you which career paths and specific jobs in those career paths are best suited to your particular background, talent, and personality traits. Typical tests include the Strong Interest Inventory (formerly known as the Strong Campbell test), which helps you get a clearer sense of how your personal preferences — your interests, what you like to do — relate to the likes and dislikes of workers in more than 100 jobs by telling you how similar your interests are to theirs.

Another common testing instrument is the Myers-Briggs test, which is designed to give you a clearer idea of your general personality traits and how those traits are likely to help or hinder you in certain jobs and professions. The test clarifies your type and tells you which of 208 jobs attract the largest percentage of workers with your same type.

The more savvy counselors are also able to give you some real-world guidance as to how marketable you are likely to be in a given job marketplace. They can teach you how to network more effectively, how to get the information you need in order to prepare for interviews, and how to handle yourself during job interviews.

Career counselors, remember, are not necessarily experts in the job market per se, which is to say that they can't tell you about the prospects for certain types of jobs in different parts of the country. Their expertise lies in the process of helping you find an appropriate career path.

Choosing a Career Counselor

The most reliable way to choose a career counselor is to get a personal recommendation from someone whose opinion you trust. If you don't know anyone who has ever worked with a career counselor, get in touch with a local school or community organization and see whether someone there can recommend a qualified counselor.

After you get a name, you can take the following steps to make sure that you've chosen someone who can help:

1. **Interview the counselor.**

   Get a feel for how the counselor works. Don't be embarrassed to ask about fees and what you can reasonably expect. Trust your instincts. If anything about the counselor gives you the creeps (for example, a boa constrictor is sleeping on one of the office chairs), find someone else.

2. **Ask about the counselor's general approach.**

   Find out how the counselor likes to work: whether the approach he or she uses relies heavily on testing or one-on-one interviewing and so forth. Don't be shy about asking what you can reasonably expect to derive from the overall experience. Ask for a description of the counselor's program — preferably in writing.

   Be wary of anyone who over-promises. Career counseling is an art, not a science.

3. **Ask for references.**

   There's nothing wrong with asking a career counselor to supply you with the names of people with whom he or she has worked. If the counselor balks, find someone else.

Steer clear of career counselors who

- ✔ Guarantee or promise that they can find you a job.
- ✔ Charge a high up-front fee.
- ✔ Subject you to a high-powered sales pitch.

TIP

If you want more information about how to select a career counselor, get in touch with the American Counseling Association. For a list of certified councelors in your region, contact the National Board for Certified Councelors.

- ✔ National Board for Certified Counselors (NBCC)
  3 Terrace Way, Suite D
  Greensboro, NC 27403
  910-547-0607

- ✔ American Counseling Association (ACA)
  5999 Stevenson Ave.
  Alexandria, VA 22304
  703-823-9800

BLOOPERS

What's in a name? You'd be surprised

As you set your sights on your next career move, and specifically on your next job title, be prepared for the fact that specialization in today's workplace has resulted in some rather diverse, lofty, and otherwise warped labels. In an independent survey commissioned by Robert Half International, Inc., executives cited some examples. (Note: You should probably avoid pursuing the "Party Chief" designation in your next interview.)

- ✔ Vice president and ombudsman of social responsibility

- ✔ Vice president, people

- ✔ Second vice president in charge of grapes

- ✔ Associate assistant to senior VP

- ✔ Deputy director of anything

- ✔ Director of direct reporting

- ✔ Procurement activist

- ✔ Supreme commander (not in a military setting)

- ✔ Director of creativity and motivation

- ✔ Party chief

- ✔ Outgoing manager

- ✔ Semi-senior auditor

- ✔ Senior special executive assistant to CEO

- ✔ Manager of artificial organs

- ✔ Vice president of retirement

- ✔ Manager of innovation

Chapter 4

Scoping Out the Market

. . . .

. . . .

*I*magine for a moment that you are in the market for a new car and have begun to shop for the car but have not yet gotten around to doing the following things:

✔ Giving any thought to the specific type of car you want to buy: something sleek and sporty that roars from 0 to 60 mph in five seconds flat, or something big and practical that will comfortably accommodate you, your spouse, your three children, and your 150-pound St. Bernard.

✔ Determining how much money you want to spend or how much you can *afford* to spend on the car.

✔ Narrowing down your choices to four or five specific models that are in your price range and that you can see yourself driving, assuming that you can work out a good deal.

✔ Deciding which options — front-wheel drive, ABS brakes, a sun roof, and so on — are important to you.

✔ Determining which dealers carry the cars that match your established criteria.

Under these circumstances, your search for a new car is not going to be a model of efficiency. You may find the search interesting and maybe even enjoyable, assuming that you enjoy browsing aimlessly from dealership to dealership and have the time to do so. But if your goal is to find a new car in the most timely and productive manner, this approach isn't "the one."

What holds true for buying a car holds true as well for finding a satisfying job in today's competitive market. Simply put, you need a *target* — a sense of focus and direction. You need to know, at least generally, where you want to end up — that is, what sort of job you want to find.

The criteria that you establish for these targets are likely to change at various times in your search. Your financial needs, your emotional state, the results you're getting in your job search efforts, the feedback you're getting from people you meet — any or all of these things can influence your targeting criteria at any given point.

Regardless of how long you have been looking for a job and how successful — or unsuccessful — you have been at uncovering leads and arranging interviews, you still need to direct your efforts toward reasonably well-defined goals.

This chapter guides you through the goal-setting process. The key concept to focus on is called *strategic targeting*.

Strategic Targeting Defined

This approach is rooted in the idea of *balance* — balance between your personal goals, values, and aspirations and the realities of the job marketplace, coupled with the pressures you may be up against at any given point in your job search.

Finding this balance isn't easy; your perceptions and attitudes at various times in your job search are subject to fluctuation. If, for example, you are not under financial pressure — that is, you already have a job or have plenty of money saved — you can afford to set targets that are heavily weighted toward *you*. Also, you don't have to worry that finding a job situation that meets your criteria could take you the better part of a year.

But if finances are an issue, your targets have to reflect that priority. You can't be as selective as you normally would be. Your target is now weighted more toward those jobs available that can alleviate that pressure.

Don't confuse thinking strategically with making *compromises*. If anything, strategic job targeting is designed to minimize the amount of compromising you have to do as you move forward in your job search. The whole process of strategic targeting is to keep you focused on what *is* and not on what *might* be, *could* be, or *should* be. Adjusting to reality isn't compromising; it's doing what needs to be done.

The process breaks down into the following steps:

1. **Assemble a rough list of job possibilities — jobs that, based on your personal and career goals, you can see yourself doing and can get excited about pursuing.**

   These jobs, incidentally, do not necessarily have to fall within the same industry (retailing, hotel and restaurant, or entertainment, for example) or even the same occupational category (manager, salesperson, administrator, and so on) — not at this early stage, anyway. And don't worry for now about *how* you go about assembling this list.

2. **Explore those rough target possibilities in more depth, with the idea of determining how *realistic* they are.**

   A realistic job target meets two criteria. The first is that there are openings and opportunities in that field in the region of the country where you would like to settle. (Translation: You don't go looking for a job as a surfing instructor in Iowa.) The second is that you can hold your own with the competition when it comes to experience and skills. (Translation: If you didn't make the cut for your high school basketball team, professional basketball wouldn't be on your list.)

3. **Assuming that there are realistic job possibilities and that you *are* a legitimate candidate, determine whether the purely practical aspects of the job or field you have targeted meet your basic financial and lifestyle requirements.**

   In other words, can you afford to accept a job if it is offered to you, given the salary it is likely to offer and the demands it is likely to place on your time?

4. **Assess your "market value" for those job possibilities by matching your personal inventory of qualifications, skills, and attributes with the qualifications, skills, and attributes that employers in those target job areas are looking for.**

   If practical, seek to shore the gap between what you can offer and what employers are looking for (which you may be able to do fairly easily by learning new skills or taking classes).

To determine which computer programs are in the greatest demand in your field, see which skills are most frequently mentioned in the classified ads in major newspapers. You can also get this information from professional associations such as Professional Secretaries International.

Before that furrow in your brow gets any deeper, here are some general observations about the strategic job targeting process.

Understand that it's not a science

Strategic job targeting is not a science. It's a *process* — and an imprecise process at that. The goal of the process, moreover, is not to conjure up the "perfect" job opportunity but simply to give you a range of options around which you can strategically organize your various job search activities.

Pay attention to sequence

The *sequence* of the steps just outlined is far from random. If you look at the steps again, you will notice that the sequence has you exploring the *opportunities* in a particular job target area *before* you begin analyzing the skill requirements. The sequence also has you determining whether you can really afford to accept an offer before you get too heavily involved in matching your own skills and qualifications to the requirements of that job.

The rationale here is efficiency. If there are simply no opportunities in a particular area that you're considering as a target (the market for cattle ranchers in New York City, for example), figuring out what it takes to be a successful candidate is clearly a waste of time and energy. And if you have determined that you cannot afford to live for less than, say, $40,000, exploring job opportunities in which the most you can expect in the way of salary is $20,000 is a frustrating and dispiriting exercise.

However, there's an exception to that rule. If that $20,000 job means enough to you, and if you can envision that a year or so down the road you could be earning what you need to earn in that field, you might consider modifying your lifestyle — at least temporarily. But that's a personal choice. This chapter assumes that you already have a fair idea of which specific features you're looking for in a job and have a good sense of your salary and lifestyle requirements. The purpose here is to add a dose of the real world to those desires — to help make sure that you are focusing the bulk of your time and energy on targets that represent genuine possibilities.

Be prepared to do some leg work

To develop strategic job targets, you need information. Lots of it. And from different sources: people, books, company literature, and anything else you can get your hands on. No one expects you to have broad, firsthand knowledge of all the various job and career possibilities lurking out there in the marketplace, particularly if you are looking for an entry-level position.

The good news, though, is that gaining access to job- and career-related information isn't difficult these days. Your library has a wealth of useful "what-it's-like-to-pursue-this-career" information, and much of that information is now available from computerized databases as well. And as this chapter will show you, it's not difficult at all to get useful, reliable knowledge from people who are currently working in jobs or fields that may represent possibilities for you.

Stay flexible

Strategic job targeting is a highly flexible process. As you move ahead in your job search, you should be prepared to modify targets, abandon targets, and add new targets in response to the results you're getting — or not getting. After two or three months of not making any headway toward a particular target, you may well have to sit down and begin the process anew.

Don't worry about having to reposition your targets. It's not a sign of failure! In today's rapidly changing job market, it comes with the territory.

Job versus Career: Which Should You Be Pursuing?

Probably the most fundamental choice you have to make in the strategic job targeting stage is whether you want your next job to be just that — a job — or whether you want it to be either the first step in a career you want to break into or the next logical step in a career that you've already begun to pursue.

This choice is important because it most certainly affects the targets you select. If you are committed to staying on a particular career path, your targeting possibilities are obviously going to be narrower than those of someone who hasn't yet launched a career or who is thinking about changing careers and is interested primarily in gaining new experiences. Your options, in this case, will probably have to do with the type of company you want to work for or the region of the country in which you want to live.

Finding a job to support a career

It is also possible that the career you hope to pursue will pretty much require you to find a job *outside* that career. The vast majority of aspiring actors, musicians, artists, and writers today, for example, do not earn their living by acting, playing music, or writing. They have other jobs — say, working in restaurants. These are "job" jobs: They pay the rent, put food on the table, and at the same time give people the opportunity to develop their craft.

This pattern, incidentally, isn't limited to artists. Suppose you have been a computer programmer for the past ten years and decide that you really want to be a teacher. This being the case, your target might be heavily weighted toward those positions that will enable you to continue to support yourself but at the same time enable you to take the classes and earn the credentials you need to launch a teaching career.

The point is that you need to think about both the short-term *and* the long-term. Don't automatically assume that because you can't afford to be choosy about the jobs you go after, you don't have long-term options. It's better to look at all the short-term options you have and decide *which* option (for the time being, at least) gets you closest to your long-term goal.

Choosing a job within a career

One final thing to think about is the degree of variation that can exist within a given occupation.

Consider the legal profession. The day-to-day life of a trial lawyer bears little resemblance to the day-to-day experience of a lawyer who specializes in tax law. By the same token, you can pursue a career in advertising but work in any number of functional specialties within that field — graphic design, copywriting, sales, or accounting, to name a few.

The fact that concepts such as *job* and *career* are not as clearly distinguished as you might think is something that you should keep in mind at all times. Above all, don't allow yourself to be locked into a mindset that limits your possibilities. Be aware that the opportunity you are looking for could exist in any number of different forms, in any number of different industries or companies, and even in any number of different jobs.

Finding Out What's Out There

In the earliest stages of job targeting, your goal is to uncover as many possibilities as you can. The more the merrier.

If you complete the exercises in Chapter 3, you should know — or at least have a general idea — what you like to do, what you're good at, and what your basic living needs are. What you may *not* know, though, is where in the vast universe otherwise known as the job marketplace you need to look for specific jobs that can meet some (if not most) of those criteria.

The following sections show you some concrete steps that you can take to broaden your perspective of the job market. By doing so, you can better establish job targets that strike a happy medium between what you ideally want to do and what you have a reasonable chance of achieving.

Read

Never before has so much information about so many job- and career-related subjects been so readily available. It would be difficult to name any field (unless it's caring for yaks in Tibet) that you couldn't become reasonably familiar with after a couple of days of basic research.

Researching job opportunities on the information superhighway is another route you may want to pursue (see Chapters 17–19). But this section applies to more traditional forms of career research.

The most obvious source of this type of information is the job and careers section of your local public library. There you can find directories and job guides in dozens of fields (including, who knows, Tibetan yak herding). True, the information in some of these directories is dry enough to put you to sleep. It isn't always as current and as real world as you might like it to be, either, and it doesn't necessarily show you what it's like to actually work in a particular industry. But this type of research is nonetheless a good foundation to build upon.

Another great source of job- and career-related information — and for obvious reasons — is the library of any local college or university. (By the way, you don't have to be a student, faculty member, or employee of a college to do research in the reference section of most college libraries, although you won't be able to check out books.)

But go beyond the directory section of your local library. Virtually every industry today has its own complement of trade magazines, many of which feature at least one or two articles an issue about job- and career-related topics. Trade magazines aren't always easy to track down — libraries tend to keep only a limited number of them in circulation — but many trade publications are accessible from on-line databases. And almost all major trade associations publish a magazine, newsletter, or journal for their members. (Your library is likely to have a directory that lists trade publications by industry. A phone call or two, coupled with a friendly request, will frequently bring you copies at no cost.) You can also get an ongoing sense of the job marketplace by reading the better known business publications, such as *Business Week, Forbes, The Wall Street Journal,* and *Fortune.*

Many libraries have CD-ROM databases on site. These are excellent for accessing data and articles on larger companies, and they may save you from wading through periodical indexes.

Other reading suggestions:

- ✔ Look for biographies and autobiographies of successful people in fields or professions that interest you — especially *recent* biographies and autobiographies. At the same time you are learning about what it takes to be successful in a particular occupation, you'll also learn about what it takes to be successful in that industry.

- ✔ Be alert to newspaper and magazine articles about companies or the people who work for or run those companies. Here, again, the payoff is current, "insider" information.

For in-depth information about library research, see Chapter 10.

Talk to people in the field

Next to being there yourself, the best way to expand your perspective of the job marketplace is to be an attentive listener — and to know who to listen to.

You don't have to go to "experts." Look around at the people you know: your friends, your relatives, your Uncle Larry, or your cousin Louise from Denver, even though the two of you fought like cats and dogs when you were kids. Write them a note. Give them a call. Interview them. Find out more about their work: what they actually *do* in their jobs, what their companies are like, and what it's like to be a professional in their particular field. Ask them to send you recruiting brochures and company newsletters. It all helps.

Don't limit your job targeting detective work to friends and family. Do you get bored at cocktail parties or other social functions? Good, because now you have an assignment. You need to seek out people, find out (politely) where they work, and then ask them to tell you about it. Most people enjoy telling other people — even strangers — about their work. Who knows, you may even get an invitation to come down and spend time at someone's company, and by doing so get an inside look and determine whether you might fit in there.

Remember, you're not looking to line up job offers or even job interviews just yet — not until you determine that a job or field represents a true strategic target, something you could see yourself actually doing. But the more people you talk to and the more job environments you can observe, the more perspective you are going to gain and the easier it will be to set job targets that make sense.

Attend trade shows

Trade shows and other events that bring large numbers of people from a single industry together in one place are another solid way to find out about the nature of work in a particular field or industry and also about job possibilities. Getting into some of these shows can be tricky since most of them are open to industry or association members only. But some trade shows — large computer shows, for example — are open to the public. And even if the trade show is closed to the public, this is not to say that you can't drop by the hotel and see if you can't engage some of the attendees in conversation. (They're easy to recognize because they're always wearing badges.)

Work as a temporary

Chapter 16 says a lot more about temporary work and how it should figure into your job hunt strategy. For now, keep in mind that working as a temp — regardless of the type of work you might be doing — gives you an opportunity to experience firsthand what it's like to work in a particular industry or company. It can also give you access to people who can broaden your knowledge of that field or who can potentially offer you a full-time position.

Get your feet wet with volunteer work

Organizations that rely on volunteers can't be terribly selective about the people they use to handle specific tasks, which opens up opportunities for nonspecialists. Suppose you have been thinking about getting out of the insurance business and have been wondering whether you could make a living writing and editing a newsletter — maybe an insurance newsletter. One way to find out whether you might enjoy newsletter writing is to write and edit a few issues of a volunteer organization's newsletter. You may find out in the end that you enjoy the insurance business a whole lot more than you enjoy writing articles. In either case, the experience will be valuable.

Attend lectures, courses, and seminars

Read your local paper or publications such as *National Business Employment Weekly* regularly to find out about lectures at local community centers, churches, and libraries. The lectures rarely cost very much and give you an opportunity to talk to people who are highly knowledgeable in fields that may interest you.

Also, look through community college and training center brochures to find out about courses and seminars in fields that seem interesting to you but that you know little about. An added benefit to taking these courses is the opportunity they provide you to meet people who are already *in* the field.

Exploring a Target: What to Ask When You Get the Chance

When you get an opportunity to sit down with someone who can give you some firsthand information about the various job and career possibilities in a particular industry, occupation, or company, do your best to capitalize on it. Don't be embarrassed about asking basic questions (as long as they're not too personal), and don't feel self-conscious about taking notes.

There are basically five aspects of any job or a career that you need to know about in order to get a sense of whether that career makes sense for you. These aspects may not be of equal importance to you, but all of them contribute to one degree or another to the "totality" of the job experience. The following sections describe these aspects.

The work itself

What do the people you're talking to do on a day-to-day basis? Do they spend most of their time in an office, on the phone, in front of a computer, in a laboratory, or on the road? Do they typically work alone or as part of a team? Is the work routine or constantly changing? Is there deadline pressure? These are just some of the very basic questions you should be asking. Feel free to add whatever questions you like and, again, don't dismiss any question because you think it's too basic. If you're curious, ask.

Available opportunities

How easy or difficult is it to break into and gain a foothold in the field, occupation, or company — especially now? How steep is the competition for jobs at your skill and experience level? Is there a demand for new people, or is there a surplus? And if there is a surplus, how big is it: 50 applicants for every opening or 500 applicants for every opening?

Moving ahead

How quickly people typically move through the ranks in a field or profession varies considerably from industry to industry, so it's a good idea to find out early on about the typical timetable for career advancement. In certain fields, such as teaching, advancement is largely a matter of seniority. In other fields, like sales, performance frequently takes precedence over tenure.

Here's a key point to bear in mind: The career path patterns in major corporations are changing rapidly with so many layers of middle management having been removed from many corporate structures. Promotions, in other words, no longer follow a predictable, hierarchical pattern. What is happening instead in many situations is that your job stays essentially the same, but your responsibilities expand.

The financial rewards

On average, what do people earn in the field, occupation, or profession you're trying to learn more about? What are the typical salaries for entry-level employees, and what do the top performers make? Keep in mind that salary ranges in any given field can vary a great deal from company to company, and you need to take into account factors like health insurance and other benefits.

In general, though, the more "glamorous" a field is, the lower the entry-level salaries are likely to be, given the basic law of supply and demand. Certain fields, too, are inherently less lucrative than others but offer their employees a level of job satisfaction that makes up for the lack of monetary rewards.

Lifestyle

Certain industries — the airline and hospitality industries, to name just two — differ from other lines of work primarily because of the lifestyle they offer. So asking questions about lifestyle should definitely be part of your interviewing strategy. Find out how much travel is involved in a typical job and where that travel is likely to take you: to Western Europe or west of the freeway. Get a feel for — and remember, it often varies from company to company — how often employees have to work nights and weekends.

Get a sense, too, for the pressure you're likely to be under on a day-to-day basis. Many people who start out in major law, accounting, and investment banking firms earn high salaries, but they have to be prepared to work long hours; it's part of the culture.

Other questions to ask people about their jobs and their industries include the following:

- ✔ Which are the dominant companies or organizations in this field?
- ✔ What qualities does it take to excel in this job, field, or profession?
- ✔ What do you like *best* about your job?
- ✔ What's the worst part of your job?

Staying on Track When Targets Don't Pan Out

After you establish job targets, any number of scenarios can unfold. Here are some of these scenarios and how you might respond to them:

- ✔ You discover early on that there are very few job opportunities in one of the targets you've established.

  Advice: Be prepared to either abandon or at least modify the target. For example, you may want to keep the geographic component of the target but be willing to expand the range of industries you're considering.

- ✔ Available job opportunities match one or more of your targets, but the competition for these jobs is intense, and you're not sure how you stack up against the competition.

  Advice: Don't be in a hurry to give up just yet. Try to get a clearer fix on what the employers in these target areas are looking for and what the other candidates might bring to the party in the way of experience, credentials, and connections. If you are convinced at this point that you are not in a strong position to compete — and, again, don't throw in the towel too soon — think about the steps you need to take (special courses, for example) to make yourself a more attractive candidate in the future.

- ✔ There are openings that match your targets, and you are a legitimate candidate for those openings, but the salary range falls below your minimum needs.

  Advice: If you see in these openings an opportunity to do something that will bring you great satisfaction and that within a reasonable period could pay you an acceptable wage, consider taking the job and explore ways to supplement your income — a weekend or evening job, for example.

Getting Yourself "Market Ready"

The assumption at this point is that you have defined a set of targets that meet your criteria. Each target, in other words, represents a job that you can envision yourself handling, offers a reasonable number of opportunities, and meets your basic requirements. The next step is determining just how "marketable" you are.

Understanding what marketability is

Your marketability is essentially a function of two things. The first is what the "buyers" in the marketplace — in this case, prospective employers — are looking for. The second is what you can bring to the table.

It goes without saying that marketability is a highly relative, not to mention subjective, notion. What makes you highly marketable in one situation or company might not make you highly marketable in another situation, never mind that the two jobs appear similar. That's because the "buyer" in each situation has his or her own idea of what's important. The fact that you lack an MBA may not mean anything to one prospective employer, but it could be the most important consideration for someone else.

Determining your own marketability

These qualifications notwithstanding, you can take some steps to develop a general sense of how attractive a candidate you're likely to be to a prospective employer.

Here's one such process. The goal of this exercise is to give you a picture of how your own strengths as a candidate match up against the criteria by which would-be employers are likely to judge the attractiveness of a candidate.

1. **On a sheet of paper, create a three-column table.**

   You can also use the spaces provided in the following table.

2. **In the left-hand column, write down the five or six factors that prospective employers in each job target area are likely to consider the most important in a job candidate.**

   If you don't have this information, try to get it by asking someone in the field or doing some research in the library.

3. **In the middle column, rate each factor according to your view of its importance to prospective employers.**

   If, for example, your research reveals that educational credentials are likely to be important to the typical employer in a particular field, you might assign it a value of 5 on a scale of 1 to 5, with 5 indicating the highest degree of importance.

4. **In the right-hand column, rate yourself in this area.**

   If, for example, your educational credentials match those that are required for the position in which you're interested, you would give yourself a 5. If you are lacking a degree that is required for the position but have a college degree, you might give yourself a 2.

5. **Repeat steps 3 and 4 for each criterion.**

6. **Add up the numbers in each column.**

7. **Subtract your total from the total of the prospective employers' column.**

What Employers Are Looking for	*Estimated Employers' Rating*	*Rating I Give Myself*
Examples:		
Written communication skills	5	3
Possession of an MBA	4	5
Total		

What you are looking for in this exercise are gaps between the importance a prospective employer attaches to each criterion and your own strengths in that area. By subtracting the sum of *your* numbers from the sum of the numbers in the would-be employer list, you end up with a rough idea of your marketability. The lower the number — the gap between what employers are looking for and what you can offer — the more marketable you are.

This exercise serves yet another function. By zeroing in on what employers care about (as opposed to what you happen to be good at), you lay the foundation for your marketing campaign. The remaining parts of this book focus on specific parts of that campaign.

Part III
The Writes (and Wrongs) of Resume Writing

In this part...

*E*veryone knows that you have to have a resume to apply for a job. This part takes you through the entire process of writing a resume that will dazzle would-be employers. By choosing the best resume style, formatting like a professional, and focusing on your specific accomplishments, you'll come up with a resume that you'll be proud to send out.

This part also explains how to write winning cover letters so that the recipient will actually *read* the resume that you worked so hard on.

Chapter 5
Resume Basics

• •

• •

A resume is what nearly everyone you approach in your job search is going to ask you to send them before they take any action on your behalf. You can think of it as the driver's license of job hunting: You can't go anywhere without it. What it is, in short, is a one- or two-page summary of your work history, educational background, and work-related personal qualifications. Its fundamental purpose is to give prospective employers a convenient and reasonably efficient way to determine, at a glance, if you warrant a closer look.

The goal of the next few chapters is to take you through a step-by-step process that will result in at least one solid resume that will hold you in good stead as you move forward in your job search. If you follow these guidelines, you'll end up with a resume that you wouldn't hesitate to send to anyone.

Great Expectations: What a Resume Can — and Can't — Do

The main thing to bear in mind about a resume is what it *doesn't* do. Regardless of how elegantly it's designed, how "brilliantly" it's written, and how professionally it's printed, a resume in and of itself isn't going to induce anyone to stop what he or she is doing, jump up and down, and say, "This is the person I definitely want to hire!" That is not what it is meant to do.

What a resume *is* meant to do is to get you past the initial screening so that you have an opportunity to be interviewed by someone who has the power to hire you.

Not that getting past this screening is easy to do. A typical classified ad for an attractive job opening in any major city can sometimes draw hundreds of responses, each response containing a resume. Someone — not necessarily the person who does the actual hiring — has to go through that vast mountain of resumes and select from it those candidates who most closely meet the basic qualifications of the position. The higher the mountain of resumes, the less time the person is likely to spend on each one. And today, the scanning is increasingly being done by computer.

This aspect of the hiring process — when someone sits down and begins to plow through a stack of resumes — is sometimes referred to as the *screening* stage. At this point, your resume faces a tough, but by no means insurmountable, challenge.

How Screening Works

Here's what usually happens. People who screen resumes typically do so by dividing them into different groupings. These groupings are based roughly on whether a candidate is considered a "definite" (someone who clearly deserves to be interviewed), a "possible" (someone who might be worth an interview), or a "definitely not" (someone whose background is clearly wrong for the job in question). The time a screener spends on each resume at this initial stage is often very brief — only a handful of seconds for each resume. Whether a resume makes it to the "definite" pile or the "definitely not" pile depends mainly on the specific criteria the screener is looking for.

That's where things get tough for *your* resume. The more resumes a screener has to go through, the more specific become the criteria used to differentiate the "definites" from the "possibles" from the "definitely nots." Here, in short, is why developing more than one resume frequently makes strategic sense. The more targeted your resume is to a particular job or company, the more likely the resume will make a favorable impression on the screener.

What employers look for in resumes

In an independent survey conducted for Robert Half International in 1994, 150 human resources managers and other executives from the nation's 1,000 largest companies were asked the following question: "Other than skills and experience, which one of the following is the most important piece of information you look for when reviewing a resume?"

Growth in responsibility: 67%

Previous employers: 15%

Stability: 11%

Other/don't know: 7%

Something else worth bearing in mind is that the people who screen resumes are usually more inclined to rule *out* people than they are to keep adding to the "definite" list — especially when the pile of "definites" begins to mount. This is why little things like typos and misspellings can often knock you out of the running, even though these little things may have nothing whatsoever to do with your ability to handle the job for which you are applying.

Keep in mind, too, that the *process* of putting together a resume is often as valuable to you as the *result* of that process. The story you tell in that resume is a story you're going to have to tell — and tell persuasively — to many people in many different situations. The more familiar and comfortable you are with that story and the more confident you are that it accurately reflects who you are and what you can offer, the easier it will be to tell the story in any number of different situations.

The 12 Cardinal Sins of Resume Writing

Before you actually begin writing your resume, it's probably a good idea to be alert to some of the more common pitfalls of resume writing. Take some time to ponder the following pitfalls, and do your best to avoid them in your own resume.

Unprofessionalism

Your resume, above all, must *look* professional. Consider the following:

- It should be printed with black ink on standard-sized, $8^{1}/_{2}$ x 11, preferably white bond paper. (Ivory and light gray are okay, too, but stay away from light pinks and blues.) The margins should be at least 1 inch all around.

- You should use one of the most commonly recognized resume formats. See Chapter 6 for more information about resume formats.

- The typeface should be simple, unadorned, and easy to read. It should *not* look like calligraphy — the typeface people use for wedding invitations. And while it is okay to boldface or underline certain phrases, keep the graphic flourishes to a minimum. Stick to a single typeface in a single size.

- The information in the resume should be presented in short, easy-to-read paragraphs. Favor bullet points over lengthy paragraphs.

- There should be no extraneous pen or pencil marks or correction fluid on the resume — and please, no gravy stains.

Carelessness

The fact that your resume is marred by typos, misspellings, and grammatical mistakes may not be an accurate reflection of how qualified you are for a particular job (unless, of course, the job was proofreader). As a rule, though, employers are neither patient nor forgiving about these things. A single typo in an otherwise well-organized and professional-looking resume may not necessarily sink you, but if the resume is riddled with misspellings and grammatical errors, you send the message to would-be employers that you don't pay attention to details. In a competitive job market, this is not a good message to send.

Cuteness and cleverness

Cute is for babies and kittens, but not for resumes. So play it straight. Forget puns and clever plays on words; they don't belong on a resume, and they don't belong on a cover letter, either. People who read resumes are not looking to be entertained. And what you might consider clever, most people — even those who may be amused by the cleverness — will not consider appropriate.

Irrelevance and fluff

The people who read your resume are interested in one thing above all. They want to know whether, based on what they read, you deserve serious consideration as a candidate. Given this priority, any information in your resume that doesn't contribute an answer to this basic question is, by definition, irrelevant. If you're a college graduate, you don't have to mention the high school you attended. And go easy on your hobbies and interests. The fact that you are a low handicap golfer or have one of the world's most extensive collections of beer cans may make for interesting conversation at a dinner party, but it's of no interest to a would-be employer — unless you're applying for a job as a golf pro or at a company that markets beer cans.

Vagueness

Vagueness occurs when you mention a job title, task, or set of abbreviations that nobody other than you and the person you used to work for are going to recognize, such as Asst. VP, RTP Div. of Corporate Reclassification of ETY Documents. It also rears its ugly head when you fail to mention specifically what you were responsible for in your last job, the number of people you supervised, the size of the budget you controlled, and so forth. Don't assume that the people who read your resume will figure out for themselves what you did. They won't.

Misrepresentation

Don't lie. It's that simple. And don't be tempted to embellish the truth. You would be foolish, of course, to include in your resume anything that is remotely unflattering. (It's one thing to be honest and another thing to be suicidal!) But the risks of fudging the truth in your resume far outweigh the benefits, particularly when it comes to specific facts, like credentials and titles.

If you were not, in fact, a vice president of whatever in your last job, don't anoint yourself with that title simply because the company you used to work for is out of business. The issue here goes beyond ethics; it is practical as well. If, in checking your references, a would-be employer discovers that you misrepresented yourself in your resume — even if the misrepresentation is inconsequential — your credibility will take a beating and you stand a good chance of losing an offer. And if your employer discovers a lie *after* hiring you, you could lose the job that you worked so hard to get.

Overkill

Overkill is the excessive use of superlatives, regardless of who or what those superlatives modify. There is nothing wrong with tooting your own horn in your resume, just as long as the notes you toot are actual accomplishments and not simply adjectives that proclaim to the reader how wonderful you are.

For example, instead of calling yourself a "dynamite salesperson" (which you shouldn't do unless you really did sell dynamite, since adjectives like *dynamite* don't belong in a resume), report that you were Salesperson of the Month for six months running.

Underwhelming

As you can come to appreciate more in Chapter 7, you need to do more in your resume than to simply list the specific functions you held in your previous jobs. *What* you did is obviously important. More important to an employer, though, is the impact of what you did — your accomplishments. The fact that you were the purchasing agent for a donut-making company is nice, but of more interest is the fact that you reduced purchasing expenditures by 15 percent in your first year.

Longwindedness

The extent to which a resume is "longwinded" has less to with how *long* it is — whether it's a one-pager or a two-pager — and more to do with the language you use when describing your past experience. Don't fall victim to the misconception that the best way to make a mundane task appear more important is to dress it up in lofty language.

If one of the things you did in your last job was to check the accuracy of invoices, think twice before you write, "Ensured the numerical veracity of documents sent to customers in order to effect the collection of funds due for purchases." If you were a short-order cook, say so. Don't say, "Assisted in daily preparation of large quantities of consumable items in a fast-paced setting."

Editorializing

Your opinions on matters such as why a particular project didn't work out or why you had to leave a job don't really belong in a resume. In other words, don't write, "Project would have been much more successful if the birdbrain I had for a boss had let me do it my way," or this gem that actually appeared: "Reason for leaving: Boss was as twisted as a pretzel." Keep your views and sentiments to yourself, as valid as they might be.

Overpersonalizing

Apart from the basics — your name, address, and phone number — do not include in your resume any information that relates to your personal life. Don't mention your age, your height, your weight, the color of your eyes, the kind of dog you own, your marital status, the number of children you have, the condition of your health, or how many push-ups you can do. Don't talk about your hobbies (unless they are career related or reveal some aspect of your personality — the fact that you run marathons, for example — that could shed positive light on your personal qualities). Don't mention your favorite author or favorite food; an employer who spends seconds looking over your resume isn't going to care.

Resumespeak

The most effective resumes are written in plain, simple language. Yes, the writing style you use in your resume should be professional and businesslike, and, yes, you should avoid slang and trendy words. But be equally wary of business jargon, and in particular go easy on businessese: words and phrases such as "assisted in the facilitation of" and "optimized."

BLOOPERS

Yes, someone actually wrote this in a resume

Before knuckling down and getting into the actual business of getting your resume written, how about a little comic relief, resume style? The following phrases are excerpts from resumes that have been submitted over the years to Robert Half, the founder of Robert Half International Inc., who collects them for a monthly column for *National Business Employment Weekly* called "Resumania" (note that certain details have been changed to protect the identity of the job seeker):

✔ "My intensity and focus are at inordinately high levels, and my ability to complete projects on time is unspeakable."

✔ "Education: Curses in liberal arts, curses in computer science, curses in accounting."

✔ "Instrumental in ruining entire operation for a Midwest chain store."

✔ "Personal: Married, 1992 Chevrolet."

✔ "I have an excellent track record, although I am not a horse."

✔ "I am a rabid typist."

✔ "Created new market for pigs by processing, advertising and selling a gourmet pig mail order service on the side."

✔ "Exposure to German for two years, but many words are not appropriate for business."

✔ "Proven abiliy to track down and correct erors."

✔ "Personal interests: Donating blood. 14 gallons so far."

✔ "I have become completely paranoid, trusting completely nothing and absolutely no one."

✔ "References: None, I've left a path of destruction behind me."

✔ "Strengths: Ability to meet deadlines while maintaining composer."

✔ "Don't take the comments of my former employer too seriously, they were unappreciative beggars and slave drivers."

✔ "My goal is to be a meteorologist. But since I possess no training in meteorology, I suppose I should try stock brokerage."

✔ "I procrastinate — especially when the task is unpleasant."

✔ "I am loyal to my employer at all costs . . . Please feel free to respond to my resume on my office voice mail."

✔ "Work History: Unsuccessfully searched for a job, incompletion of graduate program, took Bar exam and failed."

✔ "Qualifications: No education or experience."

✔ "Disposed of $2.5 billion in assets."

✔ "Accomplishments: Oversight of entire department."

✔ "Extensive background in accounting. I can also stand on my head!"

✔ Cover letter: "Thank you for your consideration. Hope to hear from you shorty!"

Chapter 6
Deciding Which Resume Style Is for You

· ·

In This Chapter
▶ The chronological resume
▶ The functional resume
▶ The combination resume

· ·

*B*efore you sit down to decide what you're going to actually say in your resume, you have to decide which type of resume you should be writing. *Type* doesn't mean the design or basic look of the resume — the color paper you choose, the typeface, and so on. It refers instead to the way you organize, sequence, and control the emphasis of the information that you include in the resume.

Fortunately, you won't have to rack you brain to make the appropriate choice. You have only three general options, each with its own rationale. And the third one is a combination of the first two. The three types of resumes are as follows:

✔ Chronological

✔ Functional

✔ Combination

Now take a closer look at each type.

The Chronological Resume: By the Numbers

The chronological resume shown on the following page lists your work experience in — guess what? — a chronological sequence — except that it's in reverse. This is, by far, the most commonly used type of resume today and the one that is the most familiar to employers.

Bambi Page
3412 Deer Path Lane
Dayton, OH 45415
(111) 555-0987

SUMMARY
CPA with 11 years' experience financial management reporting, including two years' public accounting and five years' cost accounting. Emphasis on food service industry. Extensive supervisory experience; involved with project development and network accounting systems; proficient with Lotus 1-2-3, dBASE, Paradox, and other software packages.

WORK EXPERIENCE

January 1989 - Present
XYZ Corporation/UltraFresh Food Division, Dayton, OH, Fiscal Director
Dual report to COO and CFO. Prepared operational budget of $38 million and $8 million capital budget. Maintained cost accounting system for division. Developed cost standards and variance analyses for use in company's seven geographical regions. Assisted with coding and pricing of manufacturing and marketing procedures. Accomplishments include:

• Reorganized accounting and reporting structure within division, providing enhanced analysis and control. Profits increased 21 percent in first year of program.

• Designed and implemented weekly managerial accounting seminars designed to improve fiscal responsibility of all division managers by reviewing and teaching techniques to maximize revenue and minimize expenses. Cut costs 17 percent over two-year period.

• Developed capital budget monitoring system for justifications and expenditures to ensure most beneficial use of capital funds.

July 1986 - December 1988
Worldwide Widget; Cincinnati, OH, Manager of Cost and Budget
Reported to director of financial planning. Prepared operating budget. Analyzed and recommended revenue enhancing and cost-cutting measures. Accomplishments include:

• Reduced costs by 15 percent within first year.

• Organized and taught education series of courses for non-accountants to improve fiscal responsibility of managers.

August 1984 - June 1986
Big Six Accounting, Cleveland, OH, Staff Accountant
Responsible for audit tasks; provided technical accounting assistance on management consulting engagements as part of audit staff. Clients included retailers and food companies (McJack's, Veggie King, Ola-Cola), manufacturers, government, nonprofit agencies, and others.

EDUCATION
B.S. Business, Upper State University, 1984
Emphasis on accounting

OTHER INFORMATION
- Certified Public Accountant in Ohio
- Advanced Member of Financial Specialists of America

Advantages

The principal advantage of a chronological resume is that it gives employers what they're looking for: an easy-to-follow snapshot of your work experience. Employers prefer this type of resume over others because it gives prominence to what many people consider the most important criteria for hiring: what you are doing and accomplishing *right now* — at this particular stage in your career, as opposed to what you did ten years ago or when you were a sophomore in high school. The chronological resume is especially recommended if you fall into either of the following categories:

✔ The position you are going after is in a field in which you have a solid and consistent record of progress.

✔ The strongest aspect of your work experience is reflected in your most *recent* job, especially if it is a job that you still hold or have only recently left.

Describing your work history in reverse chronological fashion showcases your qualifications and strengths to good advantage.

Disadvantages

The principal *disadvantage* of a chronological resume is that it can lock you into a sequence that may not work to your benefit in certain situations.

Say the specific aspect of your work history that has the most bearing on the job you are now applying for relates to a position that you held four or five years ago. And say that you have had two or three jobs since then. In a chronological resume, you have no choice but to position the description of the job that you want to highlight somewhere in the middle of the resume rather than near the top.

Chronological resumes can also be troublesome in the following situations:

✔ You are looking to change careers, and your most recent position has no relationship to the job for which you are now applying.

✔ You have worked exclusively in one industry and are applying for a job in a different industry.

✔ You are seeking an entry-level position and have almost no work experience.

✔ You have been a chronic job-hopper over the past several years and have less than one year in most of the jobs you would be listing in the resume.

✔ Your employment history has large gaps — significant chunks of time in which you were out of work, voluntarily or otherwise.

Note: The purpose of the resumes included in this chapter is simply to illustrate the differences in the three types of resumes. They are adaptations of actual resumes in which the names of people, places, dates, and so on have been changed. Don't concern yourself for now about the design or wording of these resumes. These matters are the focus of Chapters 7 and 8.

The Functional Resume: Use with Care

The functional resume is organized around your skills, experiences, and accomplishments and not on the specific jobs you have held at various points in your career. It omits entirely or mentions only in broad terms the jobs you've held and when you held them.

Overall, a functional resume warrants consideration if you fall into any of the following categories:

- ✔ You are an entry-level job seeker with no significant work-related experience to speak of.

- ✔ You are reentering the workforce after a lengthy absence, and little of your work history has bearing on the kind of job you are trying to find.

- ✔ You are applying for a job in which your qualifications, presented in strict chronological form, would not portray you as an especially strong candidate.

- ✔ You've held several jobs, but those jobs do not demonstrate growth in responsibility or importance.

If you are going to use a functional resume, spend extra time on your cover letter (see Chapter 9) to explain why you haven't gone into detail about your work experience.

Advantages

The chief advantage of a functional resume is that it enables you to give prominence to those aspects of your background likely to be of special interest to a would-be employer. Functional resumes also serve to shift the focus *away* from aspects of your background (long periods of being out of work, for example) that might hurt your chances of getting by the initial screening process. As the resume on the following page shows, the functional resume calls immediate attention to your accomplishments.

John E. Begood
3412 Memory Lane
Dayton, OH 45415
(111) 555-0987

SUMMARY

CPA with 11 years' experience financial management reporting, including two years' public accounting and five years' cost accounting. Emphasis on food service industry. Extensive supervisory and project development experience. Familiar with network accounting systems; proficient with Lotus 1-2-3, dBASE, Paradox, and other software packages.

EXPERIENCE

General Accounting

Have extensive experience in ensuring control over financial issues as they relate to corporate mission. Have prepared operational budgets in excess of $38 million and have played key role in reorganizing the accounting and reporting structure within divisions, providing enhanced analysis and control. Profits in one program increased 21 percent in first year.

Cost Accounting

More than five years' experience maintaining cost accounting on division level. Proven experience in developing cost standards and variance analyses for companies with regional operations. Assisted with coding and pricing of manufacturing and marketing procedures.

Management and Training Skills

Have designed and implemented managerial accounting seminars designed to improve fiscal responsibility of all division managers by reviewing and teaching techniques to maximize revenue and minimize expenses. These seminars, in one instance, cut accounting costs 17 percent over a two-year period. Developed capital budget monitoring system for justifications and expenditures to ensure most beneficial use of capital funds.

EDUCATION
B.S. Business, Upper State University, 1984
Emphasis on accounting

OTHER INFORMATION
- Certified Public Accountant in Ohio
- Advanced Member of Financial Specialists of America

BLOOPERS

Yes, someone actually wrote this in a resume

These excerpts come from resumes collected by RHI founder Robert Half, who writes a monthly column that features resume bloopers, called "Resumania," for *National Business Employment Weekly.* (Note that certain details in these resumes have been changed to protect the identity of the job seeker.)

✔ "Please disregard the attached resume — it is terribly out of date."

✔ "Insufficient writing skills, thought processes have slowed down some. If I am not one of the best, I will look for another opportunity."

✔ "Seek challenges that test my mind and body, since the two are usually inseparable."

✔ "Referees available on request."

✔ "An obsession for detail; I like to make sure I cross my i's and dot my t's."

✔ "Typing Speed: 756 wpm."

✔ "Note: Keep this resume on top of the stack. Use all the others to heat your house."

✔ "Work experience: Dealing with customers' conflicts that arouse."

✔ "Here are my qualifications for you to overlook."

✔ "Work Experience: Responsibilities included checking customers out."

✔ "I don't usually blow my own horn, but in this case, I will go right ahead and do so."

✔ "Personal Goal: To hand-build a classic cottage from the ground up using my father-in-law."

✔ "Excellent memory; strong math aptitude; excellent memory; effective management skills; and very good at math."

✔ "My experience in horticulture is well-rooted."

✔ "Experience with LBM-compatible computers."

Disadvantages

The major disadvantage of functional resumes — and it is a *big* disadvantage — is that many employers view them with suspicion. Yes, your strengths and your accomplishments are important to a would-be employer. Most employers, though, are interested in the context as well: They want to know what specific job you held that enabled you to demonstrate the skills you describe in a functional resume. They want to know how recent that experience was. They would like to see, if possible, some continuity.

CAUTION!

The less information you offer about the actual dates you held certain jobs, the more suspicions you arouse. Justifiably or not, many employers assume that if you're using a functional resume, you probably have something to hide.

The Combination Resume: A Good Mix

The combination resume — sometimes referred to as the *chrono-functional resume* — is rapidly becoming the resume of choice among many career counselors. As you can see from the resumes on the following two pages, this type of resume combines features of both chronological and functional resumes. It showcases your skills and accomplishments but also provides the reader with a clear — if thumbnail — glimpse of your work history.

The combination resume is worth considering if you fall into any of the following categories:

- ✔ You are looking to change careers and want to highlight your general skills rather than specific skills that relate to your past jobs.

- ✔ You have had no luck at all in getting past the screening process with a chronological resume.

- ✔ You are applying for a job that interests you and that you think you can handle, but the connection between your work history and that particular job could be stronger.

Advantages

The principal advantage of a combination resume is that, like the functional resume, it enables you to establish early on what you have accomplished in your career and what skills and attributes you can offer a potential employer. But because you also include in this type of resume a description of your work history, you diffuse the suspicions that often arise when this information is omitted.

Disadvantages

The only disadvantage of the combination resume is that some employers — those who prefer chronological resumes — may assume that you are attempting to conceal certain aspects of your background. All in all, however, this is not a disadvantage that you have to concern yourself with now that combination resumes are becoming increasingly common.

John E. Begood
3412 Memory Lane
Dayton, OH 45415
(111) 555-0987

SUMMARY

CPA with 11 years' financial management reporting, including two years' public accounting and five years' cost accounting. Emphasis on food service industry. Extensive supervisory and project development experience. Familiar with network accounting systems; proficient with Lotus 1-2-3, dBASE, Paradox, and other software packages.

EXPERIENCE

General Accounting

Have extensive experience in ensuring control over financial issues as they relate to corporate mission. Have prepared operational budgets in excess of $38 million and have played key role in reorganizing accounting and reporting structure within divisions, providing enhanced analysis and control. Profits increased 21 percent in first year of program.

Cost Accounting

More than five years' experience maintaining cost accounting on division level. Proven experience in developing cost standards and variance analyses. Assisted with coding and pricing of manufacturing and marketing procedures.

Management and Training Skills

Have designed and implemented managerial accounting seminars designed to improve fiscal responsibility of all division managers by reviewing and teaching techniques to maximize revenue and minimize expenses. These seminars, in one instance, cut accounting costs 17 percent over two-year period. Developed capital budget monitoring system for justifications and expenditures to ensure most beneficial use of capital funds.

WORK HISTORY

1989 - present: XYZ Corporation/UltraFresh Food Division, Dayton, OH; Fiscal Director

1986 - 1988: Worldwide Widget, Cincinnati, OH; Manager of Cost and Budget

1984 - 1986: Big Six Accounting, Cleveland OH; Staff Accountant

EDUCATION

B.S. Business, Upper State University, 1983
Emphasis on accounting

Other Information

- Certified Public Accountant in Ohio
- Advanced Member of Financial Specialists of America

HENRY HYREME
29 Turnbill Rd.
Denver, CO 89745
(111) 555-2839

SUMMARY

— Highly responsible, well organized, and self-motivated
— Dynamic leadership qualities/team player
— Excellent written and oral communication skills
— Multilingual and familiar with several cultures

ADMINISTRATION AND LEADERSHIP EXPERIENCE

— Administered and coordinated various types of government and commercial contracts including NASA and Department of Defense
— Negotiated contract terms and conditions, completed a mutual winning negotiation on the essential elements of a contract: delivery schedule, specifications, pricing, and contract terms
— Consistently received excellent rating from customers for staying within cost and schedule
— Co-chair of company's communications committee, established effective communications channels that improved the flow of information internally and externally

FINANCIAL SKILLS

— Prepared and coordinated contract budget with program and program manager, properly allocating necessary funds and work hours associated to each particular task
— Monitored contract spending on a weekly basis to ensure that expenditures did not exceed allocated funds, particularly in fixed-price contracts
— Prepared and presented monthly detailed Accounts Receivable reports of major accounts to senior management

INTERNATIONAL SKILLS

— Knowledge of diverse cultural backgrounds, including European, Asian, and American
— Experience in living and working overseas, in the Far East and in Europe
— Speak French and Japanese

WORK HISTORY

Contracts Coordinator	Felson International, Denver, CO	1989 to Present
Contract Management	First National, Denver, CO	1987 to 1989
Operations Administrator	Amityville Airport, Amityville, FL	1985 to 1987

EDUCATION

Downstate University, MBA International Business
Upstate University, BA Business Finance

BLOOPERS

Reasons for leaving

Robert Half, founder of Robert Half International, Inc., advises job seekers to refrain from including "reasons for leaving" on a resume. "The time to discuss that is in the interview," says Half. Here are some humorous examples that he has collected over the years:

✒ "The boss said the end of the world is near." (This might be a good time to take that trip to Hawaii you've been putting off.)

✒ "Was met with a string of broken promises and lies, as well as cockroaches. . . ." (That's some welcoming committee!)

✒ "Fired because I fought for lower pay." (Probably not a very popular employee.)

✒ "I was working for my mom until she decided to move." (Didn't she leave a forwarding address?)

✒ "I was gunned down in the political crossfire." (Texas. Where else?)

✒ "Extreme isolation. I worked at the bottom of the Grand Canyon and the parking lot was eight miles away." (Many great Americans started at the bottom.)

✒ "I shared an office with two heavy smokers and the plant manager's dog. It was best for my lungs and my sanity to resign."

Chapter 7
Writing Your Resume

● ●

In This Chapter

▶ Performing sentence surgery

▶ Organizing your resume

▶ Taking a closer look at each section

▶ Making your resume computer friendly

▶ Customizing: Is it worth the effort?

▶ Sending your resume to a database service

● ●

This chapter is tailor-made for you if (1) you do not currently have a resume and are preparing one for the first time or (2) you currently have a resume, but it doesn't seem to be getting you anywhere and you figure that it might be time to revitalize it. You've come to the right place.

This chapter takes you through the process of writing a resume step by step. Obviously, you have to tailor much of this advice to your own situation. But if you follow these guidelines, the overall process of writing your resume should go far more smoothly and take far less time than you might imagine. You may actually enjoy yourself. More important, you will wind up with a resume that you're comfortable with and that will serve you well in your job search.

Sentence Surgery: Five Tips for Better Resume Writing

First the good news. You do not have to be William Shakespeare to compose a solid, well-organized, professional-looking resume. All you need are the ability to express your ideas in proper English and an understanding of how a resume should be organized and written.

Being able to handle the basics of English — grammar, spelling, punctuation, proper word usage, and so forth — has become a critical skill in today's e-mail, facsimile-driven business environment. If you lack confidence in your ability to use English properly, think about enrolling in a writing workshop or community college course. Also, get a hold of the classic book *The Elements of Style* by William Strunk and E. B. White (Macmillan).

Now the bad news. You can forget most of the rules and principles you were taught when you were writing book reports and term papers in high school or college. Those principles simply do not apply to resumes. Resumes are *business* documents. They follow certain conventions that business people take for granted but that most English teachers would consider incorrect.

Following are five simple writing principles that apply specifically to resumes. All of them should come in handy when you begin to string words together in your resume, particularly when the time comes to describe your work history.

Avoid the first person pronoun

The pronoun *I* has no place in a resume — and for a logical reason: Who else would you be talking about if not yourself?

Instead of this:

I demonstrated professionalism, tact, and diplomacy while I worked with our customers in high-pressure situations.

Write this:

Demonstrated professionalism, tact, and diplomacy while working with customers in high-pressure situations.

Instead of this:

I managed a department whose chief responsibility was to oversee safety audits. I wrote all audit reports and conducted management briefings.

Write this:

Managed a department whose chief responsibility was to oversee safety audits. Wrote audit reports and conducted management briefings.

Notice that the second version of each example begins with an *action verb.* Beginning most of your sentences with action verbs may not have been standard practice when you were writing term papers, but this practice is accepted and recommended in resumes.

Keep your sentences short and don't worry about fragments

Resumes call for short, crisp statements. These statements do not necessarily have to be complete sentences; you can frequently leave out the articles *a, an,* and *the.*

Instead of this:

Spent three years working on major accounts, as both a lead generator and a closer, demonstrating proven skill in organizing and managing a territory with efficiency as well as in developing customer databases.

Write this:

Spent three years working on major accounts. Generated leads and closed sales. Demonstrated proven skill in organizing and managing a territory and in developing customer databases.

Instead of this:

I was involved in the creation and implementation of statistical reports for a large metropolitan hospital, which required the use of spreadsheet software for cost analysis and, in addition, the creation of a database to track patient visits.

Write this:

Created and implemented statistical reports for large metropolitan hospital. Analyzed costs with spreadsheet software. Created database to track patient visits.

Or try a bulleted format:

- ✔ Created and implemented statistical reports for large metropolitan hospital.
- ✔ Analyzed costs with spreadsheet software.
- ✔ Created database to track patient visits.

Use plain English

Don't be victimized by the myth that the bigger the word you use, the more impressed the reader will be with your intelligence. Keep things simple. Go easy on the adjectives. And be especially wary of those grammatical constructions known as *nominalizations* — that is, nouns that are built around verbs and become part of a bulky phrase that can just as easily be expressed in a single word. See the examples in Table 7-1.

Table 7-1	Using Plain English
Bulky Phrase	*Better*
Effected the solution of	Solved
Engaged in the operation of	Operated
Offered assistance in the facilitation of	Helped facilitate

Use bullet statements when appropriate

You usually have a choice when you are writing your resume to combine a series of related statements into a single paragraph or to list each sentence in that paragraph as a separate statement, each occupying its own line. There are pros and cons for each option, and sometimes you have to base your decision on the *amount* of information you need to get across.

Bulleted information is more readable and tends to stand out more than the same information contained within a paragraph. But bulleted information also takes up more room. Your best bet is to combine the two, as demonstrated in the work history discussion later in this chapter.

If you decide to express information in bulleted style, keep the bulleted items brief and pay attention to parallelism. That is, try to make all the items in a sequence adhere to a similar grammatical pattern.

Examples of *nonparallel* statements include

- ✔ Reconcile all statements for cardholders
- ✔ Purchases are approved
- ✔ Have experience in performing training of tellers

Examples of *parallel* statements include

- ✔ *Reconcile* statements
- ✔ *Approve* purchases for Marketing department
- ✔ *Train* tellers

Go from general to specific

Sequence the information in a section by beginning with a general statement and following it with more specific ones.

Instead of this:

Supervised training of seven toy-making elves. Responsible for all toy-making and customer-related activities in Santa's workshop. Answered customer complaints during peak season. (Note that the second of these two sentences is more general than the first.)

Write this:

Responsible for all toy-making and customer-related activities in Santa's workshop. Supervised training of seven toy-making elves. Answered customer complaints during peak season.

Section by Section: How Resumes Are Organized

Resumes should be divided into specific sections that cover different aspects of your background and qualifications. The names of the sections can vary somewhat, but the sequence stays pretty much the same regardless of the names you use. Here's a brief look at the sections of a typical resume, presented in the most common sequence:

- ✔ **Heading:** Your name, address, telephone number, and so on
- ✔ **Objective** (optional): A statement that briefly spells out the type of position or opportunity you are looking for
- ✔ **Summary** (optional): Two or three sentences that sum up key elements of your background, skills, and attributes
- ✔ **Experience:** Can also be described as professional experience or work experience; a summary of the jobs you've held and the general responsibilities and duties you performed in those jobs
- ✔ **Education:** Your educational credentials: colleges or universities attended, degrees earned, and so on

If you are a recent college graduate with limited job experience, the education section should come before the work experience section.

INSIDE SCOOP

Resume length

- 64 percent of executives believe that the preferable length for an *executive* resume is *two pages*.

- 73 percent of executives believe that the preferable length for a *staff-level* resume is *one page*.

Source: Robert Half International Inc.

- **Other:** The Other section of the resume can contain any number of things, depending on your background and the kind of position you seek. It may include special skills, memberships, computer skills, or language proficiency — anything that might enhance your appeal to a prospective employer.

- **Personal:** Years ago, it was common practice to include in your resume a short summary of personal data, such as your age, your marital status, and your health. Because of current discrimination laws, this section is no longer appropriate. Omit it.

Taking a Closer Look at Each Section

Now that you have a general idea of how a typical resume is organized, take a closer look at each section and how you should deal with it in your own resume.

The heading

The heading is nothing more than your name, address, and appropriate phone number(s). A no-brainer. Obviously, the heading goes at the top of the resume, and it usually looks better centered (see Chapter 8 for more specific formatting advice).

The only issue involving the heading of your resume that might stop you in your tracks is whether you should include your work telephone number (assuming that you are still employed). Rule of thumb: You are better off omitting the work number, even if your current employer is aware that you're looking for a job. When some employers see a work number, they may take it as a sign that you have been let go from your previous job and are simply using the offices of your former employer as your base.

The only conditions that might lead you to include your work number in the resume are as follows:

- ✔ You're not worried about your current employer finding out that you're looking for a new job.
- ✔ You cannot be reached conveniently at any other number.

If you feel that you must include it, and particularly if it's not a direct line, you can always ask politely in the cover letter that the caller use discretion when calling you at work.

The objective

Beginning your resume with a statement that spells out your *career objective* is a good idea for some people and a not-so-good idea for others.

It's a good idea if the objective you've established matches the job for which you are applying. This is why some job seekers — thanks to the miracle of word processing — customize the objective section of their resumes for the job they're pursuing.

But here's the catch: If the objective section is to work in your favor, it should be reasonably specific. It has to define your objective within a reasonably narrow frame. It also has to summarize as briefly as possible why you have chosen that objective.

Here are three examples of objectives that illustrate too much specificity (overkill); not enough specificity (underkill); and just the right amount.

Overkill

An entry-level editorial position in publishing, preferably at a publishing house that specializes in romance novels that take place in Europe during the latter part of the 19th century. This would enable me to apply the knowledge I gained about 19th century Europe through the five courses I took in college, as well as the trip I took to Europe during my senior year with my best friend, Carla.

Underkill

An entry-level position that would enable me to utilize my organizational and communications skills.

About right

An entry-level editorial position at a magazine that would give me an opportunity to apply my background in English and my three years' experience as editor of my college newspaper.

You should consider using an objective only when you are dead certain that you want only one type of job and are not interested in even talking to anyone about anything different.

You should *never* include an objective when you intend to use only one resume version but intend to send it out to a variety of companies offering a variety of different positions.

The summary

The summary (not to be confused with the objective) explains who you are and what you can offer a prospective employer. It should come at the beginning of the resume, just beneath the heading or below the objective. It can take the form of a single sentence, a paragraph, or a series of bulleted points.

You can approach the summary section in one of two ways: as a specific, highly condensed description of your professional background; or as a general description of your skills and attributes. Most resume experts recommend that — if possible — you focus on your professional background, beginning with a general statement that spells out what you do (computer programmer, sales professional, beekeeper, or whatever) and how long you've been doing it. In any case, the summary section should be brief and highly focused.

Here are some examples of summary statements that can serve as a model for you:

- *Senior training development manager with more than 16 years of experience in designing and implementing innovative strategies to effectively leverage human resources. Strong human resources generalist background with a track record of successfully driving strategies and initiatives.*

  The same information in bulleted form looks like this:

  - Senior training development manager with more than 16 years of experience in designing and implementing innovative strategies to effectively leverage human resources.

  - Strong human resources generalist background.

  - Proven track record of successfully driving strategies and initiatives.

- *Responsible, organized self-starter with strong people skills, a varied sales background. Team-oriented. Proven ability to meet monthly sales quotas.*

- *More than 12 years of administrative experience in university settings. Organized, detail-oriented, reliable. Excellent communication skills. Proven aptitude in all major word processing programs, plus Microsoft Excel, PowerPoint, and Access.*

Three guidelines for writing stronger summaries

✔ Don't be afraid to toot your horn a little bit, but avoid superlatives. They can hurt your credibility.

✔ When you send your resume to a large company, stress those elements of your background that reflect your ability to work

effectively in a large organization — that is, *teamwork.*

✔ When you send your resume to a small company, emphasize your versatility and your ability to work without close supervision.

The work history section

The work history section is, of course, the most important section of your resume and the section you need to focus on more than any other. Each position you list in this section should contain the following information:

1. The job title (if you had one)

2. The company (along with city and state)

3. When you held the job (assuming that you are writing a chronological or combination resume, as explained in Chapter 6)

4. Your general responsibilities and most important duties

5. Your accomplishments

The following sections walk you through some of the decisions that you have to make as you write this section of your resume.

Company or job title: Which should come first?

This may seem like a silly question, but the sequence can be important. The answer really depends on which aspect of your background you want to emphasize. Compare the following two examples:

THE WALT DISNEY COMPANY, Burbank, CA   **March 1990 to present**
Manager of Telecommunications

MANAGER OF TELECOMMUNICATIONS   **March 1990 to present**
Nobody-Heard-of-It Corporation, Nowheresville, NC

The first example, of course, emphasizes the name of the company. And with a well-known company like Walt Disney Studios, that name can generate some interest.

The second emphasizes the position — Manager of Telecommunications — and de-emphasizes the fact that not many people have heard of the company you worked for.

Dates: How specific should you get?

The answer to this question depends on the amount of time you actually spent on the job and becomes important when you've held a job for less than a year. If your resume says that you worked for a company from 1993 to 1994, you could have worked one week — December 27, 1993 to January 3, 1994 — or one year — January 1, 1993 to January 1, 1994. So if you held a particular job for more than, say, nine months in any given year, specify the months. If you held the job for fewer than nine months, mention only the years.

Just make sure that you're consistent. If you mention the months in one job description, do so for all job descriptions.

Job descriptions

Two principles should be foremost in your mind as you describe each job:

- ✔ Draw a distinction between the broad responsibility of the job and the specific tasks and duties that you performed as part of that responsibility.
- ✔ Describe what you actually did in a way that calls attention to your accomplishments.

Responsibilities and duties

The distinction between the broad *responsibility* you had in a particular job and the specific *tasks* you performed in that job is not always easy to draw. As a rule, though, it is a good idea to divide the general description of the job into two parts: a sentence or two that describes your overall responsibilities and a lengthier section that describes your duties and accomplishments.

Look at the following examples:

May 1992 – Present
Dining Room Manager, Dribble Dan's Restaurant, Topeka, Kansas

Responsible for training and supervision of more than 25 dining room personnel.

- Oversee all dining room operations
- Recruit and hire all dining room personnel
- Conduct orientation sessions
- Handle all training

April 1991 – March 1994
Office Manager, Bug-in-a-Rug International, Tampa, Florida

Responsible for all administrative operations in 26-person office.

- Established new purchasing system
- Supervised six administrative assistants
- Trained new employees on company software
- Developed account system for factoring

Emphasizing your accomplishments

If any one specific skill underlies the effectiveness of your resume, it is the ability to convert statements that simply *describe* the job you handled into statements that showcase your specific accomplishments in that job. The challenge here is twofold. The first challenge is to determine exactly *what* you accomplished. The second is to use wording that emphasizes those accomplishments.

You may think that you didn't accomplish anything worth emphasizing in your last job. Chances are, though, that you are underestimating yourself. Take some time to think about the positive things that happened as a result of your specific achievements in your last job.

The key to converting statements that simply describe what you did to statements that give a sense of what you accomplished lies in your choice of verbs. Some verbs, by their nature, radiate a sense of *getting something done* — like *accomplished, developed, initiated, increased, created,* and so on. Other verbs or verb phrases are static and more functional, such as *served as, was responsible for,* and *was involved in.* See Table 7-2 for examples in context.

Table 7-2	Using "Accomplishment" Verbs
Type of Verb	**Example**
Functional verb	*Served as* membership chairman for two years.
Result-oriented verb	As membership chairman, *increased* membership by 25% in first year.
Functional verb	*Responsible for* handling travel arrangements for 32-person consulting firm.
Result-oriented verb	As travel administrator for 32-person accounting firm, *reduced* travel expenses by 25% in first year.
Functional verb	*Supervised* five-person sales staff.
Result-oriented verb	*Produced* 25% increase in lead generation by introducing new tracking system to five-person sales staff.

INSIDE SCOOP

Personal best

What follows is a list of words that might help you to describe your best personal qualities in your resume.

active	discreet	practical	will travel
dependable	methodical	tactful	constructive
logical	sophisticated	analytical	hard worker
self-reliant	alert	enthusiastic	resourceful
adaptable	efficient	realistic	will relocate
disciplined	objective	talented	creative
loyal	systematic	conscientious	imaginative
sincere	ambitious	forceful	respected
aggressive	energetic	reliable	

Source: Robert Half International Inc.

The education section

The amount of detail that should go into the education section of your resume depends on two factors: how many years you have been out of school and how relevant your educational background is to the position for which you are applying. The general rule of thumb is that the further along you are in your career, the fewer details and emphasis you should put on your education.

The key guidelines are as follows:

- ✔ **Degree:** Mention the degree you earned before you mention the college or university you attended.

- ✔ **Major field of study:** Include it only if it is relevant to the position you're applying for or if you are a recent graduate.

- ✔ **Honors:** Mention grade point average (GPA) only if it is unusually high (such as *cum laude* or above). Include other honors only if they are highly regarded in your field or if you are a recent graduate.

The miscellaneous section

In the miscellaneous section (sometimes known as *interests* or *special skills*), you list information that doesn't fit into the other sections but may nonetheless pique the interest of some employers. The rule of thumb here is to stick to job-related skills, such as language proficiency or your familiarity with various computer software programs. You can also include in this section associations that you belong to — but, again, mention only those that are career related.

And what about your hobbies? Do *not* go into detail about your personal hobbies — but with this exception: when the hobby is directly related to the job you're interested in or else reveals an aspect of your personality that may be of interest to a potential employer. If you're applying for a job in a field that requires a competitive nature — sales, for example — it may not be a bad idea to mention that you enjoy participating in, say, competitive sports.

Making Your Resume Computer Friendly

Today, more than ever, there's a chance that your resume will never be read — not by a human being, at any rate. That's because a growing number of companies are now taking a computerized approach to screening resumes.

What this means, briefly, is this: Instead of being read by an actual person, your resume is read by a device known as an *optical scanner* and translated into a computer language by *optical character recognition software*. Next, specialized software, such as Resumix or ResTrac, zips through your resume in search of so-called *keywords* and, on the basis of those keywords, stores the resume in one or more databases. These databases generally are organized according to specific occupations. And when the company seeks to fill openings in these occupations, it uses another piece of software to scan the data and then screens resumes based on — and here's the brutal part — how many keywords each one contains.

The implications of this new trend are both obvious and profound. As Joyce Lain Kennedy points out in *Electronic Resume Revolution* (John Wiley, 1995), these "electronic traffic cops" (known generally as *applicant tracking systems* or *job computers*) have no interest at all in the more subtle aspects of resume writing, such as your use of accomplishment-oriented verbs. Nor are these programs interested in most of the personal qualities you would bring to a job. The fact that your resume describes you as a highly motivated, take-charge, bottom-line sort of person may carry some weight with a person who takes the time to read it, but the typical applicant-tracking software couldn't care less.

These tracking systems are programmed to look for *nouns* — more specifically, nouns that represent job titles, departments, and organizations — that reflect specific aspects of your work experience and professional background. If your field is civil engineering, for example, the tracking system designed to screen out the "most qualified" candidates may be looking for words such as Civil Construction, American Society of Civil Engineers, Preliminary Stress Analysis, and Correctional Facility. If you are a human resources specialist, keywords are likely to include any or all of the following: Defined Benefits, Disability Plans, Pensions, Downsizing, and Career Counseling.

The system as it is now evolving in many companies is far from perfect, and even the companies who represent the leading edge in this technology concede that screening candidates on the basis of specific words in a resume rather than the "story" the resume tells does indeed penalize certain candidates and doesn't necessarily produce the most qualified candidates.

For better or worse, though, the trend toward computerized screening of resumes is likely to intensify in the coming years, and you have no choice as a job seeker but to adapt. You need to be truthful, of course; *be careful that a keyword you include is an accurate reflection of your background.* But what you want to do, in particular, is make sure that when presenting an accurate account of your experience, you use words that the applicant tracking system has been programmed to look for. Here are four suggestions for putting this principle to work in your resume:

- ✔ Analyze the wording in the classified ads (especially longer ads) that relate to your occupation. Make note of those words or terms that appear most frequently. If they apply to you, make sure that those words appear in your resume.

- ✔ If you're working with a recruiter, try to find documentation — a job specifications sheet, for example — that lists some of the qualifications.

- ✔ If you know of someone in your occupation who has recently been hired, ask to have a look at his or her resume.

- ✔ Check out the sampling of keywords section in Kennedy's *Electronic Resume Revolution.*

Multiple Resumes: Are They Worth the Effort?

By now, you should appreciate that the more closely the content of your resume matches the qualifications an employer is seeking, the greater the chances are that your resume will survive the initial screening process and that you'll get a chance to be interviewed. Consequently, many job search consultants recommend that you do one of two things whenever possible: prepare not one but several resumes, each keyed to the various targets you will be going after in your job search; or compose a single resume, but be prepared to customize it to specific job openings.

On the surface, the idea of preparing multiple resumes or sending customized resumes to different employers is good advice. But it's not the sort of advice that you can follow casually — and it has limitations. Your resume, remember, is meant to be an accurate representation of your qualifications, professional and educational background, skills, and attributes. And regardless of how much you alter the sequence, wording, and emphasis of the resume's various sections, you can't change the basic facts of your background: who you worked for, what you did, where you went to school, and so on.

Other factors to consider are time, effort, and expense. Preparing multiple resumes can get expensive if you're using an outside service to format and print the resumes. And practically speaking, the only way to customize your original resume to individual inquiries is to have your resume on file on a computer that you have easy access to. Otherwise, you have to write the resume from scratch each time you want to make a minor change — not a good idea.

Does this mean that you should ditch the idea of multiple resumes or of sending out customized versions of your original? Not necessarily. If you're set up to do so and if you're in a highly competitive field in which most candidates are likely to have the same *basic* qualifications, customizing is an option that you should definitely consider. Here are some of the ways you can put the customizing principle to work:

- ✔ Make changes in the length and emphasis of specific job descriptions, depending on what the employer is looking for. For example, if you're a technical specialist and the job you're applying for includes managerial responsibilities, emphasize the managerial aspects of your background.

- ✔ Change the order of bulleted statements, depending (again) on what the job requires.

  The assumption behind this guideline is that you're *not* making anything up, but are highlighting skills that are important to the position. You should simply be rearranging a series of statements that already appear on your original resume.

- ✔ Early in the process, consider preparing two originals: one that emphasizes your professional accomplishments and another that puts slightly greater emphasis on your relevant personal attributes, such as work style. Use the professional-oriented resume for positions in which the job requirements are a close match to your qualifications. Use the other when the job opening is appealing but the match isn't ideal.

INSIDE SCOOP

Achievement test

The candidates who draw the most interest from employers today are candidates whose resumes reveal one or more of the following accomplishments in a previous job. Use this list when you're mentioning your own career achievements:

✔ Increased sales

✔ Generated new business

✔ Introduced or designed new systems

✔ Saved money

✔ Met difficult deadlines

✔ Stayed within budget

✔ Identified problems

✔ Hired and trained outstanding employees

Source: Robert Half International Inc.

Handling Delicate Situations

The assumption underlying nearly everything in this chapter is that you can write your resume in a reasonably straightforward way — without having to draw attention to aspects of your background that may not sit well with an employer.

However, some aspects of your background — long gaps of unemployment, for example — may put you in a negative light. So how do you handle these problems in your resume?

The following lists the most common problems and gives a suggestion or two for approaching them:

✔ **You have periods of long unemployment in your work history.**

If there are several short gaps between jobs, you can opt to use years only. But keep in mind that it is understandable to have a gap of a few months during which you were job hunting. If the gaps are long and numerous, use a functional resume (see Chapter 6) and explain these gaps as best you can in your cover letter.

✔ **You went to college but didn't earn a degree.**

Mention the college — and nothing else. Do not — repeat *not!* — lay claim to a degree you never earned.

> ✔ **The three or four most recent jobs in your work history bear little relation to one another.**

Use a combination resume focusing on the skills that you demonstrated and the experience that you gained from those jobs. Do your best to key those descriptions to the job you're applying for. (See Chapter 6 for more information about the combination-style resume.)

> ✔ **None of the specific jobs described on your resume are directly relevant to the position for which you are applying.**

Use a combination resume built around those skills and attributes that you want to highlight.

> ✔ **You have held the same job for a long time, and it's the only job of significance that you have held in your career.**

Try to divide the job into three or four areas of responsibility and treat each area as if it were a separate job. That is, for each major aspect of your responsibility, write out a general statement of duties followed by three or four sentences that spell out accomplishments.

What You Should Know about Resume Database Services

A rapidly increasing — and not always easy to keep track of — number of companies and organizations are in the business of gathering resumes from job seekers, sorting those resumes into occupational categories, and then using the lists they compile as a source of candidates for client companies. These organizations are known in general as *resume databases* or *resume banks,* and they fall into two general categories: those that are operated by private individuals or groups as a nonprofit service to job seekers in a particular field or occupation, and commercial databases that actively market their databases to employers.

The services operated by individuals and groups often accept your resume at no cost. Placing your resume with one of the commercial resume database services runs you anywhere from $25 to $100, with most services charging on the lower end of this scale.

A closer look

The main thing to bear in mind about resume banks is that they do not *recruit* candidates. They do not actively market you to employers or arrange interviews for you in the way that recruiters do. They generally don't know you by name — only by the information you give them on your resume — and they almost never sit down with you in person. They simply keep your resume on file as though it were a listing in a directory. Those that operate on a for-profit basis make their money by charging companies for the right to use the database as a source of candidates for job openings.

Here's how the game is played.

Employers seeking to fill positions come to database services with a set of qualifications and job specifications. The database services then run searches designed to identify those candidates in the database who meet those specifications. In some cases, the resume database service will get in touch with you and ask whether you want to be a candidate for the opening. In other instances, you will hear directly from the company.

Resume database services run their basic operations in different ways. Most of the better established services limit the resumes they keep on file to professionals in a select industry or to alumni of a particular group of member universities. Most services, in other words, concede that there isn't much point to using a resume database service if you're an entry-level candidate who doesn't have any special skills.

Another difference: Some services simply take your resume as is and sort it according to their classification system. Others send you a form and use answers to the form — as opposed to your resume itself — to create their own documents based on their search criteria.

Yet another difference is how resume database services offer their service to client employees. Some operate exclusively on-line, operating through the Internet or through the career sections of commercial on-line services. Others don't.

Is it worth it?

All things considered, the downside to submitting your resume to a database is small — with one exception. If you're currently employed, your employer might decide to use a database service on which your resume is being carried and may assume that you're actively looking for a new job, which could jeopardize your current job.

The big question, though, is whether the enrollment fee — however small it may be — is worth it. It's not an easy question to answer.

Complicating the decision of whether to use a resume database service is the fact that this fledgling industry has had a number of services that enrolled hundreds or more yearly members and then went out of business a few months later. A second problem is that no one can measure the effectiveness of these services as a job search strategy. No one to date has any reliable statistics on what percentage of people who use resume database services are actually contacted by companies.

If you're interested in getting your resume on a database service, here are some of the questions you should be asking any service that you approach:

✔ How long have you been in business? (Be wary of any resume database service that hasn't been around for at least two years.)

✔ What do you charge, and what do you offer in the way of extras, such as a newsletter?

✔ How much (if any) do you charge for each resume update?

✔ How easy (or cumbersome) do you make it to access your database?

✔ How many client companies do you have, and what arrangement do you have with those companies?

✔ How do you handle confidentiality issues? Will you guarantee confidentiality? Do you get in touch with your clients before you submit the resume to the company, or do you simply send the resume to the company? (This last question is critical if you're looking for a job while you're still employed.)

A partial list of resume database services

The following resume database services have been in business for at least two years.

Career Database

P.O. Box 626
Provincetown, MA 02657
508-487-2238 or 617-876-9521

Cost: $30 for annual membership.

Career Database is open to anyone who wants to enroll. It also offers a variety of job search-related services (career counseling, help in resume preparation, and so on) for additional cost.

Job Bank USA

1420 Spring Hill Rd. Suite 480
McLean, VA 22102
800-296-1USA

Cost: Ranges from no charge to $130 a year, depending on your affiliation.

Job Bank USA was one of the pioneers in the resume database business and draws its candidates primarily from professional and technical societies, trade associations, and alumni associations. Its members are almost exclusively professionals. Your yearly registration fee entitles you to a subscription to the company's newsletter, which covers a variety of topics relating to job searching and career planning.

National Employee Database

418 Ashmun St. Suite 2001
Sault Ste. Marie, MI 49783
800-FONE NED

Cost: $25 a year.

An on-line service (see Chapters 17–19 for more information about on-line job searching) designed primarily for professionals. When you enroll, you are asked to specify those companies to whom you do not wish your resume sent. This service operates through the Internet.

SkillSearch

3354 Perimeter Hill Drive
Suite 235
Nashville, TN 37211-4129
800-258-6641

Cost: $65 initial enrollment fee, $15 per year annual maintenance fee, which includes unlimited updates and a subscription to the quarterly newsletter.

Membership is limited to currently employed professionals with college degrees and at least two years' post-graduate experience. All members come from the nearly 40 alumni associations with which SkillSearch has established a formal working relationship.

BLOOPERS

Yes, someone actually wrote this in a resume

These excerpts that Robert Half collects for his "Resumania" column show you the types of things that *don't* belong in your resume:

✔ "I am married with no children, no house, and no furniture. I can begin working for you on very short notice."

✔ "Military service: Four years in the Army. No hero. Managed to spend all the time in offices. Never wounded. Had malaria twice and received compensation for concussion and jungle rot."

✔ "HOBBIES: Home renovation, golf, bridge, civic organizations, husband, father."

✔ "Professional Experience: Maintained payroll records for five states: Chicago, Georgia, California, and New York."

✔ "My mother lives with me; she is a CPA and can travel."

✔ "I'm relatively intelligent, obedient, and as loyal as a puppy."

✔ "Objectives: Get my employer more than happy; get my wife and children happy; drive my convertible Cadillac in the sun; live the American way."

✔ "Objective: Post as communicative expert in which coordination as an administrative responsibility in pertinence to my related background in light of the relevance to the duties are coherently applied."

✔ "I intentionally omitted my salary history. I've made money and I've lost money. I've been rich and I've been poor. I prefer being rich."

✔ "I'm extremely loyal to my present firm, so please don't let them know of my immediate availability."

✔ "Birthdate: December 2, 1052."

✔ "Work Skills: Strong on interpersonal relationships, typing, filing and reproduction."

✔ "Note: Please don't misconstrue my 14 jobs as 'job-hopping.' I have never quit a job."

✔ "Marital Status: Often. Children: Various."

Chapter 8

Getting Your Resume into Print

• •

• •

*B*ack in the Stone Age — that is, before there were computers — the only way to make sure that your resume was attractive and professional-looking was to hire a professional typist and then go to a commercial printer to have it duplicated.

You can still go this route. Most local storefront printing businesses offer resume design, formatting, and printing services that run between $40 and $100, depending on resume length and number of copies. If, on the other hand, you have access to a computer and a reasonably good printer, you can format and print the resume yourself, allowing the flexibility of multiple resumes.

This chapter shows you how to do it yourself.

A Crash Course in Resume Formatting

First things first. If you intend to design and format your own resume, the first thing to remember is that your name isn't Picasso. In other words, put a rein on your artistic impulses. Don't get mesmerized by the fact that the computer you use gives you a choice of 400 different typefaces in any number of sizes and the ability to use *italics,* **boldface**, and <u>underlining</u>.

The number one principle in resume formatting is to *keep things simple.* A resume must, above all, look neat and professional. To achieve this result, it is best to use only *one* typeface, with devices such as boldface and all caps used solely to *highlight* certain items, such as category headings and job titles.

The resume should follow generally accepted formatting standards, as illustrated later in this chapter. You can vary the basic format in a number of ways and still have it look professional. But going out of your way to make your resume look different from all the other resumes an employer may be receiving is a waste of effort, not unlike showing up for an interview with weird-looking clothing so that the employer will "remember" you.

One other point worth noting: As mentioned in Chapter 7, more and more companies now rely on optical scanners to screen resumes. The increased use of these scanners makes it more essential than ever that your resume meet certain common formatting standards. A highly ornate, script-style typeface may give your resume a distinctive look, but it might be foreign to the typical scanning program, and if the scanning program can't read the typeface, you're out of luck. (Some scanning programs have trouble with italics and underlining as well.)

Choosing a Basic Resume Format

The most widely used resume format is a two-column format in which the left column is much narrower than the right column and is used exclusively for either the names of sections or dates of employment. (You'll see examples of these formats later in this chapter.)

The advantage of the two-column format is that it produces a cleaner, airier look that makes the resume easier to read. But there are disadvantages as well. Two-column formats can be tricky to work with in certain word-processing programs. If you've never worked in the two-column format and if you are not adept at the tab and indentation commands, you can drive yourself nuts trying to get everything to line up.

Another disadvantage of the two-column format is that the extra space it creates on the page gives you a little less room to work with than the one-column format does. Consequently, you may have to use a smaller typeface or else add a page to your resume.

The choice, in the end, comes down to what works best for you. If you can handle the formatting and you're not going to run into space problems, the two-column format is the more attractive, more readable choice. Neither choice, though, is likely to have any impact on whether or not someone reads the resume.

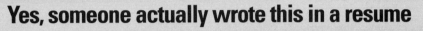

BLOOPERS

Yes, someone actually wrote this in a resume

More resume bloopers from Robert Half's "Resumania" collection show you what *not* to write in your resume:

✔ "My enclosed resume shows my critical career developments. I'm also including other important parts of me."

✔ "My inventive, versatile demeanor will astonish and dazzle the company that is smart enough to offer me full-time employment."

✔ "Self-image: An octagon with smooth, radius angles versus a plain square with sharp corners."

✔ "Size of employer: 6' 1" tall."

✔ "Manipulate cash for bank accounts."

Selecting the Typeface

Typefaces (also known as *fonts*) fall under two general categories: *serif* and *sans serif* (sometimes known as *Gothic*), with each category consisting of dozens upon dozens of different typeface families. The general difference between the two categories (serif and sans serif) is that serif typefaces tend to be somewhat more ornate and traditional. They are sometimes described as having little "hats" and "feet" at the tips of each letter. Sans serif faces, as a rule, are cleaner and more modern (they don't have little "hats" and "feet") but are not necessarily easier to read.

The differences among the families of typefaces that fall within each of the two main categories have mainly to do with the general look, boldness, and spacing of the letters. Futura, for example, is a typeface with a dozen variations: condensed, light, bold, extra bold, and so forth. But those differences shouldn't concern you. As long as you limit your choice to the most common typefaces — those that are standard among most word-processing programs — you can choose whichever one strikes your fancy.

Among the more commonly used serif typefaces are Times (known in the PC world as *Times New Roman* and in the Mac world as *Times Roman*), Palatino, and New Century Schoolbook. The most commonly used sans serif typeface is Helvetica (referred to in the PC world as *Arial*). Other good choices, if you have access to them, are Garamond (a popular serif typeface), ITC Avant Garde Gothic, and Franklin Gothic, which are slightly more distinctive than Helvetica. The following examples illustrate some of these typefaces.

This is Times Roman

This is Palatino

This is New Century Schoolbook

This is Avant Garde

This is Helvetica

This is Franklin Gothic

Sizing up the typeface

The standard range of typeface sizes in resumes runs between 10-point and 14-point. A *point,* in typesetter's lingo, represents $1/72$ of an inch, which means that a typeface measuring 10 points has a height of slightly more than $1/8$ of an inch. Some examples follow:

This is 10 point

This is 11 point

This is 12 point

This is 13 point

This is 14 point

The larger the typeface, of course, the easier it is to read, but the more room it takes up on the page, which means that you have to use fewer words in the resume if you hope to get everything on one page.

But it isn't only the size of the typeface that determines the appearance and readability of the resume. Equally important is the *leading* (pronounced *ledding*). Leading refers to how much space is between the lines. Back in the days of typewriters (remember them?), you referred to space between the lines as single-space, double-space, or triple-space. Most word processors today, though, allow you to make much finer distinctions.

Setting the leading

Unless you tell it otherwise, your word processor creates a line-to-line spacing pattern known as *automatic leading*, which means that the space from line to line is roughly the point size of the typeface itself. Automatic leading for a typeface set at 11 points, for example, is 11 points, similar to what single spacing on a typewriter gives you.

You can vary the leading in any way you want. And if you have space on your resume, it's probably a good idea to add a point or two to the leading simply to make the page look more open and inviting. If you are using a 12-point font, for example, you may want to set the leading at 14 points. Following are some examples of how sections of your resume might look using different sizes and leadings.

This is 10-point type and automatic leading
This is 10-point type and automatic leading
This is 10-point type and automatic leading

This is 11-point type and 14-point leading
This is 11-point type and 14-point leading
This is 11-point type and 14-point leading

This is 12-point type and 15-point leading
This is 12-point type and 15-point leading
This is 12-point type and 15-point leading

This is 14-point type and automatic leading
This is 14-point type and automatic leading
This is 14-point type and automatic leading

This is 14-point type and 18-point leading
This is 14-point type and 18-point leading
This is 14-point type and 18-point leading

Placing and formatting the heading

It is most common to center the heading, but you can also place it flush left at the top of the resume.

Flush left

Lawrence Edgar
1231 Edgar St.
Lawrence, MA 18392
(111) 454-7801
E-mail: le@aol.com

Centered

Lawrence Edgar
1231 Edgar St.
Lawrence, MA 18392
(111) 454-7801
E-mail: le@aol.com

If you want to make the heading of your resume stand out more, you can do a number of things:

✔ Set it all in boldface:

Lawrence Edgar
1231 Edgar St.
Lawrence, MA 18392
(111) 454-7801
Fax: (111) 454-1901

✔ Set everything in caps:

LAWRENCE EDGAR
1231 EDGAR ST.
LAWRENCE, MA 18392
(111) 454-7801
FAX: (111) 454-1901

✔ Set only your name in caps:

LAWRENCE EDGAR
1231 Edgar St.
Lawrence, MA 18392
(111) 454-7801
Fax: (111) 454-1901

Using boldface and other graphic touches

Used judiciously, graphic devices such as boldface, italics, uppercase letters, and underlining can do two things for you. One, they make your resume look attractive; two, they can help you draw attention to those aspects of your background that you want to emphasize.

Be careful, though. When it comes to these graphic devices, less is more. Here are three key guidelines:

✔ At the most, you should use no more than two devices (boldface and uppercase letters, for example) in any resume. Using more gives the resume a jumbled look.

✔ Use underlining only when you are unable to — or choose not to — use boldface.

✔ Use italics sparingly, if at all.

Highlighting (that is, using boldface, underlining, and so on) should be confined to single words and phrases — typically, the names of sections (Summary, Education, and so on) or the heading of a job description, which may include the job title, the name of company, and your years of employment.

Never — repeat *never!* — use boldface to highlight a word or phrase in a sentence, as in the following:

Set up productivity **quality control program** that reduced manufacturing rejects by **20 percent**.

Bullets and paragraphing

Bullet statements have become standard in resumes, and for a logical reason: they are easier to read than sentences embedded in a paragraph. People in a hurry usually prefer to get their information bullet-style rather than work their way through a paragraph.

You can use a number of different symbols to represent a bullet. Look at the following:

— This is an em dash.

• This is a bullet automatically formatted in Microsoft Word.

■ This is a bullet formed by a font family known as Zapf Dingbats in the Mac world and Wingdings in the PC world.

Whichever symbol you use to represent the bullet, pay attention to the alignment of sentences that run more than two lines. If you are using the Paragraph Formatting section of your word processor to set the measurements, you will probably have to set the left margin to 1 point and set the first line to -1 point. Here is the difference:

■ This is a bullet formed by a font family known as Zapf Dingbats in which the first line is evenly aligned with the first letter of the subsequent line.

■ This is a bullet formed by a font family known as Zapf Dingbats in which no attention has been paid to how the letters line up.

Punctuation and capitalization

In general, resumes follow conventional rules of punctuation, but certain issues can be confusing. Here are commonly asked questions — and the answers.

Q. Should you use periods after bullet statements?

A. If the statements are short and take the form of fragments (rather than complete sentences), you don't need to use periods. Just make sure that you're consistent throughout.

Q. Which words should you capitalize?

A. The following words in your resume should always be capitalized:

- Names of companies, persons, countries, cities, and so on
- Job titles and names of departments
- The first word in a new sentence
- The first word in a bullet fragment
- Abbreviations for educational degrees or certifications

Q. How about the little words (*in, of,* and so on) that are part of job titles?

A. Unless you have a specific reason for doing otherwise, use lowercase for these words.

Q. How many spaces should there be between a period and the first letter of the next sentence?

A. One.

Q. Should there be a comma between a title and the name of the company?

A. Yes.

A Folio of Resume Formats

Over the next several pages is a series of resumes, all of which follow a standard format. Accompanying each resume is a set of design and formatting specs. You can use these specs as the basis of your own formatting, or you can decide which format you like and give the specs to either a printer or graphic designer.

Note: To fit the pages in this book, these sample resumes had to be reduced in size. Proportionally, however, they are correct, so you can get an idea of how each typeface, type size, and leading would look.

Resume 1

Typeface: Times

Size: 12-point

Leading: 13-point

Column format: Two columns

Worth noting:

- ✔ The left column is used exclusively for section titles, which are in boldface.
- ✔ The name of the job title is set in uppercase letters, which gives more emphasis to the job than to the company.
- ✔ Uniformly aligned bullet points combine with paragraphs in the Experience section.
- ✔ Names in headings are set in uppercase letters.

CANDACE A. CANDIDATE
3412 Webster Ave.
Cincinnati, OH 10005
111-908-0987

SUMMARY

CPA with eleven years' financial management reporting experience, including two years' public accounting and five years' cost accounting. Emphasis on food service industry. Extensive supervisory experience. Involved with project development and network accounting systems. Proficient in Lotus 1-2-3, dBASE, Paradox, and numerous accounting software packages.

EXPERIENCE

FISCAL DIRECTOR   **May 1989 - Present**
XYZ Corporation/Ultra Fresh Food Division, Dayton, OH

Dual report to COO and CFO. Prepared operational budget of $38 million and $8 million capital budget. Maintained cost accounting system for division. Developed cost standards and variance analyses for use in company's seven geographical regions. Accomplishments include:
- Reorganized accounting and reporting structure within division, providing enhanced analysis and control. Profits increased 21 percent in first year.
- Designed and implemented weekly managerial accounting seminars designed to improve fiscal responsibility of all division managers by reviewing and teaching techniques to maximize revenue and minimize expenses.
- Cut costs 17 percent over two-year period.

MANAGER OF COST AND BUDGET   **Oct. 1985 - Apr. 1989**
Worldwide Widget, Cincinnati, OH

Reported to director of financial planning. Prepared operating budget. Analyzed and recommended revenue-enhancing and cost-cutting measures. Accomplishments include:
- Reduced costs by 15 percent within first year.
- Organized and taught educational series of courses for non-accountants to improve fiscal responsibility of managers.

STAFF ACCOUNTANT   **Sept. 1984 - Aug. 1985**
Big Six Accounting, Cleveland, OH

Responsible for audit tasks. Provided technical accounting assistance on a management consulting assignment as part of audit staff.

EDUCATION

B.S. Business, Upper State University, 1983

OTHER INFORMATION

Certified Public Accountant in Ohio
Advanced Member of Financial Specialists of America

Resume 2

Typeface: Helvetica

Size: 11-point

Leading: 13-point

Worth noting: All other specs are identical to those used in the preceding resume.

PETER RABBIT
3412 MacGregor Ave.
Dayton, OH 45415
111-555-0987

SUMMARY

CPA with eleven years' financial management reporting experience, including two years' public accounting and five years' cost accounting. Emphasis on food service industry. Extensive supervisory experience. Involved with project development and network accounting systems. Proficient in Lotus 1-2-3, dBASE, Paradox, and numerous accounting software packages.

EXPERIENCE

FISCAL DIRECTOR   **May 1989 - Present**
XYZ Corporation/Ultra Fresh Food Division, Dayton, OH

Dual report to COO and CFO. Prepared operational budget of $38 million and $8 million capital budget. Maintained cost accounting system for division. Developed cost standards and variance analyses for use in company's seven geographical regions. Accomplishments include:
- Reorganized accounting and reporting structure within division, providing enhanced analysis and control. Profits increased 21 percent in first year.
- Planned and implemented weekly managerial accounting seminars designed to improve fiscal responsibility of all division managers by reviewing and teaching techniques to maximize revenue and minimize expenses.
- Cut costs 17 percent over two-year period.

MANAGER OF COST AND BUDGET   **Oct. 1985 - April 1989**
Worldwide Widget, Cincinnati, OH

Reported to director of financial planning. Prepared operating budget. Analyzed and recommended revenue-enhancing and cost-cutting measures. Accomplishments include:
- Reduced costs by 15 percent within first year.
- Organized and taught educational series of courses for non-accountants to improve fiscal responsibility of managers.

STAFF ACCOUNTANT   **Sept. 1984 - Aug. 1985**
Big Six Accounting, Cleveland, OH

Responsible for audit tasks. Provided technical accounting assistance on a management consulting assignment as part of audit staff.

EDUCATION

B.S. Business, Upper State University, 1984

OTHER INFORMATION

Certified Public Accountant in Ohio
Advanced Member of Financial Specialists of America

Resume 3

Typeface: Palatino

Size: 12-point

Leading: 14-point

Column format: Two columns

Worth noting:

- ✔ The left column is used exclusively for dates.
- ✔ The resume section titles are centered and set in boldface and uppercase letters.
- ✔ Uniformly aligned bullet points combine with paragraphs in the Experience section.
- ✔ Company names are in boldface; positions are in lowercase.

JENNIFER JOBREADY
3412 Avenue Z
New York, NY 10005
111-555-0987

SUMMARY

CPA with eleven years' financial management reporting experience, including two years' public accounting and five years' cost accounting. Emphasis on food service industry. Extensive supervisory experience. Involved with project development and network accounting systems. Proficient in Lotus 1-2-3, dBASE, Paradox, and numerous accounting software packages.

EXPERIENCE

May 1988 to Present

XYZ CORPORATION, New York, NY
Fiscal Director
Dual report to COO and CFO. Prepared operational budget of $38 million and $8 million capital budget. Maintained cost accounting system for division. Developed cost standards and variance analyses for use in company's seven geographical regions. Assisted with coding and pricing of manufacturing and marketing procedures. Accomplishments include:
- Reorganized accounting and reporting structure within division, providing enhanced analysis and control. Profits increased 21 percent in first year of program.
- Designed and implemented weekly managerial accounting seminars designed to improve fiscal responsibility of all division managers by reviewing and teaching techniques to maximize revenue and minimize expenses.
- Cut costs 17 percent over two-year period.

Oct. 1985 to Apr. 1988

WORLDWIDE WIDGET, Cincinnati, OH
Manager of Cost and Budget
Reported to director of financial planning. Prepared operating budget. Analyzed and recommended revenue-enhancing and cost-cutting measures. Accomplishments include:
- Reduced costs by 15 percent within first year.
- Organized and taught educational series of courses for non-accountants to improve fiscal responsibility of managers.

Sept. 1984 to Sept. 1985

BIG SIX ACCOUNTING, Cleveland, OH
Staff Accountant
Responsible for audit tasks. Provided technical accounting assistance on a management consulting assignment as part of audit staff.

EDUCATION

B.S. Business, Upper State University, 1983

Resume 4

Typeface: Times Roman

Size: 11-point

Leading: 13-point

Column format: Two columns

Worth noting:

- ✔ The left column is used for dates and names of sections, all set in boldface.
- ✔ Job titles are in boldface and in lowercase.
- ✔ Em dashes are used as bullet symbols.

DOLLY MADISON
72-65 East Lansing Rd.
Rodeo, WA 06811
(111) 623-1835

SUMMARY   Ten years of experience in sales and sales training. Proven ability to develop and deliver sales training programs in variety of industries.

WORK EXPERIENCE

Mar. 1991 to Present

Corporate Training Consultant, Merry Melody, Inc., Seattle, WA
Research and prepare information pertaining to product lines. Conduct group seminars to train sales representatives on product information. Use products and visual aids to demonstrate quality, use, and care. Create sales videos with similar information which can be used on demand in lieu of seminars.

Feb. 1988 to Mar. 1991

Broadcast Sales Consultant, WCTB Television, Seattle, WA
On-air television salesperson, marketing fashions, jewelry, and beauty care products to approximately 10 million homes throughout the United States via a televised shopping network.

June 1985 to Jan. 1988

Training Director, Wonderland Tours, Olympia, WA
— Supervised the two-day orientation and training program for newly hired tour guides.
— Rewrote and formatted training manual.

Sep. 1984 to May 1985

Teaching Assistant, Upstate University, Department of Political Science, Upstate, MI
Prepared and delivered lectures to undergraduate students. Read and evaluated research papers.

Mar. 1981 to Aug. 1984

Sales Representative, Compton's Publishing Company, Seattle, WA
— Promoted university textbooks to a clientele of more than 500 professors in the Washington/Oregon territory.
— Attended several sales seminars and continually met all sales goals.

EDUCATION   Upstate University, Upstate, MI, May 1985
M.A., English Literature
Central Upstate College, Upstate, MI, May 1979
B.A., Major: Political Science; Minors: Russian and French

Resume 5

Typeface: New Century Schoolbook

Size: 12-point

Leading: 15-point

Column format: One column

Worth noting:

- ✔ Section titles and job headings are set in boldface.
- ✔ Job titles are in boldface and in lowercase.

DOLLY MADISON
72-65 East Lansing Rd.
Rodeo, WA 06811
(111) 555-1835

OBJECTIVE

A senior position in a corporate training company that will enable me to combine my skills as a trainer and public speaker with my experience in sales and marketing.

WORK EXPERIENCE

Mar. 1992 to Present
Corporate Training Consultant, Merry Melody, Inc., Seattle, WA
Research and prepare information pertaining to product lines. Conduct group seminars to train sales representatives on product information. Use products and visual aids to demonstrate quality, use, and care. Create sales videos with similar information that can be used on demand in lieu of seminars.

Feb. 1988 to Mar. 1992
Broadcast Sales Consultant, WCTB Television, Seattle, WA
On-air television salesperson, marketing fashions, jewelry, and beauty care products to approximately 10 million homes throughout the United States via a televised shopping network.

Apr. 1985 to Jan. 1988
Tour Director, Wonderland Tours, Olympia, WA
Traveled extensively throughout the United States, Canada, and Europe conducting group tours. Prepared and delivered, in an informative, entertaining fashion, ongoing commentary relevant to all areas visited. Responsible for maintaining a high level of interest and enthusiasm among all passengers.

Mar. 1981 to Mar. 1985
Sales Representative, Compton's Publishing Company, Seattle, WA
Promoted university textbooks to a clientele of more than 500 professors in the Washington/Oregon territory. Attended several sales seminars and continually met all sales goals.

EDUCATION

Upstate University, Upstate, MI, May 1985
M.A., English Literature
Central Upstate College, Upstate, MI, May 1979

Resume 6

Typeface: Helvetica

Size: 12-point

Leading: 15-point

Column format: One column

Worth noting: Underline is used instead of boldface.

LISA MARIE FULMER
72-65 East Lansing Rd.
Rodeo, WA 06811
(111) 555-1835

OBJECTIVE
A senior position in a corporate training company that will enable me to combine my skills as a trainer and public speaker with my experience in sales and marketing.

WORK EXPERIENCE
Mar. 1992 to Present
Corporate Training Consultant, Merry Melody, Inc., Seattle, WA
Research and prepare information pertaining to product lines. Conduct group seminars to train sales representatives on product information. Use products and visual aids to demonstrate quality, use, and care. Create sales videos with similar information that can be used on demand in lieu of seminars.

Feb. 1988 to Mar. 1992
Broadcast Sales Consultant, WCTB Television, Seattle, WA
On-air television salesperson, marketing fashions, jewelry, and beauty care products to approximately 10 million homes throughout the United States via a televised shopping network.

Apr. 1985 to Jan. 1988
Tour Director, Wonderland Tours, Olympia, WA
Traveled extensively throughout the United States, Canada, and Europe conducting group tours. Prepared and delivered, in an informative, entertaining fashion, ongoing commentary relevant to all areas visited. Responsible for maintaining a high level of interest and enthusiasm among all passengers.

Mar. 1981 to Mar. 1985
Sales Representative, Compton's Publishing Company, Seattle, WA
Promoted university textbooks to a clientele of more than 500 professors in the Washington/Oregon territory. Attended several sales seminars and continually met all sales goals.

EDUCATION
Upstate University, Upstate, MI, May 1985
M.A., English Literature
Central Upstate College, Upstate, MI, May 1979
B.A., Major: Political Science; Minors: Russian and French

Resume 7

Typeface: Times Roman

Size: 11-point

Leading: 13-point

Column format: Two columns

Worth noting: Underline is used instead of boldface as a highlighting device.

IRWIN B. INTERVEWD
72-65 East Lansing Rd.
Sacramento, CA 06811
(111) 555-1835

OBJECTIVE

A position in a corporate training company that will put to productive use my excellent sales and public speaking skills as a corporate trainer.

WORK EXPERIENCE

Mar. 1992 to Present	Corporate Training Consultant, Merry Melody, Inc., Sacramento, CA Research and prepare information pertaining to product lines. Conduct group seminars to train sales representatives on product information. Use products and visual aids to demonstrate quality, use, and care. Create sales videos with similar information that can be used on demand in lieu of seminars.
Feb. 1988 to Mar. 1992	Broadcast Sales Consultant, KCTB Television, Seattle, WA On-air television salesperson, marketing fashions, jewelry, and beauty care products to approximately 10 million homes throughout the United States via a televised shopping network.
Apr. 1985 to Jan. 1988	Tour Director, Wonderland Tours, Olympia, WA Traveled extensively throughout the United States, Canada, and Europe conducting group tours. Prepared and delivered, in an informative yet entertaining fashion, ongoing commentary relevant to all areas visited. Responsible for maintaining a high level of interest and enthusiasm among all passengers.
Mar. 1981 to Mar. 1985	Sales Representative, Compton's Publishing Company, Seattle, WA Promoted university textbooks to a clientele of more than 500 professors in the Washington/Oregon territory. Attended several sales seminars and continually met all sales goals.
Sep. 1980 to Feb. 1981	Teaching Assistant, Upstate University, Department of Political Science, Upstate, MI Prepared and delivered lectures to undergraduate students. Read and evaluated research papers.

EDUCATION

Upstate University, Upstate, MI, May 1981
M.A., English Literature

Central Upstate College, Upstate, MI, May 1979
B.A., Major: Political Science; Minors: Russian and French

The Final Stretch: Things to Do before You Go to Print

Assuming that you're happy not only with what your resume *says* but also with the way it *looks,* you may be tempted to rush to your nearest printer or high-speed copier. Not yet. Two things remain to be done. The first is to double-check and triple-check your resume for careless errors. (Have a friend give it a quick once-over, too. A pair of fresh eyes can often see errors that you've over-looked many times.) The other is to take your resume out for a "test drive" — that is, get some feedback from people in your field (perhaps a former boss with whom you're still friendly) to find out whether the resume successfully showcases your background and skills.

A short course in proofreading

There are no hidden secrets to proofreading. You simply have to take the time and effort to make sure that there are no errors. You can't simply zip through the resume the same way you would if you were reading a magazine article. You have to focus on every word in every line. The spell checker on your word processor helps, but spell checkers do not pick up words that you inadvertently left out. Nor does it pick up misspelled words that represent the correct spelling of *another* word, such as *there* and *their.*

Here are a couple of tips that may help. The first is to read the resume aloud. Do it slowly. Better still, have someone read a copy of the resume aloud as you are reading it over to yourself.

The second tip is to start at the end of the resume and read backwards. That may sound dumb, but many professional proofreaders do this routinely because it helps to dissociate them from the content so that they can pay attention to typos and misspellings. Pay particular attention to headings; errors in headings often slip by simply because your eyes tend to move quickly from the heading to the paragraph that follows it.

One final note about grammatical errors: If you do not have much confidence in your basic grammar and usage skills (quick test: do you know when to use "whom" instead of "who" and "that" instead of "which"?), find a grammar whiz to double-check your resume for blatant mistakes. Computerized grammar checkers can be of some help, but you can't rely on them entirely. The last thing you want on your resume is an indication that your communications skills may be suspect.

Getting feedback

Having someone whose opinion you trust read your resume before you go to the expense of printing it is always a good idea. Getting this kind of feedback is particularly useful if you are thinking of changing careers and are trying to position your qualifications to appeal to companies in the new field.

Be specific about what you are looking for. Ask the person or people whose opinions you are seeking to focus on the *overall impact* of the resume rather than on individual words or punctuation. In other words, have them concentrate on the big picture. The question you are seeking an answer to, above all, is this: "If the information on my resume were the only information you knew about me, what would it tell you?" If you like the answers you hear and your resume is error free, you're ready to go to print.

Getting your resume printed

The main thing to bear in mind when it comes time to get your resume printed or duplicated is to make sure that the copies you send to prospective employers or recruiters are clean and sharp. There's more at stake here than making a good impression. If the print quality is weak, the resume may not scan well.

You do not necessarily have to use offset printing to get a high-quality, professional-looking resume. A laser-quality printer with a 300 dpi (dots per inch) resolution will give you the quality you need. A high-level copy machine can do the job as well, as long as the original resume is crisp and sharp.

Give some thought, too, to the quality of the paper you use. It costs a few cents more to have your resume duplicated on higher quality paper, but the extra money is worth it.

Chapter 9

Making Your Cover Letter Count

● ●

In This Chapter

▶ Understanding why cover letters matter

▶ Developing a cover letter strategy

▶ Knowing what goes where

▶ Covering the right bases

▶ Sample cover letters

● ●

*I*t's common knowledge that the resume you send to a prospective employer should always be accompanied by a cover letter. What *isn't* common knowledge is that the cover letter in many situations is as important as the resume itself, if not more so.

Here, in brief, are a few of the reasons:

✔ A cover letter is usually the first thing the person who screens your resume looks at — your first chance, in other words, to make a good impression. If the letter looks as though your dog chewed on it or is written in a slipshod manner, you put yourself behind the eight ball right from the start.

✔ A well-focused cover letter enables you to direct the reader's attention to those aspects of your resume that are likely to push the right buttons in specific situations.

✔ A well-researched cover letter enables you to demonstrate, in ways that are impossible in a resume, your knowledge about the company you're writing to and its industry.

✔ A cover letter represents your only means of explaining aspects of your work history — such as unemployment gaps or a lack of direct experience in the field you are applying for — that might otherwise portray you as being "unqualified" for the position.

If a cover letter is to accomplish these objectives for you, you can't do what many job hunters do, which is to rattle off a few lines that basically say, "Here's the resume." Writing an effective cover letter takes time, thought, and effort — all of it highly worthwhile.

INSIDE SCOOP

Cover letters count

How important is the cover letter as compared to the accompanying resume? Sixty percent of executives in an independent nationwide survey commissioned by Robert Half International recently said that cover letters are either equally or more important than resumes.

Developing a Cover Letter Strategy

The most important principle of cover letter writing is to sit down ahead of time and think about what, specifically, you want the letter to accomplish. You should decide ahead of time the one or two key points that you want to convey.

How you answer this question depends, of course, on your particular situation, but here are a few representative strategies, one of which may apply to you. Notice that each strategy generates a letter with a slightly different focus. It can get the reader to do the following:

- Focus on two or three key points in the resume

- Ignore the fact that you may not have the exact background that he or she is looking for and consider you for an interview anyway

- Consider you for an interview even though some areas in your resume raise some questions

Looking at the Basics

Like your resume, your cover letter must look professional. It should always be typed, regardless of how good your penmanship is. It should follow a standard business format, which means proper headings, single-space typing, and block paragraphs. If you can print it on personalized stationery, all the better: Personalized stationery makes a better impression than blank paper. If you don't have personalized stationery, use a high-quality paper and try to use the same color of paper that you're using for your resume.

The following sections address the specifics of the cover letter.

Return address

If your return address isn't already printed on your stationery, it should appear at the top of the letter. You can position it in: the top left, the center, or the top right (see the sample cover letters later in this chapter for examples).

In both instances, the address should be aligned with the rest of the text in the letter. In standard business format, neither your name nor your telephone number belongs in the return address, but a cover letter in a job search situation is an exception to this rule.

Date

The date can go in one of two places: below the return address with an added space between the last line of the address and the date, or a line above the name and address section of the letter.

Name and address of the recipient

Standard procedure in business letters is to include the following information in the address section that precedes the salutation — and in the following sequence:

Line 1. The person's full name (if you have it)

Line 2. The person's title (if you have it)

Line 3. The department (use if you can't access the title)

Line 4. The name of the company

Line 5. Street name and address (or box number)

Line 6. City, state, and ZIP code

Here are some examples:

Mr. Robert Chase
Director of Marketing
Fox & Hound Inc.
125 Tree St.
Edgartown, TN 84983

Ms. Daisy Morris
Vice President
Morning Lily Enterprises
15 Ninth Ave.
Brimstone, OH 09801

Salutation

The main question regarding salutations is whether to refer to the person you're writing to by first name or to use the surname preceded by Mr., Ms., and so on. A good rule of thumb is to use the person's first name only when you've been personally introduced and have already referred to that person by first name in conversation. In either event, the person's name should be followed by a colon, not a comma, as shown here:

Dear Ms. Evans:

Dear Charles:

Dear Dr. Adams:

Ms. versus Miss or Mrs.

The use of Ms. as an all-purpose title is now standard in business. Use it.

Dr., Ph.D., M.D., and other titles

Certain titles — Dr., for example — always precede the person's name, whereas other titles — Ph.D., M.D., R.N., and Esq., for example — come after. Remember, though, it's one or the other. *Never* write the following:

Dr. Howard Johnson, Ph.D., or Dr. Howard Johnson, M.D.

President Mary Jones

Write these titles as follows:

Dr. Howard Johnson

or

Howard Johnson, Ph.D. or Howard Johnson, M.D.

Mary Jones, President

or

Mary Jones
President

If you don't know the person's name

Do your best to get the name and title of the person to whom you are sending the cover letter. It isn't always easy. There isn't much you can do when you're writing to a box number in a classified ad. And even when you have a title and the name of the company, you can't always wrestle the name from a reception-ist who works for a company whose policy is not to give names.

Incidentally, you will generally have better luck getting the right name, spelling, and title of the person you're writing to from the employees in that person's department than you will from the receptionist. And should you get in touch with someone in that department, be candid. Explain that you want to write the department manager a letter and would be grateful for the correct spelling of the manager's name and title.

Be particularly careful about spelling. More than a few prospective employers, when they see their names misspelled or their titles misworded, may assume that you are not an especially thorough person and may not be predisposed to read any further. And even if the person's name and title appear in a classified ad, it still pays to double-check, and here's why: On the outside chance that the newspaper has made a mistake, every letter that arrives is going to have the name of the person misspelled — every letter, that is, but yours.

If you have no luck at all getting a name or a title, "To Whom it May Concern:" will suffice.

Yes, someone actually wrote this in a resume

Get a chuckle at the crazy things other people came up with to put on *their* resumes (from Robert Half's *Resumania* collection), but don't feel compelled to insert this kind of humor into your own job hunting correspondence:

✔ "My complete mastery of the software interface was undermined by jealous peers. You can see the whole story when I sell the screenplay."

✔ "My name is Sam Johnson, but I now prefer to be called Michael, or at least Mike."

✔ "Am allergic to copy toner and scoundrels."

✔ "In addition to my business duties, I care for a very demanding cat, two adorable puppies, a chipper cockatiel, and three fiesty guinea pigs — all of whom insist on a share of my time and attention."

✔ "Handled incoming and outcoming correspondence."

Closing

Any of the following will do the job:

✔ Sincerely,

✔ Sincerely yours,

✔ Yours truly,

✔ Cordially,

Covering the Right Bases

What really matters in a cover letter, of course, is what it *says*. And the following guidelines are designed to help you make sure that what you say in your letter hammers home the message you want to get across.

Writing the opening

The opening paragraph of a cover letter should accomplish two things. First, it should announce the purpose of the letter (even though the purpose may seem obvious). Second, it should give the reader a *compelling* reason to read on.

If you're having trouble figuring out how to encourage the reader to keep reading, here are some suggestions.

Use someone else's name as an introduction

Whenever you can use someone else's name to make the connection between you and the person you're writing to, do so. It is by far the best way to ensure that your letter and your resume get optimal attention.

There is, of course, a catch: The connection has to be legitimate. The name you use has to belong to someone who (1) will be recognized and respected by the person you're writing to, and (2) has given you permission to use his or her name.

The person whose name you use does not have to be a close friend of yours. It can be someone you know casually, someone you met recently at a party or an association meeting, or someone who has interviewed you for a job that you didn't get. The important thing is to get permission to use the person's name. Most people will grant that permission without hesitation.

Here are some examples of openings that use names to good advantage:

- ✔ I'm writing you at the suggestion of Robert Roy, who felt that you may have a need in your company for someone with my background and qualifications.

- ✔ I had a very pleasant two days with your friend, Amy Logan, who urged me to send you the resume I am enclosing.

- ✔ I am writing at the suggestion of our mutual friend, Wally Warble, who told me that you may be looking for an assistant.

- ✔ I recently had dinner with your director of marketing, Sue Salient, who suggested that I write to you and send along my resume.

Demonstrate your knowledge of the company

This is an effective and underused way of generating interest. The idea is to work into your opening paragraph a fact or observation about the company that isn't common knowledge. Such a statement tells the reader that you've done some homework.

Here are some examples:

- ✔ I read with great interest your recent ad in the *Wabash Daily News,* and in light of the work your company is now beginning to do in gene splicing, I thought I might be able to contribute my expertise in this area in a research position.

- ✔ I have been following with great interest the success that your company has been enjoying in developing and marketing tools for left-handed people. That interest has prompted me to send you this letter, along with my resume.

> ✔ I am writing because I was taken by your recent ad in *The Wall Street Journal.* I have been interested in your company for several years and have spent a great deal of time at Jones & Co. writing research reports about your innovative approach to product development. I believe this knowledge would make me a strong candidate for the opening you describe.

Putting meat on the body of the letter

After you've taken care of the opening of the letter, you're ready to focus on the meat of the letter. This section of the letter normally consists of two or three paragraphs that do one or more of the following:

- ✔ Explain briefly your current situation — whether you're presently working, out of work, on assignment, and so on.
- ✔ Tell the reader what you're looking for and why the position you're writing about interests you.
- ✔ Expand upon or call attention to one or two points in your resume.
- ✔ Explain (if necessary) aspects of your resume or background that are not obvious and that could possibly work against you.
- ✔ Tell the reader directly what specific qualities you can bring to the job.

It's not what you want, it's what you can offer

As you write the middle section of your cover letter, one thought, above all, should be foremost in your mind: *"Here is what I can offer you."*

What this means, practically speaking, is that the letter should not focus on what *you* want and what you are interested in. It should focus on what your mix of skills and experience can contribute to the company. Consider these examples:

Here is what *I* want:

I've always been keenly interested in music, and I know I would enjoy working for a recording company.

Here's what I can offer *you*:

I've always been keenly interested in music, and the experience I've had working in bands has given me insights that would help your company attract new talent.

Here is what *I* want:

I know that I would enjoy the dynamic atmosphere that prevails in your company, and I would enjoy working with your clients.

Here's what I can offer *you:*

The dynamic atmosphere that prevails in your company is very much in tune with the atmosphere that I have always worked best in, and I know that my knowledge and passion for this field would enhance the customer relationships that are so fundamental to your company's success.

The "S" word

There's much debate on when to mention the "S" word — salary — in your conversations or correspondence with prospective employers. There are variables, but in general you should postpone salary discussions as long as possible. Only if a want ad requests salary history or requirements should you include that information in your cover letter.

One situation that may warrant a more proactive approach is when you are overqualified for a position but are willing to accept a lower salary than you would normally expect, based on your salary history. In this case, you can mention the salary range you're interested in and possibly deflect any concern that you'll be overpriced for the job.

A Folio of Cover Letters

You can use any of the cover letters that follow as a model. Notice that they all share the following attributes:

- ✔ They're written in a business letter format and have a neat, professional look.

- ✔ The first paragraph of each letter explains the purpose and generates interest, frequently by using a name.

- ✔ The body of each letter focuses on what the writer can *offer* and not what the writer wants.

- ✔ The style of the letters is conversational but still business-like. You don't need to use a lot of jargon or cumbersome sentences.

546 Mountain View Rd.
Washington, TN 28491

May 13, 1995

Mr. Tim Peters
Manager, Customer Training
ABC Inc.
431 Third Ave.
Nashville, TN 28392

Dear Mr. Peters:

I read with great interest your recent ad in the *Nashville Gazette*. From what I know about your company and the work you do in software training, I think I can bring a great deal to the position advertised.

As you can see from the enclosed resume, I am currently working for Computers Anonymous, where I manage a staff of ten people, all of whom are involved on a day-to-day basis with customer training. What interested me about the opportunity you described in your ad was the diversity of products that your company manufactures.

Because I am an incurable computer buff, I am very familiar with virtually all your programs — even your newest database program, which I have just finished teaching myself. More important, though, I understand how intimidated people who are not as involved with computers as I am can be when they encounter a new program, and I work very hard to make the people I train sensitive to this type of intimidation.

I would welcome the opportunity to meet with you in person or to speak with you over the phone. In the meantime, I thank you for your time and your interest, and I hope to hear from you soon.

Sincerely,

Helen Jobready

1823 Lincoln Ave.
Louisville, KY 43090

May 16, 1995

Ms. Julie S. Caesar
Vice President, Marketing
Harvey's Food & Beverage
123 Elm St.
Louisville, KY 00302

Dear Ms. Caesar:

I understand from your assistant, Phil Jennings, that you have an opening in your department for a director of marketing. Phil has given me a general idea of what this job might involve and seems to think, as I do, that I can bring a great deal to this position.

I am currently a brand manager at XYZ Corporation, where I have been working in its UltraFresh Food division for about six years. I have had a good relationship with XYZ, but I have now come to believe, based on my accomplishments and strengths, that my general approach to business is better suited to the kind of entrepreneurial business culture that prevails at Harvey's.

As you will see in the resume I have enclosed, the wide range of marketing responsibilities I have held during my career is quite relevant to Harvey's expansion into 15 new metropolitan areas. I have also had extensive experience in three areas — co-op advertising, regional promotions, and market research — all of which seem to be central aspects of the responsibilities I would have if I were to become part of your department. As Phil will verify, I'm an extremely hard and devoted worker, and I work well as part of a team.

If you have any questions about any aspect of my background, please don't hesitate to get in touch with me. I would also welcome the opportunity to meet with you and tell you a little more about what I think I can contribute.

I greatly appreciate your interest and your consideration. I hope to hear from you soon.

Sincerely,

Wendy Weber

105 West St.
Baton Rouge, LA 43090

May 16, 1995

Mr. Samuel Clemens
Vice President, Marketing
Harvey's Food & Beverage
123 Elm St.
Louisville, KY 00302

Dear Mr. Clemens:

A good friend of mine, May East, mentioned to me yesterday that you were
looking for a director of marketing. And my reason for writing you today is
twofold: one, to tell you that I am very much interested in this position; and
two, to tell you that I think I have the qualifications you are looking for.

As you can see from the resume I have enclosed, I have more than ten years'
experience in marketing, primarily in the food and beverage industry. In fact,
much of this work parallels the chief responsibilities of the job you are seeking
to fill.

In addition, I know quite a bit about Harvey's Food & Beverage, having dealt
with several of your salespeople several years ago when I was with UltraFresh.
I know that you have a fast-paced, entrepreneurial atmosphere and that you
place high value on teamwork and loyalty.

I know that I can bring those qualities — and more — to this job, and I would
urge you to meet with me in person so that I can tell you more about what I can
offer.

My resume also indicates that I have been out of the workforce for the past six
years — mainly because I wanted to limit myself to freelance work until my
daughter began school. Now that she is in school, I'm eager to give my all to a
full-time commitment.

I thank you for your interest and your time, and I look forward to hearing from
you.

Sincerely,

Jill Jobseeker

Note: This letter is similar to the
preceding one, but it is appropriate
for a candidate who has been out
of the workforce.

1830 Thomas Way
Winnetka, IL 32904

July 18, 1995

Mr. Henry Hireman
Director of Public Relations
The Enterprise Group
345 Fulton St.
Chicago, IL 30989

Dear Mr. Hireman:

I had a brief conversation earlier today with Rudy Fitch, the personnel manager of your company, and he suggested that I get in touch with you with respect to an opening in your department.

I am a recent graduate of the University of Illinois, and my current goal is to find an entry-level position in a public relations firm such as yours.

As my resume indicates, I was actively involved in public relations during my junior and senior years in college, so I am very familiar with the basics. I know how to write press releases. I know how to arrange press conferences. And I developed some strong relationships with the news media.

Mr. Fitch did mention to me that quite a number of people have applied for this position, but based on what I know about the Enterprise Group and my particular skills, I think I could be a great asset to your company. I also think that I could begin making a contribution almost immediately.

Please feel free to call me at any time. I would welcome the chance to meet with you personally.

Thank you so much for your interest and consideration.

Sincerely,

Bradley Quicklerner

Part IV
Drumming Up
Job Leads

FOR GEROME, GETTING HIS FOOT IN THE DOOR WAS
ONLY *HALF* THE BATTLE...

In this part...

You can't very well find a job without job leads, so this part shows you the various ways to find those leads. You'll see how to do effective research, network like a champ, and decipher the want ads. This part also shows you how to wage a targeted mailing campaign at the companies you come up with, get help from recruiters, and temp your way into full-time work.

Chapter 10

Digging Up Information: The Basics of Effective Research

*I*n most instances, the one activity that has more bearing than any other on how quickly you find a good job — apart from your qualifications — isn't what most people think. It's not how solid your resume is or how brilliantly you write your cover letters. It's not how drop-dead marvelous you look when you go on interviews. And it's not how smoothly and convincingly you answer interview questions. What it is, in a word, is *research*.

Research is digging up information. And being good at it gives you an enormous edge in the job market. The right research helps you uncover job leads that wouldn't normally come to your attention. And it helps you get more mileage out of the job leads that you do uncover. (Job leads, remember, aren't like apples. You don't pluck them or shake them from a tree branch. You have to dig them up.)

And after you dig up a job lead, diligent research increases your chances of making a strong impression when you're either arranging interviews or being interviewed. The more you know about the company and the person interviewing you, the more intelligently you can answer interview questions and the less likely you will say something that inadvertently sinks your chances.

Like all the other aspects of job hunting, however, research isn't quick and easy. You have to approach your research efforts in a logical, systematic manner. You have to set priorities and be resourceful. And you have to manage your time effectively. Above all, you should have a clear idea of what information you need — and where to find it.

Finding Your Way Around Your Local Library

As mentioned in Chapter 4, the best source of job search information is — where else? — the library. True, now that online databases are multiplying like rabbits, the library is no longer the *only* place that you can effectively handle the research aspect of your job search. But your local library remains the most *cost-effective* place to do your research (downloading from online databases can get expensive if you're not disciplined, but more of that in Chapters 17, 18, and 19). Regardless of how cyber-smart you are, you need to be library-smart as well.

What a library can offer you

Any public library worth its salt should be able to give you access to the following information, all of which can prove invaluable to you in your search:

- Job openings listed in want-ad sections of newspapers and other publications that you wouldn't normally be able to access

- Directory information, articles, and books about companies where you either have set up interviews or are tracking down job leads that could materialize into interviews

- Articles and books about companies and industries that may hold job possibilities

- Information about specific people in companies that you are currently talking to or are hoping to approach

- Information about up-to-the-minute trends and issues in your industry or profession

The following sections tell you how to gather this information in the most intelligent and efficient way.

Seven ways to get the most out of library research

Here are seven guidelines for efficient and effective research.

Pick the right library

Assuming that you have a choice of libraries, bigger is usually better. There's no mystery here. Larger libraries have more room for business- and career-related reference materials and more money to spend on directories and computerized reference aids.

But factors other than size should influence your decision as well. How far do you have to travel to get to the library? How busy is the library? How up-to-date is it when it comes to CD-ROM equipment and other computerized aids? And how friendly and accommodating are the people who work there? The last thing you need when you're looking for a job is to have to ask for help from people for whom *customer service* is an alien concept.

If you live in an area in which there are several libraries to choose from, it's not a bad idea to spend a day traveling from library to library. Get a feel for each one. Make your decision, in the end, based on the following factors:

✔ Hours of operation: Are they open during the evening and on weekends?

✔ The number and variety of newspapers and periodicals the library keeps on file

✔ The number of publications (trade magazines and directories in particular) that cover your industry or profession

✔ The size and scope of the business reference section

✔ The general atmosphere — whether the staff seems friendly

✔ The presence of state-of-the-art research equipment (for example, CD-ROMs)

Ask for help

Librarians in general — and reference librarians in particular — tend to be helpful by nature, not to mention the fact that helping people is what they're paid to do. So don't be bashful about asking for help, and don't think that you're being a bother whenever you have a question. Here are some tips for helping librarians do a better job of helping you.

✔ When asking for help, be as specific as possible about the information that you're looking for. Librarians are not career counselors, but they can direct you to the sources you need.

> ✔ Be sensitive to the pressures that reference librarians are under (many libraries today are understaffed). Be reasonable, show your gratitude, and don't "hog" reference materials that you don't need.

Set up a schedule

Library time should be a fixed part of your job search schedule — something you do on a regular basis, as opposed to something you do whenever there's nothing good playing at the movies. Even if you are working at a full- or part-time job, you should be prepared to spend a minimum of three to four hours a week doing library research — particularly if you are not generating job leads in other ways.

Try to schedule your library time during those hours when the library isn't teeming with students racing to finish their term papers or reports at the last minute. Peak hours at most libraries are late afternoons and weekends throughout the year. If you can work out a schedule that puts you in the library during nonpeak hours, you'll get more done in less time.

Establish a routine

The library can be a pleasant place to hang out, but you're not there to relax or socialize. You have digging to do. So it's to your advantage to set up a routine. Assuming that you don't have a specific research task to complete — like finding out more about the company with which you're interviewing tomorrow — you may want to divide your library time into segments: for example, a certain amount of time scanning the classifieds of newspapers; a certain amount of time reading business or trade publications in your field; and a certain amount of time gathering directory-related information about specific companies.

Stay on track

Getting sidetracked when you're doing research in a library is an easier trap to fall into than you may think. You've just finished reading a newspaper article about a new company planning to open a branch in your town, and you're about to write down the name of the person you need to get in touch with. Suddenly, though, your eye catches a heartwarming story about a baby whale that got stuck in somebody's tuna net somewhere in the Pacific, only to be saved by a kindly, heroic captain. Compelling reading, but it's not going to dig up job leads.

The best way to stay on track is to set goals for each library visit. A typical goal might be to get the name and address of a contact person for mailings at, say, ten companies you've never approached. Another goal might be to uncover at least four general articles about a company with which you've scheduled an interview. Yet another goal might be to come away with at least two career or job possibilities that you've never thought about before.

Set up a system for taking notes

Note-taking is generally the most tedious part of library research. But it's a necessary evil, and you need to go about it systematically. Whenever possible, try to take advantage of CD-ROM databases (assuming that your library has them); that way, you can usually print out what you want with a single keystroke. Using a portable tape recorder can speed things up, too, but remember that you have to transcribe those tapes when you get back home, and that's double the work.

A portable computer? Not a bad idea, except that battery capacity on most portables is two to three hours maximum. Then, too, if you're doing your research in a large library, you can't very well leave the computer sitting there at the reference table while you go to the photocopy machine.

Speaking of which, the most *tempting* way to record the information you need is to use the coin- or card-operated photocopy machines that are now a fixture in most libraries. Why go to all the bother of writing things down when a machine will do the job for you in one-tenth the time?

Show some discipline, though. People have a tendency to *over*gather when there is a copy machine handy. You collect so much information that you never get around to looking at it.

If you're going to gather information the old-fashioned way, with pad and pen, buy a loose-leaf notebook and divide it into sections based on the different categories of information you're gathering. And don't forget to take some small sticky notes with you; they come in handy when you want to designate certain pages in a book to photocopy.

Directory Intelligence

The number of directories containing information that may be of value to your job search has mushroomed over the past five years — so much so that most libraries no longer have the room or the money to keep themselves fully supplied with the newest directories.

Choosing the most appropriate directory with the least amount of hassle is no easy task. That's because many directories that focus on the largest companies tend to cover the same territory, albeit with different emphasis. Some directories, such as *Moody's,* tend to be financially focused. Others emphasize the people in the corporations more than the corporations themselves. Still others focus on the types of businesses the company is in and the brands it sells.

Generally, the more information a directory gives you about individual companies, the fewer companies it tends to list. Indeed, one of the ongoing problems of using many of these directories is that they don't have much to say about the tens of thousands of small, private companies that are currently the fastest-growing segment of the job market. To get information about these companies, you have to rely on industry-specific directories or directories that are keyed to a certain locale. **Rule of thumb:** The broader the scope of the directory, the less likely it will cover smaller companies.

In any event, the best way to find out which directories are best suited to your needs is to talk your situation over with the reference librarian. Give the librarian a general idea of your needs. Get the names of several directories that seem applicable, and then take some time to browse through each directory. You should be able to tell fairly soon which ones have the information you need and how easy that information is to access.

In the meantime, here is a list of directories that are well worth checking out. They are grouped into three general categories: directories for (1) job seekers; (2) general business audiences (these directories list companies but are still useful to job hunters); and (3) special interest groups.

When you're using directories as a source of information, always verify independently — as best you can — any of the names listed. It's especially important to do so whenever you're working with a directory that is more than a year old.

Directories designed specifically for job hunters

The number of directories geared specifically for job hunters is on the rise. Here are a few that you should be able to find in most libraries.

The Almanac of American Employers

This one-volume directory lists 500 companies, devoting one page to each firm. Each listing offers the following information in addition to the basics:

- The name (when available) of the college recruiter
- Recent financial performance, including percentage growth in profit
- Salaries and benefits (along with a rating number that enables you to compare how the salaries and benefits compare to those offered by other companies)
- Regional presence
- Brands and divisions

> ✔ Specific academic backgrounds that the company tends to look for in candidates
>
> ✔ Plans for future growth

Each listing in this directory attempts to give you a sense of the company's corporate culture. The barometers it uses include everything from the tuition reimbursement policy to that for subsidized child care. **Publisher: Corporate Jobs Outlook.**

D&B Employment Opportunities Directory — The Career Guide

A one-volume directory, published annually, that lists employment-related information about more than 5,000 companies throughout the United States. Apart from the basics (company names, addresses, and so on), each listing includes information that would be of specific interest to a job seeker, such as a summary of the educational specialties that the company values, the most promising areas of employment, and a brief description of the company's insurance plans. Companies are listed alphabetically but are indexed geographically and according to industry. **Publisher: Dun & Bradstreet, 3 Sylvan Way, Parsippany, NJ 07054, 800-526-0651.**

Job Seeker's Guide to Private and Public Companies

This multivolume directory is organized according to region and describes more than 17,000 American companies. The typical listing gives you the basics (name, address, and so on), the date the company was founded, the number of employees, human resources contacts, and application procedures. **Publisher: Gale Research, 835 Penobscot Building, Detroit, MI 48226, 800-877-GALE.**

Directories that offer general company-related information

The following directories are directed to general business audiences as opposed to job seekers, but the information they contain can be valuable in all phases of your research.

America's Corporate Families and International Affiliates

Volumes I and II of this Dun & Bradstreet guide list more than 11,000 U.S. parent companies and more than 76,000 domestic divisions and subsidiaries. Volume III lists more than 3,000 U.S. parent companies and their nearly 18,000 foreign subsidiaries, plus nearly 3,000 foreign ultimate parent companies and their 11,000 U.S. subsidiaries. The key numbers in each listing are the number of sites and the company's net worth. Most of the listings also include the names of key people at the division and subsidiary level. **Publisher: Dun & Bradstreet.**

Directory of American Firms Operating in Foreign Countries

Not every library carries this directory, and it isn't published on a regular basis. But this three-volume directory is a useful guide for people looking to hook up with American companies that do business throughout the rest of the world. It lists some 3,000 American corporations that have factories and branch offices covering some 36 countries. It also lists key personnel, although the information might be dated. **Publisher: UniWorld Business Publications, 257 Central Park West, Suite 10A, New York, NY 10024, 212-496-2448.**

Reference Book of Corporate Management

A very good source for basic biographical information about senior managers in major American companies. A typical listing includes the manager's name, business address, phone number, and educational background, as well as memberships and political activities. The point of plowing through this information is to see whether you can get a read on the company's culture. **Publisher: Dun & Bradstreet.**

Dun & Bradstreet Principal International Businesses

Some 50,000 companies in more than 130 countries are listed here — and in four languages: English, Spanish, French, and German. The companies are grouped alphabetically, by geographic location, and by product. **Publisher: Dun & Bradstreet.**

Dun & Bradstreet Million Dollar Directory Series

This five-volume series lists 160,000 companies in alphabetical order. It is the most extensive list of its kind available and is indexed in a variety of ways. The information, though, is sketchy — little more than name, address, phone number, key executives, and some financial statistics. The bang you get for your buck here is the sheer number of companies listed, plus the fact that it includes subsidiaries not mentioned in other directories. This is a useful directory for job seekers who intend to launch a targeted direct-mail campaign (see Chapter 14). **Publisher: Dun & Bradstreet.**

D&B Million Dollar Directory — Top 50,000 Companies

This volume lists the largest 50,000 companies of the 160,000 listed in the *Million Dollar Directory*. **Publisher: Dun & Bradstreet.**

Hoover's Handbook of American Business

This two-volume set includes profiles of 705 companies containing operations overviews, company strategies, histories, key financial data, lists of products, executives' names, headquarters addresses and phone and fax numbers. Also has more than 60 pages of business lists, including the *Fortune 500* list of the largest U.S. corporations and the *Forbes 500* list of the largest U.S. private companies. **Publisher: Hoover's Inc., 1033 La Posada Dr., Suite 250, Austin, TX 78752, 800-486-8666.**

Hoover's Handbook of World Business

A companion guide to the *Hoover Handbook of American Business,* offering the same general information and the same format but focusing instead on 250 companies headquartered outside the United States. **Publisher: Hoover's Inc.**

International Directory of Company Histories

This multivolume set is published annually and consists of article-length histories of more than 1,200 major companies in a variety of industries. Each history is straightforward — mainly a chronological account of key events and key people in the company's history — but you get a good sense of how the company got to where it is today. You also get a fairly accurate picture of the company's fiscal health. **Publisher: Gale Research.**

Standard and Poor's Register of Corporations, Directors and Executives

This familiar three-volume directory is published annually and covers roughly 55,000 public and private companies. Volume 1 provides basic information about the companies. Volume 2 offers thumbnail sketches of key executives. And Volume 3 indexes the companies according to their S.I.C. or industry classification. **Publisher: Standard & Poor's Corporation, 25 Broadway, New York, NY 10004, 800-221-5277.**

Thomas' Register of American Manufacturers

This monolithic guide — 26 hardcover volumes — profiles more than 150,000 manufacturers, listing major products and services. It's geared primarily to vendors seeking to sell goods to manufacturing companies, but it lists basic information about smaller manufacturing companies that the major directories don't cover. **Publisher: Thomas Publishing Company, 5 Penn Plaza, New York, NY 10001, 800-699-9822.**

Special-interest directories

The following directories are published by Gale Research (835 Penobscot Building, Detroit, MI 48226, 800-877-GALE).

Directories in Print

Yes, it has come to this: A directory that lists nothing *but* directories, giving names and publishers of thousands of directories and a brief description of each. A good place to start your directory research.

Encyclopedia of Associations

Probably the best source for the names, addresses, and key people in professional associations throughout the United States. Some 20,000 trade and professional associations are listed.

Worth buying

One of the most useful books for job hunters is *Jobs 98*, by Kathryn, George, and Ross Petras (Simon & Schuster). More than a directory of companies, this guide offers career outlooks in 15 different professions (everything from accounting to managers, writers, and editors) and analyzes employment trends in 21 different industries. Additional features include lists of associations, directories, and industry-specific periodicals. The book is available in most reference libraries and costs about $15.

Although many of the business directories found in libraries sell for several hundred dollars, you can sometimes get a hold of one for a fraction of that cost. The only catch is that it will probably be one year out of date. Many libraries, once they get the new edition, will virtually give away the older directory. You shouldn't care, though, because most of the basic information in major directories doesn't change all that much from year to year. However, be sure to verify spellings of names and check addresses personally before sending correspondence.

Gale Directory of Publications and Broadcast Media

This three-volume directory lists virtually every newspaper, magazine, and radio station in America and is probably the best source of information currently available for industry trade publications and local community newspapers. Listings are organized regionally — by state and by cities within each state — but the index groups listings are organized according to specific categories (retailing, restaurant industry, and so on) as well. Each listing gives you the name, address, and telephone number of the publication along with a one-line description, the name of the editor and publisher, the size of circulation (paid and unpaid), and subscription rate.

Trade Catalogs

Trade catalogs are industry-specific or profession-specific directories that are published mainly for buyers and sellers in a particular industry — and there are zillions of them. None of these directories offers more than the sketchiest of information about the companies — name, address, telephone number, a key name or two, and sometimes the number of employees. What makes trade catalogs valuable is that they often list smaller companies that are not mentioned or described in other directories.

Getting the Most Out of Periodicals

Keeping current on key issues and new developments in your profession or industry and in the business world at large is key if you want to advance in your job. The need to stay on top of things, however, doesn't diminish when you are looking for work. If anything, it becomes even more critical.

If you are not already doing so, you should be making three types of periodicals part of your regular reading diet: (1) general business publications that are the most widely read among senior managers and other key decision makers; (2) trade publications that cover your particular field; and (3) local newspapers and business publications.

General business publications

Some of the most important and widely read periodicals geared to business people are the following. They are all worth scanning, particularly the sections that focus on people who have recently taken on new jobs.

- ✔ *Business Week*
- ✔ *The New York Times* business section
- ✔ *Forbes*
- ✔ *The Wall Street Journal*
- ✔ *Fortune*
- ✔ *Inc.*
- ✔ *The Journal of Commerce*
- ✔ *The Economist* (published in the U.K.)
- ✔ *Barron's*

It's hard to imagine any library that *wouldn't* have these publications on file. So at the very least, you should be zipping through at least some of these publications on a regular basis for articles and features that are relevant to your job search. In particular, look for the following:

- ✔ Key business and economic trends
- ✔ Companies expanding or relocating
- ✔ Key trends in your particular profession or industry
- ✔ Companies in your industry (and in particular, those companies in your region)

National Business Employment Weekly: Essential for job hunters

If you're not already doing so, you should be reading — on a regular basis — a publication called *National Business Employment Weekly*. Published by Dow Jones, this is the only weekly publication written exclusively for job seekers. A typical issue brings together the want-ad advertisements from all the regional editions of the *Wall Street Journal*. These ads are geared primarily to mid- and upper-level professionals, but each issue also offers a mix of how-to articles and features that cover virtually every aspect of job hunting for all levels. Also, each issue has a regionalized calendar of events — seminars, meetings, support groups, and so on.

✔ People in companies who you might want to approach or would need to know about if you were to interview at those companies

✔ Advice on job hunting and career advancement

How to cover more ground when you read periodicals

The first place to turn when you're looking through one of these periodicals is the table of contents (or in the case of newspapers, the story index). The title of the article and the description that follows the title should give you enough of a taste so that you can decide whether you want to read the entire story. If you're not sure, thumb to the article itself and look over the headline and subheads.

After you make note of which articles (if any) are worth a look, go next to the section of the publication entitled "Index to Companies" and look for mention of companies that you currently may be researching. If the publication has a section devoted to people, give that section a quick glimpse as well.

Keep in mind your objective. You're not *reading* the magazine or newspaper; you're doing research. The difference is one of focus, curiosity, and patience. The key to research is having a reasonably well-defined sense of what you're looking for.

When you find something that might be useful

If you come across an article that looks as though it might be useful, make a note of the article (and page number) or use a sticky note to mark the page in the magazine. In other words, don't spend time on any single article or feature in a publication until you've scanned the entire publication.

The reason is priorities. Assuming that you don't have an unlimited amount of time to spend on articles, you should choose the articles that you intend to read with care. You may find, for example, after you look over the contents of a particular publication, that four or five articles might be worth reading. At that point, you need to decide whether you want to read them at that moment, make a photocopy of one or two of the articles so that you can read them later, or go out and buy the publication if the issue is current.

When you are researching a specific topic or company

When you have a specific research target in mind — that is, a specific topic, company, or person that you want to find out about — your best bet is to go directly to a publication called the *Business Periodicals Index.* This guide, like its companion and non-business-specific directory, the *Reader's Guide to Periodical Literature,* lists the names, authors, and publications of articles that have appeared in hundreds of publications. The articles are arranged according to subject, and broad subjects are often divided into smaller categories. The only downside is that you may not be able to access some of the publications listed in the directory at your local library.

Two other resources to tap when you're looking for information about specific business issues or reasonably large companies are the *New York Times Index* and the *Wall Street Journal Index.* As with the *Business Periodicals Index,* the articles here are listed according to subject. Chances are, too, that your library has these articles stored on microfilm or on CD-ROM.

Researching Trade Publications

Virtually every industry, business, and profession — including industries you probably never knew existed — has at least one publication devoted exclusively to it, and many, like the chemical industry and hospitality industry, have dozens more — some national, some regional, and some local. Given the fact that they focus on one industry, trade publications are probably the most valuable research resource you can tap. The problem, though, is that trade publications in general are far more difficult to access than general-interest magazines. The *Business Periodicals Index,* for instance, covers articles published in only a fraction of the thousands of trade publications that come out each month, and it's the rare library that carries more than a few dozen of the largest trade publications.

Trade publications become especially important when you're having no luck at all uncovering information about a company that is too small to be of much interest to publishers of major directories or of major business publications. This means that you'll have to step up your digging efforts. Two directories could be useful to you: the *Gale Directory of Publications and Broadcast Media,* described earlier, and the *Standard Rate & Data Service Business Publications Directory.*

Your goal when you consult either of these directories is to get the name and number of a local trade publication. You can then call and ask whether the publication has written anything about the company you're interested in.

Community Newspapers and Publications

Don't overlook either community newspapers or small, regional business publications — particularly if your research interest is in small, local companies. Here again, though, don't look for well-organized directories or CD-ROM indexes. Any local publication that covers business issues or runs articles about companies and their management teams should be a regular part of your library reading agenda — more important, in many ways, than the national publications. The "people" sections in these publications in particular can give you clues to what's happening at local companies. (You can also use the fact that you saw someone's name or picture in the paper as a pretext for sending a letter of introduction along with your resume.)

If you need information about specific companies that may have been written about in earlier issues of these publications, your best move is to call the publication directly.

Other Sources of Information

Here are some other resources for research information:

Annual reports

Annual reports are yearly publications that publicly owned companies are obliged by law to send to shareholders. The typical annual report gives you a bird's-eye view of the various businesses the company is in, its divisions, its board members and key management, and its financial performance. These reports can be invaluable for researching a prospective employer.

Recruitment and marketing brochures

These brochures (when you can get your hands on them) can, like annual reports, give you an in-depth view of the company. They're useful but should never be your sole source of information about a firm.

10-K and 10-Q reports

The annual 10-K and quarterly 10-Q reports are filings that public companies must make with the Securities and Exchange Commission. Their principal purpose is to describe the company and its financial position in detail. They also alert potential investors to problems that could affect the company's bottom line, such as lawsuits pending, changes in raw material availability, and any marked change in the company's debt structure. You can generally get a company's 10-K or 10-Q report from its investor relations department or from any stock brokerage firm.

Abbreviations

The following is a summary of the most common abbreviations found in corporate directories:

AMEX: American Stock Exchange

CEO: Chief Executive Officer

CFO: Chief Financial Officer

CIO: Chief Information Officer

COO: Chief Operating Officer

EPS: Earnings per share

ESOP: Employee Stock Ownership Plan

FY: Fiscal year

HR: Human resources

NASDAQ: National Association of Securities Dealers Automated Quotations

NYSE: New York Stock Exchange

IPO: Initial public offering

P/E: Price-to-earnings ratio

Chapter 11
Networking 101

• •

In This Chapter

▶ Why you can't afford *not* to network

▶ The "pyramiding" factor

▶ The three biggest myths about networking

▶ Establishing a contact base

▶ Cross-referencing: Setting up a database

• •

*I*magine the following scenario.

Someone you've never met or even heard of has precisely the sort of job you would love to find and holds that job in a company you don't even know exists. This person wakes up one day to learn that he or she has won the state lottery. The person goes to the president of the company and says in so many words, "I'm history."

What this means, of course, is that an opening for a job that you would love to have and might well be hired for now exists. There's only one problem: You may never hear about the opening. Or by the time you hear about the job, somebody else will have been hired.

Now change the script around to produce a happier ending. Same situation, same job, same lottery winner, same "I'm history." In this scenario, though, a close friend or relative of yours happens to work at this particular company and is so well connected that nothing goes on that he or she doesn't hear about it. More important, this friend or relative knows that you are looking for a job, knows that the newly created opening is something that would interest you, and wants very much to help. After all, years ago you did this person a favor, and there is very little that this person wouldn't do for you.

Question: How long do you think it would take before you found out about that job?

And that's just *one* company. Imagine how many job leads — good, solid leads — you could have heard about if you had friends and relatives working in dozens of companies, each of your contacts aware of what you're looking for and all of them keeping their eyes and ears open for an opportunity that might work for you. Think for a moment about the kind of edge that you would gain in your job search.

All of which underscores the importance of the subject that is the focus of the next two chapters: networking.

What Networking Really Is and Why You Can't Afford Not to Do It

Networking is a trendy word that means *making connections*. To be more precise, it is making connections with people whom you may not yet know but who might be helpful to you in your job search. The very notion of networking is built around a simple but far-reaching principle: namely, that it is easier to get information and help from people who either know you or know someone who knows you than from people who have never heard of you.

It is certainly *possible* to find a job in today's job market without having to rely on personal connections. And it's true, too, that connections alone aren't enough to get you hired; you still have to demonstrate at some point that you can handle the job. And after you're hired, you have to be able to perform the job.

But connections clearly help. It's been estimated that between 70 and 80 percent of all jobs that get filled today are filled by people who first heard about the job through word of mouth: Someone *told* them about the job or told someone who told someone who told someone about the job.

That's why networking is so important. It puts eyes and ears in places where you yourself can't look and can't listen. The larger your personal network is (in other words, the more sets of eyes and ears in places that may be sources of job leads), the more likely it is that you'll find out about job openings when they materialize.

The "Pyramiding" Factor

The fact that such a high percentage of jobs go to people who originally hear about jobs through personal connections may not seem fair to you — especially if you don't know a lot of people to begin with.

Bear in mind, though, that you don't need all that many personal connections to launch an effective networking campaign. The whole point of networking, remember, is to make connections that you *haven't yet made.*

Consider the following lesson in geometry.

Assume for the sake of argument that if someone asked you to come up with a list of people you know who might have some business connections, the most you could come up with was four, including your two brothers. (Chances are that you can come up with a lot more than four, but make this truly a worst-case scenario.)

Granted, a four-person network isn't very impressive. But what if each of those 4 people could give you the names of 4 people *they* know. Suddenly, the potential of your network jumps from 4 to 20: the 4 original names plus 16 (4 times 4) new names. And assume for the sake of argument that those 16 new people, once you get a chance to talk to them and demonstrate to them what a terrific person you are, can give you just 4 names. Now you have 64 new names to go along with the 20 you had before, which means that the puny original list of 4 has now mushroomed to more than 80.

This little exercise demonstrates a basic networking principle known as *pyramiding.* Pyramiding means that each new contact you make does more than simply add *one* new person to your network of personal connections. Each new contact gives you the potential of adding dozens more.

But it doesn't just happen. The network of people who are in a position to hear about job openings and help you get interviews for job openings doesn't grow on its own. *You* are the force that keeps it growing. And the minute you stop feeding the network, the network stops growing.

Networking Isn't as Difficult as You Think — You Just Have to Do It

Yes, networking can be hard work — especially if you break into a sweat at the very thought of asking people you don't know for favors. But networking isn't *difficult* in the sense that playing a Brahms piano concerto is difficult. In other words, you don't need special skills or training to network effectively. It helps, of course, to be organized and systematic. And when you're face to face with someone whose help you are seeking, you must be able to introduce yourself and explain your situation in a brief, cogent way that puts people at ease (see Chapter 12 for information about composing your "sales pitch").

But above all, the one thing you need to network effectively is the *will* to do it. You can't allow yourself to be hamstrung by the hesitancy that might normally prevent you from introducing yourself to strangers who could possibly prove helpful to you. You have to face the possibility that, yes, some of the people you approach aren't going to be as helpful as you would like — including people you think you can rely on.

But here is what you must never forget: The *worst* thing that can happen in your efforts to create and build a personal network is that someone you approach won't be willing or able to help. That's it. On the other hand, as you'll come to appreciate more and more, most people you approach will, in fact, be willing to help. The connections are there to be made. In many instances, all you have to do is pick up the phone or extend your hand.

The Three Most Self-Defeating Myths of Networking

Before moving on to the nitty-gritty of networking, look briefly at some of the common perceptions that frequently interfere with your ability to get the most out of networking. Listed here are the three most pervasive — and most self-defeating — misconceptions about the process.

> ✔ **The only people you should focus on in your networking efforts are people who are in a position to offer you a job.**
>
> This notion is probably the most common and self-defeating misconception about networking. True, your *ultimate* goal when you network is to gain access to people who are in a position to offer you a job. But networking itself is all about making connections with people who, indirectly or directly, can increase your likelihood of gaining that access.
>
> The lesson here is simple: *Don't set limits on who should — or shouldn't — be part of your network.* Virtually everyone you know or might meet, regardless of what he or she does for a living, could be in a position to hear about a job opening. Don't minimize your chances by underestimating the potential value of anyone you know.

✔ **You have to know the "right people" to network effectively.**

There is certainly an element of truth to this statement, but it is nonetheless misleading. The basic purpose of networking, remember, is to *gain access* to the so-called "right people." And if there is a single key to effective networking, it lies in your ability to create a *set* of connections that will eventually give you access to the people who are in a position to offer you a job.

Networking is very much a step-by-step process. You meet one person, who gives you a name of someone else, who gives you yet another name, and so forth until you have a connection with a key person. Not having immediate access to that key person doesn't lock you out of the process: It simply forces you to be more resourceful and more patient.

✔ **Strangers resent it when you ask them to help you in your job search.**

Okay, it's not a perfect world. Every once in a while, you're going to call someone or meet someone at a function who will try to make you feel bad simply because you have the *audacity* to ask *him* for help in your job search. Happily, though, most people — even people you don't know that well — will be surprisingly cooperative, as long as you approach them properly and make *reasonable* requests.

Getting Started with the Networking Process

The easiest part of networking, believe it or not, is getting started. All you need is something that you can write names on — a tablet or computer screen, for example.

But first things first. Before getting to the business of which names to write down, consider why you're writing these names down in the first place. The obvious answer, of course, is that they can help you. But what, exactly, does *help* mean? You can look at this word in terms of what various people may be in a position to do:

✔ Offer you a job right now

✔ Offer you a job in the near future

✔ Introduce you to someone who is currently looking to hire someone — or may be looking to hire someone in the near future

✔ Inform you about a job opening or situation that could produce a job opening

✔ Give you information about a particular person or company and, by doing so, increase your chances of converting a job lead into an interview or converting an interview into an offer

Notice that each of these points is keyed to one of two objectives: (1) to uncover leads to job openings, and (2) to help you convert those leads into offers. You need to keep *both* objectives in mind as you launch and manage your networking campaign. And you also need to keep in mind the relationship of quantity and quality.

Quantity, of course, refers to the number of people who actually become part of your network — it is obvious that more is usually better. The more people who know that you're looking and are in a position to hear about openings, the more likely it is that you will get a jump on job leads that you might not otherwise hear about.

But *quality* is important, too. Some people, for any number of different reasons, are in a better position to help you than other people. It has to do with who they are, the position they hold in a company, the people they know, and their willingness to go to bat for you.

Quantity and quality are *both* important when it comes to developing your personal network. You need numbers, but you also want to make sure that included among those numbers are people who can make a difference. What this means in practical terms is that you have to manage the time and effort you devote to networking in a strategic, intelligent manner. In general, the more "quality" there is to someone who might become part of your network, the more it is worth your time and effort to make the connection and to cultivate that contact. At the same time, though, you don't want to become so preoccupied with making one specific connection that you neglect the network as a whole.

Strive for balance. Look to expand the sheer number of people in your network through activities that do not require an enormous amount of time and effort. Equally important is to improve the quality of your network through more targeted efforts.

Putting a List Together

One of the things you have to do a lot of in your networking efforts is compile lists of names. And the more organized and systematic you are in this seemingly mundane aspect of networking, the more success you are likely to have.

The first step is to develop a strong *primary list,* which is nothing more than a list of everyone you know who, in any way — directly or indirectly — could be of help to you in your job search. It's a good idea to divide that list into three broad categories: level I, level II, and level III.

Level I

Your level I list should consist of the people you would feel the most comfortable approaching for contact names. This list should include your closest friends and relatives. These are people you see or talk to regularly — people you know you can count on. Write down the names of as many of these people as you can think of, and, if you grew up in a very large family or are so popular that you have dozens of close friends, narrow down the list to the 15 or so people who are likely to have the most connections in your target job areas.

Level II

Your level II list should consist of people you would describe more as colleagues or acquaintances than as close friends. These are people you see occasionally and wouldn't normally call upon for a favor — people you see now and then in your neighborhood, at your health club, or at your local Kiwanis meeting. But they know you and presumably wouldn't hesitate to help. Included in this list should be the people you deal with on a professional basis: your doctor, lawyer, and dentist, for example.

Level III

Your level III list should consist of people you have yet to meet but whom you have good reason to believe could be helpful to you. You may hear about these people in a number of ways. Someone from your level I or II list may tell you about them. You may read about them in the newspaper or get their names from a directory.

How you get in touch with these people can vary. In some cases, you may be able to arrange an introduction through someone on your level I or II list. Or you may choose to contact this person directly, using the name of a level I or II person as a connection. In some cases, though, you may have to make the connection entirely on your own.

Prioritizing Your Contact List

For information about what to *do* with your lists after you compile them, skip to the next chapter. For now, you have to *prioritize*. This means determining, as best you can, how valuable a person on your primary list is likely to be in your job search — valuable in terms of what he or she can offer and how connected he or she is to people you want to add to your network.

You can use any rating system you want in making this determination, but the simplest thing to do is to rate each name an *A, B,* or *C.* Use *A* to designate any person who is very well connected and in a very good position to give you information and help. Use *B* to identify people who are somewhat less well connected than *A* people and less able to give you information and help. Use *C* for people whose value lies primarily in their ability to hear about possible job openings or give you names of other people.

For example, you would probably write the letter *A* after Masie Fields, your cousin, because she is a big-time lawyer with loads of connections. You would put a *B* after Harley Evans, your former boss who is now retired, living in Phoenix, and not as well connected as he used to be; and the letter *C* after Dr. Irving Drillmaster, your dentist.

The purpose of these priority symbols should be fairly obvious: to help you get the most mileage out of your networking efforts. Generally speaking, you should approach the As on your primary list before you approach the Bs and Cs. This is not to say that you should ignore the Bs and Cs. Not at all. But if you decide to go out to lunch with someone on your primary list, your time is better spent with your cousin Masie than with your dentist.

Incidentally, you should maintain this system of priorities with every person you add to your list — assuming, that is, that you know enough about the person to rate him or her as an A, B, or C.

Setting Up a Networking Database

If it's at all possible, try to set up your networking list on a database. Databases give you the capacity to cross-reference, which can save you an enormous amount of time when you're tracking down a specific name or fact. Assume, for example, that you hear about a job opening at the Great American Box Company and vaguely remember that, at some point, someone gave you the name of a person who works there. The only problem is that you now have more than 250 names on your network list and can't remember for the life of you who gave you the name.

If you've set up your database properly, there's no problem. You run a search for Great American Box Company and, presto, within seconds you learn — wow! — that the president of the company is one of Dr. Drillmaster's patients.

If you're setting up your list by hand, the way you organize your database (or your notebook or note cards) can vary. Here are some of the fields or categories that you might want to include, assuming that the information is available:

- Name of person
- Title
- Company
- Business address
- Home address
- Telephone number
- Fax number
- E-mail address
- Nature of connection (friend, introduced by someone else, and so on)
- Other companies (names of companies in which this person knows people)
- Additional names (names, titles, and companies of people whose names this person has given to you)
- Level (I, II, or III, based on how well you know the contact)
- Priority (A, B, or C, based on how valuable the person might be to you in your job search)
- Comments (Use this space to record meetings with the person, letters sent, and so on)

If you find databases or computers in general terribly confusing, IDG Books Worldwide publishes ...*For Dummies* books on a number of popular database programs, including Access, dBASE, and FoxPro.

BLOOPERS

College grad antics

Looking for work is a task that is especially overwhelming for recent graduates and other job market newcomers who haven't yet learned the "rules of the road." Here are some real-life examples of new grad naiveté collected by Robert Half International Inc. founder Robert Half. After reading them, you may feel a little better about your own interview or resume blunders. It could be worse — a lot worse!

✔ A college graduate's resume stated the following objective: "To specialize in corporate run-arounds." It passed the spell checker with flying colors, but what this candidate really hoped to specialize in was corporate *turnarounds.*

✔ While interviewing a recent graduate and trying to put him at ease, one manager noticed several tags on the left sleeve of the candidate's crisp, new suit. The manager had trouble concentrating on the interview because she kept wondering how to tell the nervous grad about the tags.

✔ A recent graduate interviewing with a large company was scheduled to meet with several line managers when the last manager seemed to have lost him along the way. In searching for him, the manager found the applicant in an empty office asking, "If it's okay, I'll take this office." (He was serious!)

✔ A job hunt novice brought his family and babysitter to watch the children in the lobby of the firm. After the interview, the children asked questions, such as when their dad would be able to start work.

✔ One applicant had in his possession prewritten answers to interview questions that came from the college placement office.

✔ A candidate brought to the interview transcripts and by-semester grade reports spanning a four-year period.

✔ A graduate interviewing for an entry-level accounting position was doing very well until the end of the meeting. That's when she said she'd be ideal for the job since she would need a year of this kind of experience before starting her *own* company.

✔ A grad remarked to the interviewer that, coincidentally, two separate firms she had talked to that day had "ink" in their corporate names.

✔ A candidate sent the hiring manager a resume along with a mock shoe filled with M&Ms. A note attached said, "Now that I've got my foot in the door, won't you see the rest of me?"

✔ A female applicant was applying cosmetics right outside the door of the manager's office. When the manager left his office to use the water fountain across the hall, he nearly knocked her over.

✔ A male candidate brought his wife to the interview to interpret and analyze how his answers to interview questions came across.

✔ One female candidate who was told to "make a lasting impression" in the way she dressed showed up dressed in sequins from head to toe.

✔ A recent grad told the interviewer that gumchewing relaxed her. She then proceeded to put piece after piece into her mouth during the course of the interview.

✔ Resume colors seen from recent grads: tie-dye colors, purple, pink, and stripes.

Chapter 12

Getting the Most Out of Networking

Compiling a list of people who could prove helpful to you in your job search is one thing. Getting the people on that list to give you the kind of help you need is another. And here, really, is the key to successful networking: not simply gathering names but making sure that you get as much mileage as you possibly can out of each connection you make.

Now, *this* aspect of networking — how you actually work the list you compile — isn't easy to pull off. But the difficulty has less to do with the process itself and more to do with the difficulty that some people have in introducing themselves to folks they don't know and, more important, asking them for help.

You can't reinvent your personality by reading this chapter. And there is no getting around the fact that your networking efforts will be more difficult if you're not comfortable with the idea of meeting new people and asking people you know only vaguely to help you. Then again, this chapter may convince you that you are far better than you think at building a contact list and developing relationships with those people on it.

Developing Your Basic Sales Pitch

One thing you have to do repeatedly in your networking campaign is to tell people who you are, what you're looking for, and how they can be of help to you. You should be able to get this message across in no more than 25 seconds when meeting face to face.

Where to begin

Start with the basics. Your in-person 25-second sales pitch should communicate the following information:

- ✔ Your name
- ✔ Your profession, trade, or occupational specialty (that is, what you have been doing for most of your business life)
- ✔ Your current situation (whether you are currently working, were let go because of downsizing, are changing careers, or whatever)
- ✔ What you're looking for in the way of job opportunities
- ✔ What you can offer an employer that sets you apart from other candidates

At first blush, cramming all this information into one 25-second pitch might strike you as impossible — unless you can talk at warp speed. Here are a few examples of 25-second sales pitches that cover all the bases just mentioned. (Keep in mind that telephone pitches may have to be somewhat shorter, which means that you'll have to pare down some of the information you try to convey. Generally, your initial phone pitch should last no more than 10 seconds.)

When making your pitch by phone, it's usually a good idea to do it in two stages. In the first stage, simply identify yourself, let the person know how you came across his or her name, and then ask for a few seconds of his or her time. After you capture the person's attention (if only briefly), you can present the rest of the pitch. Here are some examples:

- ✔ "My name is Brad Hopkins, and I got your name from Larry Dennis. Do you have a minute or two to talk with me?" [After getting permission to move ahead.] "I've been an advertising account executive for more than ten years, working mainly in pharmaceutical companies. My former firm, PPT&W, went through a reorganization a few months ago and disbanded my department. Now I'm looking to join a medium-sized agency that handles health care accounts. I have a lot of contacts in this industry, and I know I could help an agency build its business."

- ✔ [Following the opening.] "I graduated from college last June with a degree in business and have spent the past four months temping for a variety of companies. I'm looking for an entry-level position in a corporation that does a lot of clothing business in Latin America. I'm fluent in Spanish and, because I lived for several years in Argentina, I have a good sense of how you do business in South America."

✔ [Following the opening.] "I'm a nutritionist by training, and for the past eight years I've been working mainly in hospitals in and around Detroit. My husband has been transferred to Dallas, and I'm looking to change the focus of my career and move into the training aspects of nutrition. I love teaching, and I'm very good at working with small groups."

Pay special attention to the sequence of the information in these sample pitches. Generally, it's best to begin with a brief description of your background.

You can use the following space as a framework for your own sales pitch:

My name is _____. I got your name from

_____. For the past _____ years, I have been working as a

_____ and have specialized mainly in _____.

Right now I am _____, and I'm looking for _____

_____. What I have to offer is _____.

Feel free to vary the wording in the preceding sales pitch in any way that suits your situation. The important thing is to be able to articulate your message naturally and with confidence. After you write it down, practice the message over and over. Say it to yourself when you're driving or taking a shower. If you have a tape recorder, record it. Keep practicing it until you're satisfied that the message comes across clearly, without hesitation, and without a trace of embarrassment or defensiveness.

Getting the Word Out

After you put together some sort of network list, your number one priority is to let as many people know — and as soon as possible — what your situation is and what you're looking for (again, if you're employed, use discretion).

The easiest way to accomplish this objective is through a targeted mailing. Compose a one-page letter that describes your situation in brief and send it to all the people on both your level I and level II lists. (See Chapter 11 for information about creating level I, II, and III networking lists. See Chapter 14 for more information about targeted mailings.)

Putting together a mailing of this size may seem to be a monumental task, but it's a piece of cake if you have access to a computer and know how to work the mail-merge features of your word-processing program. Remember, you can write the same basic letter to everyone on the list and customize only the opening paragraph. Addressing the envelopes is easy, too, assuming that you have input your names in a database and know how to use the label-printing feature.

If you don't have access to a computer, you can hire an individual or a company to duplicate, personalize, address, and even mail the letters, but doing so can get pricey. The way to keep costs down is to do most of the routine work yourself (typing names and addresses, stuffing the envelopes, putting on the stamps, and so on).

Resist the temptation to send out nonpersonalized "Dear Friend" letters, even though doing so enables you to send out a mass mailing without having to fool around with mail merges. The information you're conveying to your mailing audience is crucial. Don't diminish its impact with a depersonalized "junk-mail" greeting.

Most people by now recognize computerized letters (even though their names are on the letter). To personalize the letter, hand-write a short message to the people on the list whom you know very well and are likely to contact first. Doing so can make people pay a little more attention to the letter.

When you're sending the letter to close friends, use their home addresses. With business associates, use business addresses.

Writing the Letter

What follows is an example of the kind of letter you might write to the people on your contact list. The key points to bear in mind about this letter are that it

- ✔ Lets the reader know in the opening paragraph what the letter is about (that is, that you're looking for help in your job search).
- ✔ Explains your situation in a direct, upbeat way.
- ✔ Asks for the specific kind of help you want.

June 12, 1995
Mary M. Webster
324 Spelling Ave.
Minneapolis, MN 84938

Dear Mary:

I'm writing to let you know that some unexpected changes are taking place in my career, and I would like to be able to call on you for help, if possible.

My situation is this: Carlton Industries, where I have worked for the past eight years, was recently taken over by Pendleton Industries, which is moving the company's operations from Minneapolis to Huntsville, Alabama.

I was given the opportunity to move to the Alabama headquarters, but Leslie and I decided that we didn't want to uproot the family — especially since we love the area and have so many friends here, and also because both our boys are so involved with high school athletics. So as of July 1, I will be officially unemployed for the first time in my professional career.

You could be of help in a couple of ways.

First of all, if you know of any high-tech companies that need a marketing specialist, or if you hear of any situation that might be suitable for me, I would greatly appreciate your letting me know about it as soon as possible. Secondly, I would like to be able to call you over the next week or so to see if we can get together or talk over the phone. What I'm looking for specifically are names of people I might want to get in touch with.

I have mixed feelings about my situation. On the one hand, I'll miss all my friends at Carlton. But on the other hand, I'm looking forward to the challenge of a new job with a new company. I know I have a great deal to offer in the way of marketing expertise to small to medium-sized high-tech companies, particularly since this area has become such a key ingredient to success in many high-tech industries.

I have taken the liberty of enclosing my resume, and I plan to give you a call over the next few days. If you have any ideas in the meantime, please give me a call. Thank you in advance for your help!

Sincerely,

Patrick A. Wordsmith

This letter is more appropriate for a close personal contact than for a business associate you know only casually. When writing to people you don't know well, you generally shouldn't (1) ask directly for references to jobs (with contacts, you can ask for names of people who could be helpful), or (2) send a resume.

Lining Up People to Give You Help

You don't have to be a psychologist to know that you're much more likely to get help from people who know you and like you than you are from people with whom you share little or no personal history.

But once you get beyond that circle of close friends and relatives, lining up people to help becomes a more imposing challenge. People who know you only casually are not going to be as accessible or as predisposed to helping you as close friends will be. This is not to say that you can't make the connection or cultivate the help of these people. You simply have to change your approach.

Getting help from these people — that is, people on your level II and level III network lists — is usually a two-step process. Step one is making the connection. Step two is getting a chance to meet or talk with them over the phone.

Here are some guidelines to keep in mind when you are trying to establish the connection with these people.

Be prepared

Never try to make contact with anyone on your networking list — especially people you do not know especially well — before taking a few moments to determine what, specifically, you want that person to do for you. The specific reason could be any of the following:

- You simply want the person to be aware of your situation so that he or she will get in touch with you in the event that he or she hears of an opening.

- You want the person to set up an introduction or send your resume to a particular person in his or her organization.

- You want the person to meet or talk with you over the phone so that you can get some names of people to get in touch with.

- You want to meet or talk with the person over the phone to get some ideas about how you might better tailor your job search strategy to a particular industry or company.

Don't beat around the bush

Always let the people you call or write know early on in the conversation or letter that you're looking for help. Don't be embarrassed about asking for it, either. Looking for a job is nothing to be ashamed of. You didn't commit a chain-saw murder or run off with the funds of an orphanage. As soon as you dispense with the hello and how-are-you pleasantries, explain your situation.

The following are some examples of how you might launch a conversation with a networking contact:

- ✔ "Hi, Alice. This is Leslie Gump, a friend of Marcia Allen's. Is this a good time to talk?" [Assuming it is.] "I'm a graphic designer, and the reason I'm calling is that my company has decided to disband its graphic design department, and I'm looking to join an advertising agency that specializes in computer graphics. I'd like to talk with you for a couple of minutes and tell you a little bit about what I can offer, and see if you might give me some names of people I could call."

- ✔ "Jeffrey, my name is Paul Arnold. I don't know if you remember me, but we sat next to one another at lunch two weeks ago at the Pharmaceutical Conference in Philadelphia. [After the connection is acknowledged.] The reason I'm calling is that our company is cutting way back, and I'm looking to make a change. What I'd like to be able to do — and we can do it by phone or, if convenient, I can visit you — is to take a few moments of your time and get some ideas and maybe some names of people I might get in touch with."

Be specific

The more specific you can be when asking people for help, the better. Again, it's up to you — not the other person — to specify the kind of help you need. Ideally, you should know ahead of time if the person is in a position to help you. But if you're not sure, there's no harm in asking, as in the following examples:

- ✔ "I understand that you worked for several years at Amalgamated International, and I was wondering if I could sit down with you, tell you a little bit about myself, and maybe get the names of some Amalgamated employees I might get in touch with."

- ✔ "You've been in this industry a long time, and I can't think of anyone who would be in a better position to give me some advice on how I might make the switch from what I'm doing now to your industry."

Make it easy to say yes

If you approach people in the right way, you're going to be surprised at how cooperative and helpful they can be — even if they don't know you. But you have to do your part. The easier you make it for that person to help you — that is, the less time and effort that person has to put forth — the more likely you are to get the help you seek. Here are some specific suggestions:

- ✔ Let your contacts know that while you would prefer to meet with them in person, you would be more than willing to get the information you need over the phone.

- ✔ If your contacts whom you meet with need time to think about possible names, ask if you may leave behind a sheet designated for that purpose and include with that sheet your fax number or a self-addressed, stamped envelope.

- ✔ When people are giving names and addresses, don't expect them to give you the *complete* address. If you have the city, you can usually phone the company for the address and ZIP code.

Dealing with Voice Mail

Voice mail and other automated answering systems have added an obstacle to networking that didn't exist as recently as five years ago. They have also raised a troublesome question: What do you do when you're calling someone you do not call routinely and get transferred to that person's voice mail? Do you hang up and try again, or do you leave a message? And if you leave a message, how specific should it be?

Job search specialists are split down the middle on these questions. Some people recommend that you *never* leave a message for someone you don't know well — and, even more important, never ask someone you don't know to call you back.

Others see nothing wrong with leaving a message and your number, just as long as you're up-front about your reason for calling.

One thing everybody agrees on, however, is this: You should never simply leave your name and number along with a request for a callback with no clue as to why you're calling. This tactic is frequently used by bill collectors, fund-raisers, and aggressive salespeople fishing for new customers. And while it may be an occasionally effective way to get in touch with people who might not otherwise want to talk to you, it is basically rude and is not recommended if you're trying to get help from someone you don't know.

So what do you do? Well, if it's the first phone call and you have no personal connection with the person, you're probably better off leaving no message at all and calling back at a later time. If you've called numerous times and haven't had any luck getting in touch with the person, you can try the following:

1. **Identify yourself to your contact and then immediately give your telephone number.**

2. **Explain how you got his or her name.**

3. **Let the person know why you're calling.**

4. **Explain that you will be getting in touch at a later time.**

5. **Thank the person in advance for his or her time.**

Here is an example of this approach:

> "Nancy, my name is Phil Ford, and my number is 464-555-9877. I'm calling at the suggestion of your cousin Doris. The reason I'm calling is that I'm looking for a job in retailing and am trying to get the names of some people I might get in touch with in Chicago. I'll try to reach you sometime tomorrow afternoon. Thanks so much for your time."

If you get the answering machine or voice mail when you call a second time, you can shorten the message somewhat, again mentioning the connection and reminding the person that you called last week.

You may make several attempts to get in touch with someone and never get past the person's voice mail. If the best you've been able to do is to leave messages, try this: Get the person's address from the individual you know and write or fax a short note spelling out what help you would like. If you send the note by mail, include a self-addressed, stamped postcard on which the person can write the names and numbers for you. If you fax the note, add an extra page for that information, and remember to include your fax number (or a fax number that you have access to).

Getting the Most from a Networking Meeting

Assume that you've successfully navigated the initial stage of the networking process. You've gotten someone to agree to meet you in person or talk with you over the phone. The challenge now is this: How do you get the most out of the meeting? The following sections give you eight key points to bear in mind.

It's the little things that count

Before you sit down for the first time with any person whom you're approaching for networking help, do some research on the person and try to bring to that meeting something small that might be of value to him or her. It could be a book, an article, or even a report that you did at school or in your previous job. Even if the article isn't something the person is interested in, the simple fact that you've gone out of your way to do something nice will create a strong impression and will make that person a little more eager to go to bat for you.

Look your best

If you are going to meet personally with the people on your contact list (as opposed to talking to them on the phone), treat the meeting as if it were, in fact, a job interview. True, the people you're meeting aren't going to be evaluating you for a specific job. But the impression you make on them will determine how eager they'll be to give you names of other people or to recommend you for possible job openings.

Get to know the gatekeeper

If the person you're meeting has an assistant or receptionist who screens phone calls and arranges appointments for that person, introduce yourself and, without pushing things, try to establish a relationship. Get the person's name. Make sure that he or she knows *your* name so that when you call the next time, you won't have to reintroduce yourself.

Be prepared

Being prepared for the meeting or interview itself obliges you to go through the same preparation process you go through when you set up the interview in the first place. Make sure that you know (1) what you want from the other person, and (2) whether that person is capable of giving you what you want. If you're meeting the person simply to gain information about a specific industry or company, draw up a list of questions before you go into the meeting.

Verify how much time you have for the interview

Verifying how much time the person is prepared to give you before you actually begin your conversation is always a good idea. Don't make a big deal out of it. Just ask directly, "Roughly how much time do we have? I don't want to interfere with your schedule." Keep track of the time as the interview or the conversation proceeds. If the person begins to appear restless, or you've used up your time, *you* should offer to bring the conversation to a close.

The reason is twofold. First, it avoids the awkwardness you may feel when the other person has to tell you, "I'm sorry, I don't have any more time." Secondly, it conveys the right message by showing the other person that you value his or her time. If you have to go back to that person for help, he or she will probably be more willing to say yes.

Take notes

Taking notes during your meeting — as long as you do it in a relaxed, natural way that allows you to maintain eye contact — is a good idea for two reasons. The obvious reason is that doing so helps you to retain the information you gather. The less-than-obvious reason is that notetaking flatters the person giving you the information.

Be careful, though. Don't allow the note-taking process to interfere with the person's efforts to answer your questions. Listen attentively and write down key ideas. You'll have time immediately after the interview to convert your rough notes into a more finished form.

Remember that it's common courtesy to ask whether it's okay to take notes. Very few people will say no.

Don't talk about your problems

The purpose of a networking meeting is to get information and at the same time to make a favorable impression so that if this person does hear of a job, he or she will not be reluctant to recommend you. So regardless of how discouraged you might feel about your job hunting prospects, don't wear your heart on your sleeve. Be upbeat, positive, and enthusiastic. The last thing you want from the person you're talking to is pity.

Ask for names

If you accomplish nothing else, try to come out of any informational meeting with at least one or two additional names of people you can contact — and with that person's permission to use the names. The best time to ask for those names is at the end of the conversation, after you have established some rapport and have won over the person's confidence. Here again, the direct approach is usually the best, as in, "Do you know of any others who might be helpful for me to talk with?"

Show your gratitude

Always — repeat, *always* — send a short thank-you note to everyone who gives you their time, either in person or over the phone. Always do so within a day or two. Ideally, you should send the letter via regular mail on your personal stationery or send a handwritten note. Less desirable choices are to send it via e-mail or fax because it may appear impersonal, obligatory, or rushed.

Here's a longer-term suggestion. If, for example, the two of you discuss a subject in which the person is clearly interested, and you come across a magazine article the person might be interested in, send a copy. This shows that you're reciprocating the favor and keeps your name visible.

Getting Help from Perfect Strangers

The biggest challenge in networking is getting connected to people you neither know nor have access to. But the challenge is well worth accepting. Remember, this particular group of people — people you *don't* know — represents the largest potential source of network contacts. They're tougher to reach than people you know, but making them part of your network isn't as impossible as you may think. The next few sections give you some suggestions.

Write to them directly

Believe it or not, one of the best ways to get a perfect stranger to agree to help you is the most obvious: through a well-written, highly personalized letter. The trick is to find some pretext for writing and to demonstrate how that person's input will help you directly.

Your reason for writing can be just about anything. It can be a quote the person gave in an article you've read. It can be a speech the person gave at a gathering you attended. Or it can just be the company's reputation and the pivotal role the person or the person's department plays in its success. The letter should be brief (one page) and should *not* include your resume. It should ask for help concisely and directly. Here's an example of this type of letter:

June 12, 1995
Darlene Jobs
Associate Producer
WBJE
14 Studio Place
Buffalo, NY 01202

Dear Ms. Jobs:

I was in the audience last Thursday evening when you gave your presentation to the Association of Women in Media, and I was taken by the account you gave of how you were able to secure your first job in broadcasting.

My current situation is very much like the situation you described in your talk, and that is why I am writing to you. I graduated from Syracuse University last June with a degree in communications. Since then I have been working at a series of temporary jobs at radio and television stations.

I know how busy you are, but if at all possible, I would like to speak with you over the phone for a few minutes.

What I am looking for, in addition to advice, are perhaps the names of a few people I might get in touch with. I have a good knowledge of television production, having worked on several programs that were televised regularly at the University of Minnesota.

I would like to give you a call later in the week as a follow-up to this letter, and I thank you in advance for your help.

Sincerely,

Barbara Fisher

Become active in associations

Association meetings and similar events are an excellent way to add to your network people you might not otherwise get a chance to meet — and for an obvious reason. People are far more approachable at meetings, civic events, and social events than they are when they're working at their desks.

If you're going to association meetings as a networking strategy, prepare for them by gathering as much information as you can about the key players. If the association has a newsletter, for example, try to obtain past issues. Read the articles. Make notes of the people whose names are mentioned the most frequently. Chances are, they're the most active members.

Bring plenty of personal business cards to these meetings as well as to one-on-one meetings to facilitate more incoming networking calls!

If you would like to meet someone in particular at the meeting, your first step should be to find someone who can introduce you to that person. If that doesn't work, you'll have to make the introduction yourself. There's no secret here. You simply wait for what looks to be an appropriate time. Then excuse yourself, introduce yourself, and ask if the person has a moment or two. Once you reach this point, the next step is to ask permission to get in touch with the person at a *later* time. Do not try to force the issue at that moment — unless the other person invites you to do so.

Again, the best approach is the most direct approach. Use your sales pitch, let the person know what you want, and don't be embarrassed. Ninety-five percent of the time — maybe even more — you'll get what you want. Keep that in mind when you run into the occasional sourpuss who turns you down flat.

Do volunteer work

Getting involved with volunteer organizations is a great way to network simply because you're meeting people who share common values and goals. Be careful, though. Your principal focus in doing volunteer work should be on the work itself and on the people you're helping, not on the people you're trying to meet in order to expand your network.

If you're an eager volunteer, you probably won't have to make the first move. People will come to you, ask you questions, and, more often than you might think, offer to help without your having to come out and ask for it. That's not unusual, considering that people involved in volunteer organizations tend to be helpful by nature.

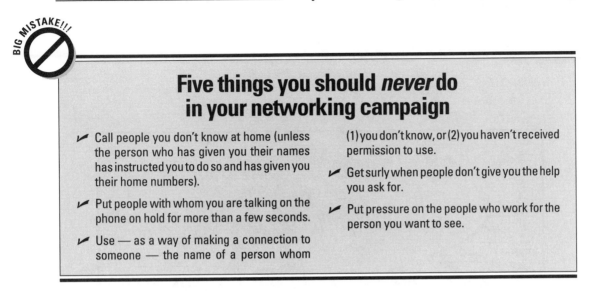

Five things you should *never* do in your networking campaign

✔ Call people you don't know at home (unless the person who has given you their names has instructed you to do so and has given you their home numbers).

✔ Put people with whom you are talking on the phone on hold for more than a few seconds.

✔ Use — as a way of making a connection to someone — the name of a person whom (1) you don't know, or (2) you haven't received permission to use.

✔ Get surly when people don't give you the help you ask for.

✔ Put pressure on the people who work for the person you want to see.

"HELLO, IS THIS THE NETWORKING CRISIS HOTLINE...?"

Chapter 13

Creative Reading: Scouring the Want Ads

*W*ant ads are the most obvious and easily accessible source of job leads. They're conveniently located in the same newspaper that tells you what's going on in the world and what's playing at your local movie theater.

The problem, though, is that focusing your job search activities on want ads alone is not the best job search strategy you can pursue.

The reason is numbers. Only about 15 to 20 percent of the job openings that get filled on any given day are advertised in the help-wanted sections of newspapers and other publications, and a good chunk of these jobs are entry-level or part-time positions. If you do happen to come across a help-wanted ad that sounds interesting and attractive — especially a job in middle management — the resume and cover letter that you submit are likely to have plenty of company.

But enough doom and gloom. While help-wanted ads may not be the primary source of job leads, many companies, especially smaller ones, rely on the classifieds to find qualified candidates. So *ignoring* the want ads would be unwise. The trick is knowing how to approach this aspect of your search logically, systematically, and creatively.

This chapter shows you how to do it.

It's Not a "Numbers Game"

Answering want ads isn't like playing the lottery. You don't increase your chances of "winning" (that is, converting your response to a want ad into an interview) by increasing the number of ads you respond to. You increase your chances of winning by focusing on the following three fundamentals:

- ✓ Concentrate on those publications that are most likely to yield openings keyed to your job targets.

- ✓ Take a disciplined, prioritized approach to determining which ads you respond to.

- ✓ Customize your responses to enhance your chances of surviving the initial screening process.

The following sections take a closer look at each of these fundamentals.

Knowing Where to Look

The vast majority of help-wanted ads are published in the classified sections of large-circulation metropolitan newspapers — particularly the Sunday editions of those newspapers. Depending on the type and level of job you're looking for, however, other classified ad sources may be worth pursuing, such as the following:

- ✓ Trade magazines and association publications that cover trends and events in your specialty or profession

- ✓ National business publications, such as *The Wall Street Journal, National Business Employment Weekly,* and so on (**Note:** *National Business Employment Weekly* is published by the same company that publishes *The Wall Street Journal* — the Dow Jones Company — and lists a week's worth of help-wanted advertisements from all regional editions of *The Wall Street Journal*)

- ✓ Major metropolitan dailies whose classified sections focus not only on jobs for their respective cities but also on national and international jobs, including *The New York Times,* the *Chicago Tribune,* and *The Washington Post*

- ✓ Small-town newspapers that cover communities within commuting distance of where you currently live or might be willing to relocate (these publications are good sources of jobs being advertised by small companies located in or around these communities)

- ✓ Online classified listings (for more information, see Chapter 18)

You may have to do some legwork to find some of these publications. Only a small percentage of trade and professional publications are sold on the news-stands or carried by local libraries, for example. If you want to follow the classifieds in these publications, you have to subscribe or have someone who subscribes send you the classified sections. To find out the names of trade publications that cover your field, consult either the *Gale Directory of Publications and Broadcast Media* or *Standard Rate & Data Service Business Publications Directory.*

Gathering local community weeklies and biweeklies can also be tricky. These newspapers typically cover a single county or town, which means that the only places you're likely to find them are at newsstands and libraries in that area. To follow the classifieds in these newspapers, you have to do one of the following:

- Make periodic visits (every two weeks or so) to the local library that subscribes to the publication or check the news racks at your local supermarket.
- Become a subscriber.
- Get friends or relatives who live in these communities to clip the classified sections and send them to you each week — devoted friends and relatives, that is.

Of course, not all these sources are necessarily worth the time and effort it may take to find and read them. But in the early stages of your job search, you should be looking through as many different types of publications as possible. Over time, you can narrow down the list to those publications most likely to list suitable openings. The ultimate test is the number of ads that are genuinely worth pursuing, based on how closely those jobs match your job targets.

When you're scouring newspaper classifieds in a library, don't limit yourself to the most current editions of those newspapers. Go back to the issues published several weeks before. The reason: The person the company hired may not be working out, and by getting in touch with that company, you could position yourself to become that person's replacement.

The Art of Reading Want Ads

The word *art* may seem like a silly word to use when talking about a task as mundane as reading through want ads, but there is more to reading the want ads than meets the eye. The following four tips can help you get the most from the time and effort you invest.

Set aside a fixed time

Tracking the want ads in a strategically selected group of publications should be a fixed part of your weekly job search routine — not something you do while you're watching *Jeopardy* or sitting in your car going through the car wash.

How much time you devote to reading and responding to want ads each week will depend on the number of newspapers and publications you intend to cover. Regardless of that number, try to do your want ad tracking on a regular basis. You may want to set aside an hour or two on Monday morning, for example, to go through the ads that appear in the Sunday classifieds. You may also want to set aside a certain day of the week — perhaps Wednesday — to go through publications that you don't get at home.

Instead of answering the ads that you come across one by one, pull together a group of them and then set aside a certain time each week to do nothing but write and mail your responses.

Become headline smart

Want ads are typically arranged alphabetically according to job titles, but some employers prefer to list their openings under a specific industry or profession rather than under the specific job category. As a result, you're likely to find openings for the same type of job under a half-dozen or so different listings. The lesson: Don't limit your reading to jobs listed under one category. Scan the entire classified section, especially in the beginning stages of your search. Get a sense early on of the range of categories that may apply to you in different publications.

Read between the lines

Even if you don't uncover any openings that warrant a response, reading through the want ads can still be useful. A careful reading of the Sunday classified section of your local newspaper can give you insight into which companies in your area are hiring, which specialties are in demand, and how salaries shape up in fields that you may want to enter. Reading the want ads can also give you a clearer sense of what specific qualities employers are looking for in candidates, and that information can help you learn how to make yourself more marketable.

Keep track of the ads you respond to

Set up a system that enables you to keep track of the ads you respond to. You can store this information on your computer (as a word processing file or in a database) or in a loose-leaf notebook. Make a copy of every cover letter you send and store it either in a separate file on your computer or in your notebook.

The following form (or some variation thereof) may work for you.

Name of the publication in which the ad appeared: _____

Date on which the ad appeared: _____

Name of company (if mentioned): _____

Person to whom you sent the response (if specified): _____

Company's address (if listed): _____

Phone number: _____

Fax number: _____

Date you responded: _____

Material sent (If you're using multiple resumes, keep track of which resumes you send to each company. At some point, the company may ask for an additional resume):

_____

How you responded (phone, mail, or fax): _____

Response from company: _____

Additional letters you write or calls you make to the company: _____

_____

Also, attach a copy of the ad or write down the exact ad copy.

Deciding Which Ads to Answer

A common temptation when you're looking through the want ads is to respond to *every* ad that describes a job that interests you — never mind that you are not qualified or are way overqualified. You figure that, except for the postage, you have nothing to lose. And, hey, you never know: You could get lucky.

Put a blanket on this impulse. Discipline yourself to apply only to those jobs that meet the following criteria:

- ✔ The job, as described, genuinely interests you.

- ✔ Your qualifications, background, credentials, and skills match up reasonably well with those that the position requires, based on the way the ad is worded.

- ✔ If you were eventually offered the position, you would be in a position to accept it, given the salary it pays and the special requirements (travel, for example) it entails.

The reason you need to take all these criteria into account when you are deciding which ads to answer can be summed up in one word: efficiency. It makes no sense whatsoever to pursue any lead for a job that, for whatever reason (such as salary or travel requirements), you are not going to be able to take. And it is equally foolish to squander time and effort (not to mention postage) responding to job leads when you do not have the credentials or skills specifically mentioned in the ad.

In both the short run and the long run, you're much better off focusing your time and energy on leads that are truly worth pursuing — jobs that interest you, that you would be in a position to accept, and for which you possess the majority (if not all) of the credentials and skills required. Think *quality,* not quantity.

Responding to an Ad

How you actually respond to a want ad usually depends on what the ad asks you to do. Occasionally, you're given a name and a number ("Call Zeke at 912-555-9088"). More often, though, you're asked to send or fax your resume (and sometimes your salary requirements) to a company. Sometimes you're given the name of the person to whom you should write. More often, though, you're given a title or department. This being the case, try your best, within reason, to get the name of the person to whom the title belongs or who runs the department. (See Chapter 14 for more information about getting that contact name.)

Tailoring your response

Your number one objective when you respond to a want ad is always the same: *to demonstrate to whomever reads the ad that you possess the basic qualifications and qualities that the employer is looking for.*

If the match isn't there, don't force it. Misrepresenting yourself *may* get you by the initial screener. Sooner or later, though, someone is going to get wind of the fact that in spite of what you said in your letter, you're really *not* proficient in the particular spreadsheet that you claimed to be an expert in and that people skills are *not* really your strong suit. All you accomplish by not telling the truth is to waste everyone's time and to trash your credibility in the process.

Adhering to this principle is especially important when it comes to what most people refer to as "hard" qualifications — that is, specific, verifiable aspects of your background: how many years of experience you have in a field, what degrees or certifications you hold, and how proficient you are in specific programs or systems, for example. If the ad is loaded down with these requirements and you don't meet them, case closed. Don't waste your time. Don't try to convince the employer that your "intangibles" more than make up for these shortcomings.

Here are two examples of ads that are heavy with "hard" qualifications:

- ✔ Programmer Analyst. Design, develop, and implement insurance and finance systems by using operating systems such as UNIX & ORACLE & languages like C++, Windows, APL, Visual Basic, Power Builder, FoxPro & MicroFocus Cobol. Requirements include bachelor of science or engineering with at least one year of experience as a project or systems analyst. Must have 6 mos. experience in using ORACLE, C++, Windows, APL, FoxPro, MicroFocus Cobol.

- ✔ Social worker. Manhattan. Provide individual group and family counseling to Chinese families. Requirements are a MSW and the ability to read, write, and speak Mandarin & Cantonese.

There are exceptions, though. You may come across ads in which the qualifications are a mix of hard requirements and softer, more subjective qualifications — qualities such as "organized," "energetic," and "motivated." In these situations, you can fall somewhat short of the harder requirements and yet still be a legitimate candidate, assuming that you are strong in the attributes described.

Here's an example of this type of ad:

> EXECUTIVE ASSISTANT. Multicultural advertising firm seeking executive personal & professional assistant with min. 2 years experience. Mac knowledge a must. High visibility position requiring daily client contact, executive phone skills. Must be detail-oriented with excellent organizational and writing skills. Must be independent, articulate, versatile, and discreet. Willing to work long hours if necessary. Your job is to make the executive's job easier.

In this ad, you see two "hard" requirements ("2 years exp." and "Mac knowledge"), but most of the requirements fall into the "soft" category. The best thing to do in this situation is to begin by stressing all the attributes you possess that match the hard requirements. If you don't have two years of experience (perhaps you have only one), mention it, but don't dwell on it. If you don't have Mac experience but are familiar with IBM-compatibles, make that point, emphasizing the fact that you are good with computers in general and would have no trouble getting up to speed on a Mac.

Either way, you don't want to take anything for granted. If you do meet the key qualifications spelled out in the ad, state this fact in the first sentence or two of your cover letter, as illustrated in the following examples:

✔ My three years of experience in public relations, coupled with my knowledge of desktop publishing, qualifies me for the position of public relations assistant that you advertised in last Sunday's *Bay City Gazette*.

✔ "Strong people skills," "Detail oriented," "Self-starter": These are phrases that virtually everyone I have worked for over the past ten years would use to describe me. And the fact that you stress the importance of these qualities in your recent ad tells me that the position advertised is one to which I could contribute a great deal.

Timing your response

Don't fret if you're out of town for a week or two and miss an ad. The hiring process for most mid- to high-level jobs, for example, usually takes weeks. Even if you submit your response a week or so after the ad originally appears, someone will take the time to read over your resume and cover letter.

However, with the flood of resumes now pouring in in response to many jobs, some companies review only resumes sent in the first week or so following the listing.

A good rule of thumb is to mail your response two or three days after the ad appears. Doing so keeps your response separate from the avalanche of responses that typically arrive one or two days after the ad appears but still ensures that it will arrive soon enough to warrant serious consideration. The lone exception to this rule is a position in which the ad clearly communicates a sense of urgency. In these instances, though, the ad usually lists a phone number — not an address.

If your current strategy of analyzing and responding to want ads isn't working, get a hold of issues of newspapers that date back three months before you began following the classified sections and look for ads that interest you. Chances are, those positions have been filled, but there's a possibility that the people hired for some of these jobs aren't working out, in which case your letter and resume could arrive at a propitious time. Also, when you respond to ads that ran several weeks earlier, you're not going to be competing with hundreds of other letters and resumes.

Dealing with salary requirements and history

Ads that specifically instruct you to indicate your salary requirements or history in your response can be troubling, particularly since you're generally advised to postpone discussions about salary until you've had a chance to present your case and find out more about the job. The obvious downside to mentioning your salary requirements up-front is that you might be asking for less or more than the company is willing to pay. On the other hand, by *not* indicating salary, you could hurt your chances for getting an interview.

You can relax on this one. The only circumstance in which providing the requested salary requirements or history could hurt you is when the starting salary you're seeking far exceeds what the company either wants or can afford to pay, in which case it's probably better to find out sooner than later. Depending on your situation, here are some approaches:

- When asked for salary *history,* be honest and specific. Employers are generally looking for your most recent salary.
- When asked for salary *requirements,* give a range of what you're looking for.
- If you're concerned that you may be overpriced for the position you're interested in, come right out and say that, if the job is right, you are willing to negotiate salary.

Red Flags: Ads to Think Twice about before Answering

Simply because an ad describes a job that looks to be right up your alley doesn't necessarily mean that it deserves a prompt response. In certain situations, you may be better off *not* answering the ad, regardless of the job it appears to be offering. Here's a brief description of the kinds of ads that fall into this category and what you need to watch out for.

Something-for-nothing ads

Be wary of short, vague ads that try to conceal the least attractive features of a job with euphemistic wording. Table 13-1 gives a sampling of phrases you may find in an ad (left column) and what the phrase may mean.

Table 13-1	Translations for Ambiguous Ad Phrases
Ad Copy	**What It May Mean**
"Earn up to six figures with no experience"	No salary, commission only.
"Challenging environment"	Bring your antacid.
"Applicant must be highly flexible"	Your office (if you have one) could well be a tiny cubbyhole next to the air conditioner compressor.
"Unlimited opportunity for the right person"	One in a million can succeed at the job.

Blind ads

Blind ads describe the job but don't mention the name of the company (you respond to a box number instead). Companies have their own reasons for placing blind ads. In some instances, they're looking outside the company to fill a position and don't want employees to know. In other instances, the company knows that it has a bad reputation and doesn't want to scare away applicants.

Whatever the reason, you should treat blind ads with care — especially if you're looking for a job while you're still employed. It's possible that your company may have placed the ad. (And one of the surest ways to get yourself fired is to give your company reason to believe that you're looking to leave.)

Chapter 14

Jobs by Mail: Conducting a Targeted Direct-Mail Campaign

● ●

In This Chapter

▶ What is a targeted mailing, anyway?

▶ Discovering the hidden benefits of targeted mailings

▶ Identifying target companies

▶ Writing the letter

▶ Following up on the letter

● ●

You can skip this chapter if any of the following apply to you:

✔ You have more job leads than you can handle right now.

✔ The fact that you haven't generated a significant job lead in six months doesn't bother you in the least because you figure that the law of averages is bound to shift in your favor sooner or later.

✔ You would rather walk on hot coals than do research on companies and write letters.

✔ You would rather walk *very slowly* on hot coals than send letters to people you have never met and then follow up those letters several days later with a phone call.

✔ You would rather *stand* on hot coals than make calls, even occasionally, to people who have already told you that they would keep your letter and resume on file.

If, on the other hand, you are *not* generating solid leads, despite your networking and the time you spend reading the classifieds, and you're willing to take a more aggressive approach to your job search, this chapter warrants special attention. Its purpose is to spell out a successful strategy of generating job leads through *targeted direct mail*.

What Is a Targeted Mailing, Anyway?

A targeted mailing is exactly what it sounds like — a mailing directed to a specifically targeted group of companies. In some instances, you may have some connection to the person you are writing in that company. More often than not, however, the person you're writing wouldn't know you from Adam, and you have no personal connection.

A *targeted* direct-mail campaign is different from a so-called "blitz" or "broadcast" letter direct-mail campaign. In a blitz campaign, you send the same basic, "Here-I-am-folks-make-me-an-offer" letter to the human resources departments of hundreds of companies, hoping that one or two of them might (just might!) bite. You don't worry too much about sending the letter to a specific person, and you don't follow up the letter with a call. It's essentially a numbers game. You send out hundreds and hope for a response rate of 1 to 2 percent.

Targeted campaigns are different. In a targeted campaign, you select a relatively small group of companies, do research on each company, and send an individualized letter to a *specific person* in each company. You then follow up the letter with a phone call and, if necessary, additional calls thereafter.

If you think that this sounds like a lot of work, you're right. Targeted mailings involve considerable effort and thought — and with good reason. You simply can't take a casual, now-and-then, when-the-spirit-hits-you approach to a targeted mailing — not if you want to achieve results. You need to be organized, focused, and persistent. And you need to have faith in the process, never mind that you have no way of knowing whether (a) anyone will take the time to read the letter; (b) the person who reads the letter will talk to you when you call; or (c) the person who talks to you (assuming that you actually talk to someone) will have anything to say to you other than "Thanks, but no thanks."

It's worth it. An estimated 10 percent of all hirings originate from an unsolicited letter sent directly to a company. But for job seekers who launch an aggressive, highly focused direct-mail campaign, the odds of landing a job are generally vastly improved.

The Hidden Benefits of Targeted Mailings

The benefits of targeted direct-mail campaigns go beyond helping you uncover job leads that you might not otherwise hear about. You get another bonus as well: the sense of control and direction that the process itself gives to your overall job search efforts.

When you launch a targeted mail campaign, *you* take over the controls. Instead of waiting around each week to see if anything looks promising in the Sunday classifieds, you take the initiative. The fact that you're spending a certain percentage of your time each week identifying, researching, and writing to companies and then following up with them helps to keep you focused and motivated.

And consider how much you learn in the process. Each new industry you investigate and each new company you study gives you a broader understanding of the job market. Each contact you make along the way expands your network. Without making a conscious effort, you learn more and your confidence grows, making you a stronger job candidate during eventual interviews.

Identifying Target Companies

No factor will have more bearing on your ability to generate job leads through the mail than the quality of your target list. That's why it is impossible to overestimate the importance of setting priorities during the selection stage. The key is establishing a set of criteria that are somewhat narrower than "anyone who will offer me a job."

The specific criteria you use to determine which companies are worth pursuing and which aren't will vary according to your general job targets. And remember, there's a difference between a *job* target and a *company* target. Job targets refer to the kinds of positions you're looking for within specific industries or types of companies — large or small, for example.

Certain professions and occupations, such as sales, marketing, law, accounting, and public relations, lend themselves to jobs in a variety of industries. Other professions and occupations — nursing and hotel and restaurant management, for example — are largely industry dependent, with fewer companies to choose from. The narrower your job targets are, the fewer the companies in your target company universe. But even if your job targets are fairly narrow, you still need to establish a means of prioritizing those companies.

The following criteria will help you prioritize. Bear in mind, though, that you may not be able to obtain *all* the information in these categories:

- ✓ **Location:** Is the company located within commuting distance of your current home, or is it somewhere that you would consider moving to?

- ✓ **Size:** How many employees work for the company? In smaller firms, you may be able to advance more quickly than at larger companies; however, the latter may provide more training opportunities.

✔ **Financial stability:** Is the company doing reasonably well, or is it hanging on by a thread?

✔ **Hiring patterns:** Is the company adding employees or cutting back? If the company is cutting back, how are the cuts affecting the department in which you're looking for work?

If you choose to, you can add still more criteria, such as the corporate culture, benefits package, and so on. But don't make the mistake of setting up *too many* criteria; otherwise, you won't assemble enough companies to make the campaign worth pursuing.

Getting Started on Your Target List

The best places to look for the names of target companies are the business reference directories listed in Chapter 10 or in the on-line sources described in Chapter 18. Bear in mind, though, that the better-known directories specialize in fairly large companies, whereas the biggest growth area in the job market is among companies with fewer than 100 employees. Unless you have a specific reason for doing so, don't limit your search to large companies.

Good sources for the names of smaller, local companies include the following:

✔ Regional business association directories

✔ Chamber of Commerce directories

✔ Local business publications

✔ Help-wanted ads

A reasonable target to shoot for in the beginning is 25 companies. That number may drop after you investigate a little further and remove companies from your list, at which point you can go back to the directories and add some more. The important consideration is balance. The more legitimate target companies you contact, the better, but you don't want *so* many that you don't have the time to do adequate research or make follow-up calls.

Set up your own system for capturing basic information about the companies appropriate to your target list. It could be a page in a loose-leaf notebook or an index card. When you first start out, write down the name of *every* company that looms as a potential target candidate, even though you may not know whether the company meets your other criteria until you do further research. You can always narrow down the list later.

Finding Out Who to Contact

After you assemble a list of companies, you're ready to start researching in earnest. Your first step is to get the name of the person you're going to be writing. The *ideal* person to write is not the Director of Human Resources but the person who will be doing the hiring.

You will often find the person's name — especially at a larger company — in the directories that you use to identify companies. Even so, it pays to call the company to verify that the person is still with the company.

If the person's name is not listed, call the company directly. Don't play games. When the operator answers, explain what you want: "I'm writing a letter to the Director of Marketing, and I would like the spelling of that person's name. Could you help me?"

If, for whatever reason, the person on the other end of the line acts as if you're asking for the president's private line, don't force things. Call back in a few days and simply ask to be connected to the department you want, at which point you can ask for the name of the person you seek. Department staff, in general, are usually more inclined to give out information than are receptionists.

If, after several attempts, you still can't get the person's name, you can do one of two things. Try to locate someone in your network database who has a connection to that company, or simply forget about the name and use the person's title instead. It's not the best way to approach the company, but at least it's a start.

Getting Your Contact to Take Notice

Apart from having a specific name you can write to, information that will motivate the reader to pay attention to you is the next most important thing to have. That you happen to be interested in a job doesn't constitute powerful motivation to a busy person who doesn't know who you are and is not concerned with whether you find a job. But if you can communicate in your letter that you understand the company's needs and have something to offer, you greatly increase the chances that your letter will be noticed and that your follow-up call will lead to at least a conversation.

What you are looking for, above all, in this phase of research are *recent developments* or *current trends* in the industry or the company (or both). If you have been keeping up with your research in general, you should already have a pretty good feel for this. The challenge is to determine how the specific company you've targeted is likely to be affected by these developments.

Here are some sources to tap when you're looking for recent information that is company-specific:

- ✔ The business sections of major local papers
- ✔ Trade publications
- ✔ Regional business publications
- ✔ *Business Periodicals Index*

Your efforts to get the current information you need may not bear fruit — especially if the target company is very small. This being the case, you may have no choice but to use your network sources to get more information. Keep plugging away.

Writing the Letter

A direct-mail letter is similar in many ways to the typical cover letter that you might write in response to a classified ad, and similar, too, to the letters that you might send to people to whom you've been referred by a network contact. (For details, see Chapter 9.) It should follow a standard business-letter format and be organized as follows:

- ✔ An opening paragraph sets the stage, capturing the interest of the reader and explaining why you're writing.
- ✔ Two or three paragraphs elaborate on the story you began to tell in the first paragraph. Here, you can add the information that you've gathered through researching the company.
- ✔ A concluding paragraph lets the reader know that you will be following up the letter in a few days with a phone call.

The main difference between a direct-mail letter and a want-ad response letter is the opening. Your opening here must be focused on the company you're writing — not on you. It should demonstrate that you have been doing your homework, that you have identified a need, and that you can offer something that can fill that need.

Here are three openings that illustrate this principle:

✔ "The fact that Snap-Its recently announced plans to market its line of left-handed tools in Latin America suggests to me that there may be a need in your company for people who are not only sales-oriented but also fluent in Spanish. I meet both of these criteria and, in addition, know a great deal about the hand-tool business, given the fact that my family owned a large hardware store in Dallas, Texas."

✔ "The bottom-line pressures in today's medical systems business have undoubtedly created new challenges for your sales staff — challenges that conventional sales training can no longer meet. I have a solid background in sales training and also have a good understanding of today's medical systems market, and I think I can make an immediate contribution to your company."

✔ "As one of *Commerce Magazine*'s 'fastest growing companies in America,' Stuff Shirts, Inc. is probably facing a problem that has become increasingly common among young, successful companies — figuring out a way to customize computer systems without disrupting day-to-day operations. My specialty is helping small companies get the most out of state-of-the-art technology, and from what I know about Stuff Shirts, Inc., I think I can make an immediate contribution."

Following Up with a Call

In a perfect world, following up your direct-mail campaign letters with a phone call wouldn't be necessary. Two or three days after you mailed the letters, you would be besieged with phone calls from the people you wrote — all of them begging you to come in for an interview as soon as possible.

In an *almost* perfect world, your follow-up phone call would put you in direct touch with the person you wrote. That person would not only recognize your name immediately but would say something along the lines of, "Yes, I got your letter, and we're *very* interested in you. When can you come see us?" Better still, "We'll send a limousine."

However, what is *most* likely to happen when you make a follow-up phone call is one of the following:

- ✔ You'll get the person's voice mail.

- ✔ The phone will be answered by the person's assistant, who will ask what you want and, after you explain, will say, "Yes, we've received your letter, and we've put your material on file."

- ✔ The person you're trying to reach will answer the phone but

    A. Will be too busy to talk with you right now.

    B. Won't remember having received your material.

    C. Will remember having received your material, will thank you for sending it in, but won't express any interest in seeing you right away.

Don't allow these possibilities to depress you. As anyone who does cold calling for a living can tell you, you can expect to be rejected more than 95 percent of the time. Each rejection, in other words, doesn't represent failure. It's a logical consequence of the process. If, out of every 100 letters, you can generate a dialogue with as few as six or seven people, you're doing twice as well as you would do with a standard broadcast letter (that is, a letter that you wouldn't customize to companies).

The real question to ask yourself is how hard you should push when you run into resistance. The answer depends on how comfortable you are with pushing people to do things they're not all that fired up to do. The following sections give you some ideas for overcoming the resistance.

When you get voice mail

If you're calling a person for the first time and you get voice mail, the best approach is to leave your name, telephone number, and a short message telling the person that you will get back to them, not unlike the approach with networking contacts. Again, the reason for leaving your telephone number at the same time you're telling people, in effect, "It's not necessary to call me back," is this: You give them the option of calling you back but, at the same time, you're keeping the ball in your court. You're not forcing yourself to wait around for the phone to ring.

Whether you should leave a message after subsequent calls is primarily a question of how frequently you call. If you're calling every other day, *don't* leave messages — you'll come across as a desperate pest. But if your calls are at least a week apart, you can leave a second message, keeping it brief and upbeat. If, after repeated attempts, you still haven't reached the person, you may want to leave a lengthier message, acknowledging that the person must be very busy but that you would like to talk to him or her for only a few minutes at any time that's convenient. If you can fax that message, do so. Even better, if the person happens to be on e-mail, send the request via your computer.

When the assistant answers

If the assistant who answers the person's phone is a gatekeeper — that is, responsible for keeping people like you from talking to the person — you'll undoubtedly be asked to explain why you're calling. If you're asked, be up-front. Playing it cagey won't work; it will only make the gatekeeper more suspicious and more reluctant to be of help. You might try something like, "I sent Mr. Jenkins my resume last week, and I'm calling to see if I can set up an appointment. I only need five or ten minutes. Can you help me?"

This approach may not work, either. But asking the gatekeeper to help you is often a good way to build rapport. Most people like to feel needed.

If, despite your appeal, the gatekeeper gives you the brush-off, don't force things. You have other people on your list to call. Fighting gatekeepers is a battle you're not going to win.

When the person answers

The drill here is simple:

1. **Introduce yourself quickly, explain why you're calling, and ask if the person has a moment to spare.**

2. **Tell the person what you're looking for — an opportunity to meet so that you can talk about job opportunities at that company — if not now, then sometime later.**

If you're lucky, the person will agree to meet with you, at which point you should set the date, say thank you, and get off the phone. *Do not* try to sell yourself during a phone conversation after the person has agreed to see you.

More typically, the person in this situation will do one of three things: tell you straight out that he or she is not interested in talking with you and that there is no point in calling back (at this point, don't push it); hedge the refusal by saying something along the lines of, "Well, I'm not sure if it would be worth your time to see me. We don't have any openings here and I don't see any materializing in the near future;" or tell you that he or she doesn't remember seeing your material.

The third of these possibilities is the easiest to deal with. Issue an apology (even if it's not your fault), double-check that you have the right name and address, and tell the person that you will remail the package.

When it comes to possibilities two and three, you have a choice: You can either push for the interview or back off. According to conventional wisdom, you should always push, the idea being that an *interview* is always worth pushing for. If it doesn't lead to an offer, it at least can help you expand your network.

Maybe so. If the person works for a company that ranks high on your target list, it is definitely to your advantage to set up an appointment — even if it's a ten-minute conversation over the phone. The trick is to push in a way that doesn't come across as pressure, as in this example:

> "I realize that you may not see any reason to talk with me, and I can appreciate how busy you are. But it would be extremely helpful to me in my job search if I could talk to you for a few minutes. I'm sure you would have some very valuable advice. We could do it by phone, at your convenience."

If the person turns down this request, don't push any further. Thank the person for his or her time (and do it graciously), and get on with the next call.

What if the company is *not* high on your list and is a pain to get to? And what if you have a lot of other people to get back to? Should you still push as hard? Probably not. In this situation, you're better to say the following:

> "I understand. What I'd like to do, though, if it's okay with you, is to get in touch with you at a later date when things aren't as busy."

This leaves the door open for a future conversation (at which point you might choose to push for a meeting).

Chapter 15

The Recruiting Game: Getting Outside Help

. . . .

In This Chapter

▶ Who does what: Looking inside the recruiting industry

▶ What you can expect from recruiters

▶ Understanding how recruiters operate

▶ Contacting recruiters by mail

▶ Working with recruiters

▶ Picking the firm that's best for you

. . . .

*T*housands of companies throughout the world are in the business of matching job hunters to businesses and other organizations that need to fill job openings. The people who work for these companies are known, in general, as *recruiters,* but you will sometimes hear them referred to as *headhunters, search consultants, placement counselors,* and *recruiting managers.*

Recruiting specialists are contacted by employers of all sizes to find suitable candidates for specific job openings, which run the gamut from entry-level administrative jobs to CEO positions. Recruiters then seek out candidates, handle the screening, interviewing, and so on, and then arrange company interviews for those candidates whose qualifications best match the needs of their clients. Companies make the final hiring decisions but frequently rely on the input of recruiters when making the choice.

Recruiters will serve one principal function in your job search: They will give you access to job leads that you wouldn't otherwise hear about. This chapter shows you how to get the most out of this relationship.

Note: Throughout this chapter, I'll be using the term *recruiter* to encompass both search and recruitment firms.

Who Does What: Looking Inside the Recruiting Industry

The recruiting industry is divided into two broad categories: executive search firms and employment or recruitment firms. Typically, executive search firms focus on the most senior-level positions and are paid a retainer fee by the client company. Recruitment firms and employment agencies, on the other hand, work on a *contingency* basis — they are paid a fee when and if the candidate they refer is hired. They can represent candidates for entry-level to senior-management positions.

But how a recruiter gets paid doesn't generally affect you one way or the other — except that you yourself should never be responsible for any portion of the fee. It didn't always work this way. Not too many years ago, if you found a job through some employment firms, a percentage of your first year's salary was applied to the fee. Fortunately for you, that practice has pretty much disappeared. Today, any company that hires you through a recruitment firm should be responsible for the entire fee.

What You Can Expect from Recruiters

Regardless of which type of firm you work with, you can save yourself a good deal of time and frustration if you keep in mind the following observations:

✔ Even if you're using a recruiter to get access to leads, you still have to do the bulk of the heavy-duty work preparing for interviews. (See Chapters 20–22 for interviewing tips.)

✔ Recruiters are generally of more value to job hunters who have a stable background in a specific field, as opposed to candidates who have job-hopped or are switching careers. The reason: Job-hoppers and career-switchers are much harder to "sell" to client companies. This doesn't mean that recruiters won't look at you if you don't have the most stable work background. It simply means that they may have to work a little harder to find situations for which you're qualified.

✔ The number of interviews that a recruiter sets up for you doesn't necessarily determine how good the recruiter is or how hard the recruiter is working on your behalf. The more experienced and knowledgeable recruiters are, the better able they are to judge — *before* you go on an interview — whether the company is likely to view you as a serious candidate. Good recruiters don't waste your time (or their clients' time) by sending you on interviews for jobs that you're not really qualified to fill. And good recruiters do not pressure you into going on interviews for dead-end jobs that don't meet your basic requirements.

✔ Always view the job leads that you get through recruiters as a bonus to the leads that you generate through networking and other strategies. In other words, don't allow the fact that you're working with a recruiter induce you to cut back on your lead-generating activities. You're still in control. You have to maintain the initiative.

While the main function that recruiters serve is to open doors to job openings, they can also be an invaluable source of information about job trends in your industry, such as which areas are hot and what current salary levels are. Be sure to ask broader questions about your search.

How Recruiters Operate

Executive search firms often hold the key to the highest level positions available in the job market. The question is how you go about positioning yourself so that you have a shot at those jobs that you're qualified for.

It's a challenge, but not an insurmountable one.

For one thing, you have to be more than *routinely* qualified for most of the positions that executive recruiters are retained to fill because recruiters frequently set their sights on top performers who are currently employed. Your competition for these jobs, in other words, is not confined simply to people who are actively looking for jobs but now includes people who wouldn't otherwise have been potential candidates.

Search firms can afford to be ultra-choosy. After they get an assignment, they don't have to worry about other recruiters beating them to the punch when it comes to delivering an attractive candidate to a client. And because executive recruiters generally work on a retainer (that is, a guaranteed fee), they don't have to rush. They can afford to consider only those candidates whose qualifications are an almost perfect match for the client company's requirements.

Regardless of whether you're working with an executive search firm or an employment firm, and even if your background and skills seem to qualify you for a position that a recruiter has been retained to fill, you run into another problem: gaining access to the recruiter who has the assignment. Unless you are privy to inside information, finding out which assignments recruiters are working on at any given time and whether those assignments represent legitimate opportunities for you is tough.

Executive recruiters in particular play it close to the vest when it comes to the specifics of their assignments. They don't typically place want ads for the positions they're trying to fill. (And if they do, they almost always place a *blind ad,* which is to say that it doesn't mention either the employer or the recruiter.) And they tend to work quietly and behind the scenes, relying on their own contacts and devices to find suitable candidates.

More important, search firms prefer to initiate contact with candidates they've already checked out before responding to candidates who get in touch with them. All of which explains why establishing a dialogue with recruiters you don't know can be so difficult, regardless of your qualifications.

Networking Your Way to a Recruiter

The first thing you need if you hope to use networking as a way to make contact with recruiters are the names of those recruiters who specialize in jobs in your field. A good source for this information is a directory that lists executive search firms and their specialty areas. See Chapter 10 for a list of directories that give you this information, or pick up a copy of *The Executive Job-Changing Workbook,* by John Lucht. It has a section devoted exclusively to search firms, their specialties, and their key personnel.

Better still, get on the horn with other people in your field — people who may have been contacted themselves at one time by recruiters.

After you identify recruiters who are likely to handle searches in your field, go back to your network list and try to find people who know those recruiters personally. Finding such a person may take time, but the effort is well worth it. Don't forget: You are always better off trying to establish contact with a recruiter indirectly — through someone you both know — than to try to make the connection on your own.

And What If You're Unemployed?

Don't let the fact that you're out of work discourage you from pursuing a relationship with a recruiter. Being unemployed may not *enhance* your attractiveness as a candidate, but neither does it hurt as much as it used to. Many recruiters used to be more reluctant to work with unemployed candidates, the theory being that they were a tougher "sell" to the client company. A few dinosaurs in the recruiting business still subscribe to this view, but in light of corporate downsizing over the past ten years, being out of work no longer carries the stigma it once did. The important thing is to be able to give the recruiter a solid reason why you and your former employer parted company.

How to get "discovered" by a recruiter

Practically speaking, there are only two ways you can initiate contact with a recruiter who hasn't gotten in touch with you first. The first and more effective way is to have someone introduce you, particularly at higher levels. The second is to write a strong cover letter — and then follow up.

What about cold calling? Depending on your background and available openings, you'll get anything from an invitation from the receptionist to send in your resume to an appointment.

Contacting Recruiters by Mail

One strategy for gaining access to recruiters — a long shot but sometimes worth the effort — is to send out a mailing to a targeted group of firms that specialize in your field. Because mailings take time and can get expensive, give this strategy some thought before you forge ahead. And bear in mind that recruiters at first are primarily interested in your professional experience and credentials.

The package that you send to each firm should include your resume and a cover letter. The letter should ideally be printed on personalized stationery. It should spell out, preferably on one page, what you have to offer and what you're looking for. The opening paragraph is crucial and should explain who you are and why the recruiter should be interested in you, not unlike the cover letters described in Chapter 9. The following are examples of good opening paragraphs:

- "I am a senior-level chemist with nearly 20 years' experience in the pharmaceutical industry. During this time, I have managed laboratories consisting of more than 500 people and controlled budgets in excess of $3.5 million."

- "For the past seven years, I have been the CFO of a $7 million restaurant company that was recently purchased by the Hammerhead Corporation. If one of your clients is a hospitality company in need of a financial specialist who understands the special needs of this industry, you may want to get in touch with me."

> ✔ "I am a senior-level human resources manager with more than 15 years' experience in Fortune 1,000 companies. In my most recent position — Director of Human Resources of the Feelgood Corporation — I managed a staff of 35 people and developed a quality awareness program that earned our company the number three ranking in the new book, *The 100 Most Quality-Oriented Companies in North America.*"

Notice how specific each example is. Specific numbers. Specific dollars. Specific names. That's the kind of "hard" data you must communicate to recruiters, especially in today's job market.

The remainder of the letter should be heavy on specifics as well. It should document specific accomplishments and explain — clearly and without equivocation — your current situation. It should also include your salary requirements and whether you would be willing to relocate. Keep the style simple and direct. And just as you would in any cover letter, make sure that the focus is on what you can *offer* and not on what you *want*.

Keep your expectations in check. Your goal in this exercise should be to elicit two or three responses out of every 50 letters you send. And remember, not getting a response doesn't mean there is anything wrong with you. It simply means that the firm you've written to does not have an assignment that matches your qualifications.

If you are currently employed, mass mailings to recruiters (and employers, for that matter) could result in your employer finding out that you're looking to move on. Use discretion!

When the Recruiter Calls

If you end up pursuing a job lead through a recruiter, the initial contact is likely to come in the form of a phone call.

Usually, the recruiter introduces himself or herself, mentions that your name came to his or her attention, offers a vague picture of the job that needs to be filled, and then begins to ask questions. Don't expect the recruiter to tell you the name of the company, and don't take it personally if the recruiter is evasive when you probe for details. At this early stage in the process, the recruiter is on a simple scouting mission.

Don't misrepresent yourself

Misrepresenting any aspect of your background or skills to a recruiter does you no good at all. Considering the detail in which most recruiters check your credentials, it's inevitable that any misrepresentations you make will surface, at which point you will lose out in two ways: one, you will no longer be a serious candidate for that job; and two, the recruiter is likely never to call you again.

Meeting the Recruiter

If you pass the initial phone screening, the next step in the process is a meeting with the recruiter. The meeting usually takes place at the recruiter's office, or it could be over breakfast, lunch, dinner, or cocktails. Here again, you can expect a battery of questions. At this stage of the game, the recruiter is generally verifying that the list of accomplishments on your resume is a genuine reflection of your abilities.

Many of the questions you are likely to be asked at this stage require specific answers: number of people managed, size of budgets controlled, and so on. Try to answer each question as directly as possible. The more vague you are, the less confidence you inspire.

What happens next depends on a number of factors, most of which are within your control at this point. If the recruiter thinks that you're the greatest thing since sliced bread, and your references check out, you'll probably get an opportunity to interview with people at the company that's hiring. Chances are, though, that you'll be competing at this stage with *several* candidates and may be asked to come in for several interviews. Don't try to force the issue; it won't work as a strategic ploy. You can certainly keep the recruiter informed about other developments in your job search, but you can't expect the recruiter, or the client company, to act according to *your* timetable.

Choosing the Best Firm for You

As a rule, recruitment or employment firms tend to specialize in entry-level to mid-management jobs (although they *can* extend to executive-level positions). This being the case, they are far easier to approach and cultivate a relationship with than are executive search firms. They typically have a number of positions to fill, so attracting a wide field of qualified candidates is to their advantage. Consequently, they're much more approachable.

Most recruitment firms operate pretty much the same way. The differences among them have to do with the types of jobs they offer, the quality of their personnel and candidates, and how specialized they are.

The first decision you need to make if you intend to go this route is which type of firm you want to work with: one that offers a range of jobs in a variety of fields or one that specializes in certain industries or fields. The advantage of working with a specialized firm is that it is likely to have far more opportunities in your particular field than does a generalist. If, on the other hand, your targets are not limited to a single field or industry, you may be better off with a firm that offers positions in a variety of fields.

In either case, try to pay attention to the *level* of jobs being offered. Some recruiters specialize almost entirely in entry-level positions — clerks, word processing specialists, and so on. And while these firms may have an excellent record of placing entry-level candidates, they may or may not be appropriate for you.

The simplest way to determine which firm is best suited to your needs is to spend some time with the Sunday classified section of your metropolitan newspaper. As you read through the ads, take note of those firms that seem to offer the kinds of jobs that you would like to pursue. You don't have to limit your search to those firms, but they're a good start. Another good approach is to ask friends and contacts to recommend firms with which they've worked.

Establishing the relationship

You can establish a relationship with recruiters in one of three ways: by answering an ad, by calling them, or by visiting their offices.

The busiest days of the week in most firms are Mondays and Tuesdays — the heaviest response days for Sunday ads. If you're not applying for a specific position but simply want to establish a relationship with a firm, plan to visit later in the week.

Generally, if you have good credentials, you won't have to jump through many hoops to get a face-to-face meeting with someone who has the authority to send you on interviews. If you have the background and experience that clients are looking for, you'll be more than welcome. A good recruiter should be able to give you an idea of your marketability. You'll learn early on if there's a reasonable match between what you want and can offer and the kinds of jobs the agency normally fills. If there isn't a match, a recruiter — without giving you full-fledged career counseling services — may be able to look at your background and experience and offer suggestions that may not have occurred to you.

On your initial visit, you're asked to fill out an application form and to verify, by your signature, that everything you said on the form is true. For certain types of jobs — entry- to mid-level accounting positions and word processing-related jobs, for example — you may be asked to take a skills or software-related test. For more information about testing, see Chapter 24.

You may also be asked, at some point, to sign an *exclusivity agreement.* This agreement represents your commitment to work with only that particular firm for a specified period. Whether an exclusivity arrangement works to your advantage is difficult to say. If you're a highly qualified candidate, an exclusivity agreement can be a disadvantage to you.

In any event, don't allow yourself to be *pressured* into signing an exclusivity agreement. If you do sign one, set a time limit of no more than a few weeks.

When the recruiter offers additional services

Some recruiters who specialize in entry-level positions offer other services, such as training on certain equipment, resume writing, or general career counseling. In some instances, the training is free; in others, fees are involved.

Generally speaking, you should be wary of any firm that offers services for a fee. This is not to say that agencies charging fees for services not directly related to placement are necessarily disreputable. Fees for certain services — resume copying, for example — may be legitimate, as long as you're not paying more than you would pay to have the same service performed elsewhere.

However, be particularly wary of any firm that wants a hefty up-front fee for vaguely worded services, such as "career counseling." And head for the nearest exit if anyone "guarantees" you a placement after you go through this training. The one thing you can be guaranteed of in the employment business is that there *are* no guarantees.

Making the relationship productive

Establishing a productive relationship with an employment firm shouldn't be a problem — not with the better ones, at any rate. The successful firms in this industry go to great lengths to provide a supportive, upbeat atmosphere. They're willing to work with you and give you constructive feedback.

The keys to a productive relationship, from your perspective, are comfort and trust. You have to feel comfortable when you're in the firm's offices and when you're talking to staff members over the phone. You shouldn't be reluctant to check in every now and then (as long as you're not doing it every two or three hours) just to talk to your recruiter to see whether anything is on the horizon. If the people you have to deal with are insensitive or unprofessional, find a firm where you're treated with respect.

Of course, it cuts both ways. When you ask a recruiter you're working with, "Why didn't you give me a chance to interview for that job?" and he or she responds, "Because it wasn't right for you," you need to trust that recruiter's judgment. Good recruiters, of course, will do more than simply tell you that a job isn't "right" for you — they will explain why. And they should also give you constructive feedback if you've gone on interviews but haven't received an offer.

Some Final Thoughts about Recruiters

To repeat a point raised earlier in this chapter, recruiters, whether they specialize in finding CEOs or in placing entry-level assistants, are not miracle workers. They can give you leads on jobs that you may not otherwise hear about and can help you prepare for interviews, but they can't manage your job search for you. Nor is it to your advantage to ask them to assume that role, even if it were possible. Recruiters are one of many resources that you should call upon in your efforts to find the job you want. Use them wisely.

Chapter 16

Temping and Other Ways to Get Discovered

In This Chapter

▶ Why temping makes sense in today's job market

▶ Understanding how the temporary services industry works

▶ Choosing the best temporary staffing service for you

▶ Doing your best on the temp job

▶ Temping and keeping your job search going at the same time

---

*T*emping, which is shorthand for taking a job on a temporary (as opposed to full-time) basis, was until about ten years ago largely associated with clerical positions and entry-level jobs. But all that has changed. Companies of all sizes and in virtually every industry throughout the world are now using temporaries for positions requiring higher skill levels. A rapidly increasing percentage of the millions of temporary employees throughout the United States today are college-educated, mid- to high-level professionals: accountants, lawyers, managers, engineers, computer programmers, teachers, physicians, nurses, and even CEOs.

The assignments that these temporary workers take on can last for a few days or for several months. And according to industry statistics, 38 percent of temporaries today have been offered full-time jobs at companies where they were on assignment. This chapter gives you a look at the most common source of temporary jobs — temporary help services.

A number of people at all levels of experience and in many professions are currently working as temporaries not because they are unable to find full-time employment but because they have made a conscious choice to work on a variety of projects with different companies for specified lengths of time. They like the challenge, flexibility, and exposure to prospective employers. They also like the opportunity that temping gives them to develop new skills.

Then again, temping isn't right for *everyone*. If you're the sort of person who doesn't take to new surroundings and new people very easily, for example, you may not be very suited to the temping experience. But if your personality lends itself to working on a variety of projects and in different jobs, temping can become a job-seeking strategy unto itself. For some job hunters, in fact, getting temporary work assignments represents the single most productive strategy for finding a full-time job.

The Benefits of Temping

If you're not convinced at this point that temporary employment represents a job search strategy worth your serious consideration, consider the following ways that temping can help you in your job search.

Ease financial pressure

The money you earn in a temporary job can help reduce the financial pressures that come with the territory when you're out of work for any length of time. With less financial pressure, you can afford to be more selective about the kinds of job leads you pursue and the offers you accept. At higher levels, you can often match or exceed the salary for the full-time equivalent of the position.

Develop a clearer sense of your job targets

What better way to find out whether you are cut out for a particular kind of job, a particular field, or even a particular company than to spend time actually doing that job in a real-world situation? As with internships, temporary assignments frequently give you access to companies where you wouldn't otherwise be able to get a foot in the door. Indeed, if you're not really sure about "what you want to be when you grow up," you can do yourself a big favor by postponing decisions about a full-time job until you have a chance to sample a variety of different work experiences through temporary assignments.

Beef up your qualifications

Many temporary assignments give you work experience that makes you a much stronger candidate for full-time employment. This experience can be especially valuable if you have a one-dimensional resume — that is, you have spent most of your career doing pretty much the same job for the same company — and you want to shift career gears. If you've spent most of your career with a big-name, Fortune 500 company, for example, a series of successful temporary assignments at smaller firms may help to reassure a smaller company that you don't need the support and structure of a big company to handle the position they need to fill. And if you've *never* worked for a big company, temporary assignments at large companies can reassure a larger employer that you can adjust to its structure and environment.

Expand your network

Temping is one of the best — and easiest — ways to expand your network. Each temporary assignment you take on puts you into the trenches with people you probably wouldn't otherwise get a chance to meet. And if you're temping in the field in which you eventually want to end up, you get a chance to observe and learn from those who are successful.

If networking is one of your goals, look for shorter assignments that give you more exposure to more companies. However, if you come across a great company and opportunity, let your temporary service know that you would like to work there as long as possible, and eventually in a full-time capacity.

Keep your morale high

The mere fact that you're getting up in the morning, getting dressed, going to work, and spending your day doing productive things (and getting paid for it) is one of the most reliable ways to keep up your morale during your job search.

The value of temping

Percentage of human resources managers and other executives who consider a long period of consistent temporary work comparable to full-time work: 78

Percentage of human resources and other executives who believe that it is valuable to have a prospective executive assistant or secretary work on a temporary basis before a full-time job is offered: 80

Source: Robert Half International Inc.

How Things Work in the Temporary Employment Business

Although some companies advertise and recruit temporary workers on their own, the vast majority of temporary assignments are handled by temporary service firms, some of which are specialized divisions of recruiting firms whose main business is recruiting full-time workers. Many firms that specialize in temporary help are national companies that have local branches; others are locally owned and operated. Many firms specialize in certain fields, while others offer more generalized service.

Regardless of their size and the kinds of jobs they offer, temporary service firms operate in pretty much the same manner. Like recruiters, temporary services get assignments from client companies and then recruit qualified people to fill those assignments. And as with most reputable recruiting firms, you, the employee, don't have to pay a fee.

The big difference, however, is that unlike search firms and employment agencies, temporary help services do the actual hiring. After you register with a temporary help service, you become *its* employee while you are on temporary assignments. Its employees sign your paycheck. And after you've been with that service for a set length of time, you may be entitled to perks, ranging from paid holidays, vacations, or bonus pay to tuition reimbursement and discounts on various services and products.

Here's a closer look at some of the specific perks you may be able to get, depending on the service you sign up with:

Medical coverage

When you register with any corporate member of the National Association of Temporary and Staffing Services (NATSS), you immediately become eligible for discounted medical coverage. You're responsible for the premiums, but the rates are lower than they would be if you were to apply for coverage as an individual. Some temporary services offer no such comparable plan, while others are beginning to offer their own plans. As with most medical plans, you usually have a variety of options to choose from.

Some temporary service firms also offer prescription benefit plans to temporaries who have worked a designated number of hours.

If you recently resigned from or were terminated by an employer where you held a full-time position and received medical coverage, by law you can opt to continue that coverage for 18 months after you depart. The law is called COBRA, and while you must make the premium payments, it saves you from any administrative hassles in finding insurance during this uncertain period.

Holiday and vacation pay

After you work a specified number of hours for certain firms within a specified time period, you often become eligible for holiday pay. You may also be eligible for vacation or bonus pay after a certain period, depending on the temporary service with which you're registered.

Choosing a Service That's Right for You

The temporary service business is competitive, especially among the firms that handle a variety of jobs rather than specializing in a single field. There's a good chance, in fact, that you will have a number of temporary services to choose from. And make no mistake about it, it pays to shop around.

Your number one consideration when choosing a temporary service to work with is *your* motivation — that is, what you hope to get out of the temporary work experience. If your main priority — for now, at least — is nourishing your anemic bank account, and you're not all that particular about the type of temporary jobs you get, the two key questions you should ask yourself when comparing services are: one, how much work they can give you; and two, how much money you can make. (Bear in mind, though, that the income you earn as a temporary employee, just as in full-time employment, depends primarily on the market value of the work you perform.)

If, on the other hand, your goal is to turn a temporary assignment into a full-time position, the nature of temporary assignments now available becomes critical — as do the companies you may be assigned to. If this is the case, you obviously want to find a service that specializes in the type of job you're looking for and, even better, that already has relationships with companies for which you would like to work.

The following sections give you six specific suggestions to help you make the best choice.

Evaluate the company's reputation and stability

Find out how long the service has been in business. Call trade associations that relate to the service's specialty area for input. Try your local Chamber of Commerce, too.

Get a personal recommendation

Some of the most reliable sources of information about temporary help services are people you know who have actually worked with one or more services. They'll be able to tell you whether the firm offers a good selection of assignments and benefits, and they may even be able to recommend a contact person at a specific firm.

Call companies that are likely to use temps

You don't have to be cagey. Simply call the appropriate department in one of the large companies in your city (ideally, a company that you would like to work for on a full-time basis). Explain to the person who answers the phone that you're thinking of signing up with a temporary help firm and that you would appreciate it if he or she could recommend one or provide the names of services that the company uses. If the person can't help you, he or she may be able to direct your call to the person who does work with them. And don't ignore smaller companies, either. The majority of future jobs — both temporary and full-time — are going to be with employers of 100 or fewer workers.

Analyze the Sunday want ads

And not just *one* Sunday, either. Study the ads for several consecutive Sundays. Ignore the flashy headlines and jazzy promises in the ad copy. Focus instead on the *specific jobs* being offered, and favor firms that offer specific jobs over those that simply invite you to come on down and sign up.

Check out the Yellow Pages

This is obviously the least effective way to make a value judgement, but at least you'll find some names. Virtually all temporary service firms advertise in the Yellow Pages, and their ads usually list the types of temporary jobs they offer.

Don't get discouraged if you can't find any firms listed under the heading "Temporary." Most Yellow Pages group all full-time and part-time employment services under the heading "Employment Agencies" or "Employment Contractors – Temporary Help."

Call or visit the firm in person

Don't hesitate to call or pay a personal visit to the temporary help services you may be considering. Pay attention to how the phone is answered, and, if you go there personally, to the surroundings. Are the employees pleasant and professional, or does being there make you uncomfortable? A good time to visit the firm is on payday (assuming that you can find out which day of the week it is). That way, you can meet some of the temporaries who already work for the service. While you're there, pick up brochures and ask questions about the firm's counselors, their level of expertise, and so on.

Signing Up with a Temporary Service

After you come up with a list of firms that seem to offer what you're looking for, try to meet personally with a counselor or representative from each service. Getting an appointment shouldn't be a problem if you have relevant experience; all it usually takes is a phone call.

Handling the interview

During the interview itself, you'll be asked some routine questions about your skills, the kinds of assignments you're interested in, and your availability. The person who interviews you will want to know how long you are prepared to work, the length of assignments you can commit to, and how flexible you can be. Another subject that is almost certain to come up is whether you're looking to convert a temporary position into a full-time position or are interested in exploring different types of jobs.

As it is when you're talking to full-time job recruiters, candor is essential. Don't misrepresent your skill levels; you'll be exposed sooner or later. And be honest about your motivations. If your goal is to convert the temporary job to a full-time job, tell that to the placement specialist. If you're looking for longer assignments, say so. The better temporary services go out of their way (within reason) to offer you assignments that meet your criteria, but you have to communicate those criteria early in the game.

✔ Don't be embarrassed to talk about money. On a typical temporary work assignment, you're paid an hourly fee, but the amount you receive may vary from one assignment to the next, even though the jobs are similar. The reason is that fees paid to temporary workers are frequently subject to market pressures, and sometimes special situations — weekend work, for example — warrant higher salaries. You may have *some* room to negotiate with the temporary service you're working with — but not much.

✔ Depending on the kind of temporary assignment you're looking for, you may also be asked to take a skills test that is designed to measure your proficiency in, say, a particular software program like Lotus 1-2-3 or Microsoft Word. Don't be insulted if you're asked to take such a test even though you've indicated on your resume that you are a whiz in this program.

✔ Don't be shy about asking questions yourself. Get a feel for how much you might be paid for a typical assignment, how soon you can expect to be called, and how much work you can reasonably expect. Most services will level with you.

Signing up with more than one service

Nothing is stopping you from signing up with as many temporary services as you want. Just bear in mind that if a temporary service calls you repeatedly and you are unable to fill assignments, the service is likely to lose interest in you. Your best bet is to start with one or two firms and wait to see how frequently they call you. If you're not getting as much work as you want, you can then try other services. You'll probably end up with one that you work with regularly.

Doing Your Best on the Temp Job

Generalizing about the type of work experience you can expect to have on your temporary assignments is impossible, other than to say that no two situations are alike and that you should never take anything for granted. Seasoned temporary workers have long since learned the best approaches to take when going on temporary assignments for the first time. The following sections outline these approaches.

Get a thorough pre-job briefing

The temporary service you're working for should give you a thorough briefing before you go on any temporary assignment for the first time. You'll know how to get to the company you've been assigned to, when they expect you, whom to get in touch with when you get there, and what sort of work you can expect to be doing. You'll be told, too, about lunch hours and any other special consider-ations (sign-in procedures, for example) that you need to be aware of. If you're *not* given this information, ask for it.

And while you're at it, see if you can dig up any more information that might be valuable. Is there anything unusual about this assignment, this company, or the person you'll be working for that you should know about before you show up?

Adopt a full-time mindset

The fact that you are working as a temporary employee in no way lowers the standards you will be expected to meet in the job. You should show up for work well groomed and appropriately dressed. Your placement representative should be able to tell you about the company's dress code, but if you're not sure, play it safe. Your appearance becomes particularly important if you're hoping to convert the temporary assignment into a full-time job. Don't underes-timate the importance of first impressions.

Keep in mind, too, that companies who rely frequently on temporary employees often request specific people who filled earlier assignments. The more a company requests you specifically, the more valuable you are to the temporary service you work for, and the more money you can expect to earn.

Clarify expectations

Even if you have been well briefed ahead of time, it's still a good idea to spend a few moments with your supervisor on the job assignment just to make sure that you understand the assignment and what is expected of you. Try to get a sense of not only what you'll be doing but also the bigger picture — and how what you're doing fits into that picture. If the assignment involves a number of tasks, ask your supervisor to set priorities for you. Don't be afraid to ask questions about anything you don't understand, and always take notes.

Be adaptive — to a point

One thing you have to get used to early on as a temporary employee is that you can't expect your working conditions to be tailor-made to your preferences. Your workspace may not afford you the privacy or the quiet you're accustomed to. The equipment you're obliged to work on may not be state-of-the-art. You may not have access to job tools you normally use, but do your best to adapt.

What you are *personally* accustomed to shouldn't be an issue, albeit with one exception: when conditions *prevent* you from doing the job you've been assigned to do. In that case, you should let the person you're working for know what you need. If that doesn't work, you should get in touch with your representative at the temporary service.

Practice diplomacy

Some companies for whom you work as a temporary employee are not necessarily going to do things in ways that you consider intelligent or productive and may even do things in a way that you consider — well, dumb. But don't be in a hurry to criticize. And whatever you do, don't make a fool of yourself by telling everyone how much "better" *your* way (or another company's way) is. After you prove yourself and come to know the company better, you will have plenty of time to make recommendations. Even then, it's best to be *asked* first.

Don't force things

As a temporary employee, you won't be "one of the gang" — not until you've been there for a while. So don't take it personally if the full-time employees don't go out of their way to make you feel at home.

Also, if you're hoping to convert a temporary assignment into a full-time job, there's no need to share that with everyone on staff. Focus instead on learning as much as you can about the company and the job. If you prove yourself, the opportunity to work there full-time will probably evolve — but on the company's timetable, not yours.

Stay in touch with your representative

If you run into problems that you can't handle on your own, don't hesitate to call your placement representative. Doing so is especially important if you are asked to perform duties that you were not hired to perform — such as duties that call for higher-level skills that would normally command a higher fee. In that case, still do everything in your power to put in a full day's work. After you meet that initial obligation, you can let your representative work out any problems.

Temping and Keeping Your Job Search Going at the Same Time

Temporary work provides you with a stream of income and puts you back in the workforce in the path of potential job opportunities. However, while working on a temporary assignment, you need to be prepared to make some adjustments to your job search program. Depending on the number of days you're doing temporary work, you may have to do your library research in the evenings. And you'll have to schedule job interviews for early morning or after work — which, by the way, won't harm your chances.

The biggest obstacle you face is making phone calls during working hours. As a temporary employee, you should *never* make job-related calls on company time or, for that matter, on company phones. It isn't ethical, and it could cost you future assignments. If you need to make calls, make them on your lunch hour on a public telephone outside company offices. If that approach doesn't work for you, then try to arrange with your temporary service to work no more than three or four days a week, and schedule your phone calls for those days when you're not working.

Part V
Taking Your Job Hunt OnLine

In this part...

The information superhighway is a fairly new addition to the job hunting process, but it can be extremely helpful to you in your search. This part shows you what resources are available on "the Net" and briefly explains how to use them. And because on-line researching and job hunting are not for everyone (it's perfectly okay to admit that you're a complete technophobe and prefer conventional methods), this part also helps you to decide whether you want to "surf the Net" at all.

Chapter 17

Online Job Hunting: The Basics

● ●

In This Chapter

▶ Online 101: A crash course in the basics

▶ Why online job searching makes sense

▶ Okay, there's a downside, too

▶ Should you make the leap?

● ●

*C*yberspace. The information superhighway. The Internet. Web sites. *Pick up almost any business publication today, and you can bet that somewhere in it you can find either a story or a blurb dealing with the growing popularity of the Internet.

This phenomenon is generally referred to as the *electronic information revolution* — so named because tens of millions of people throughout the world today are spending more and more of their work and leisure time "online." What they are doing, in short, is using a computer, modem, and phone line to conduct business, personal, and recreational activities that they would otherwise handle in person, over the phone, or by mail. They're catching up on the day's news; checking stock quotes; making purchases; setting up hotel and airline reservations; playing rotisserie baseball; swapping homeopathic cures; finding out how hot it is in Delhi, India; and taking part in discussion groups with people they've never met before about topics of mutual interest.

Online computing isn't simply a flashy trend. It has become common practice. For many professionals, going online has become as routine an activity as using the fax machine. People are asking themselves — as they did with fax machines — "How did I ever get along without this?"

What does all this have to do with job searching? Quite a bit. If you own a computer and a modem, it is now possible to go online for many basic job search tasks. You can network, exchange correspondence, gather research on companies and industries, search for job openings in your field, get career advice from professionals, and, in some cases, actually be interviewed online by prospective employers.

Why do it? Two reasons, mainly:

- ✔ Productivity, as measured by your efficiency and your ability to respond quickly to opportunities.

- ✔ Convenience — you can conduct online job search activities at virtually any time of the day or night (as long as the coffee holds out!) without having to leave your home.

Is there a catch? Sort of. In order to take advantage of the resources available on the Internet, you need the right equipment, which means a computer, a modem, and a phone line (preferably a second line so that you can keep your main line free for calls). You also need to learn to navigate the Web, which, depending on how familiar you are with computers, can take some time. And you have to be willing to spend some money — Internet service providers (ISPs), including commercial online services, charge either flat monthly fees or hourly rates. These fees, by the way, do not include additional charges you may incur through your regular phone service. Remember, each time you go online, it is like making a phone call.

It's important to bear in mind, too, that the Internet isn't the silver bullet of job hunting. It can't uncover job openings that don't exist, and it doesn't change the basic package of qualifications, skills, and personal attributes that you yourself bring to the marketplace. In short, the Internet is simply a tool — but a remarkably valuable one once you successfully incorporate it into your job search strategy. This chapter and the two that follow show you how to use the Internet to your advantage.

Online 101: A Crash Course in Going Online

If you have never sat in front of a computer and heard that distinctive, cavernous sound (a raspy "ahhhhh") followed by a faint "pop" that lets you know that you are officially online, the Internet can seem like a strange and bewildering place.

Think of the Internet as a series of interconnected networks that link together businesses, individuals, schools, government agencies, nonprofit organizations, and the news media worldwide. The Internet was originally developed by the military, and later became a central communication vehicle for the academic community. Today, the Internet, particularly the World Wide Web, has become an invaluable tool for business communication and research. The typical online user pays a monthly subscription fee to an Internet service provider or commercial online service such as America Online. Commercial services provide access to the Internet but also offer exclusive features such as movie reviews, shopping and travel services, research databases, and online versions of popular newspapers and magazines available only to subscribers.

The question you face when you decide to take your job search online is usually, "Where do I begin?" Commercial services offer a good introduction to online computing. They provide a user-friendly graphical interface — including a Web browser — that lets you "point and click" on areas of interest. In some instances, these services also offer 24-hour technical support should you encounter any problems while online. If you arrange for direct Internet access through an ISP, you'll likely spend most of your time browsing the World Wide Web, the graphical portion of the Internet that uses hypertext to link documents. With today's advanced Web browsers, such as Netscape Navigator and Microsoft's Internet Explorer, navigating your way through the vast amounts of information located on the Internet is easier than ever. The Web is where you can find corporate and media sites as well as myriad other Web pages, ranging from those hosted by private individuals to sites sponsored by universities and government agencies.

To help you sort through the online maze, the following sections take a quick look at some of the names and terms you should become familiar with before you take your job search online.

Search engines

Consider search engines to be your own personal research assistants. Depending on which engine you use (there are several), you can instantly find information about a particular company or industry simply by typing in a few keywords. The more specific you are, the better your chances of getting a good match. For example, if you type in "jobs," you'll likely receive thousands of potential matches, all of which you have to browse through to find precisely the types of jobs you're looking for. On the other hand, if you enter key words like "advertising jobs in Toledo, Ohio," you may have much better results. To be sure, using search engines efficiently takes practice, and sometimes there's no way to avoid sifting through dozens (a conservative estimate) of potentially useless links before you find what you need. Be patient, though. With a little resourcefulness, you can locate information that helps you immensely in your job search efforts.

Online discussion groups

Sometimes referred to as *chats* or *communication forums,* online discussion sessions give you an opportunity to communicate, via your computer, with people who either share your interest in a subject or have expertise that you want to tap into. Career-related Internet sites, as well as commercial online services, typically host online discussions for job seekers.

What generally happens in these forums is this: You select the live discussion group in which you want to take part and are then connected to that group. An on-screen graphic tells you how many people are currently participating, and you're invited to join the discussion simply by typing your user name or any other name you choose to use. Once you're part of the group, you can ask questions or make observations to the group as a whole or to other individuals (their names are usually listed on the menu), and you can leave the group any time you wish.

You can also capture to your own file any of the information exchanged during the session. In addition, many career sites archive past discussions. Job hunters typically take part in these sessions for one of three reasons:

- ✔ To network
- ✔ To share information and war stories with other job seekers
- ✔ To get information from specialists in different fields

Online databases

Online databases are precisely what the term suggests: databases that you access online. For example, Dun & Bradstreet's Companies Online, available on the World Wide Web, contains extensive information about more than 100,000 companies. The number and variety of databases that may be valuable to you in your job search is enormous and getting larger all the time. You may have to pay a fee for downloading articles and other information, but many databases provide information at no charge.

Newsgroups (Usenet)

Newsgroups are special interest groups located on the Internet. They act as electronic bulletin boards, and a growing number are dedicated to helping people find jobs.

The best thing about newsgroups, in general, is that they give you an opportunity to tap an information source that is focused on your particular interest and career objective as it relates to your geographic area. Keep in mind, though, that the quality and timeliness of the job-related information that you can gather from these sources varies greatly from one newsgroup to another. So you have to be prepared to sift through a lot of chaff before you get to the wheat.

The best place to start is with a Web site called DejaNews (`www.dejanews.com`), which catalogs all the newsgroups and allows you to search them by subject.

What's in It for You: A Closer Look at the Benefits

Exactly how quickly your own job search can benefit by your ability to tap into online resources is tough to say. A lot depends on the kind of job you're looking for, and how fast you can get up to speed with search techniques. Using the Internet as part of your job search strategy has the potential to bring you the following benefits.

Vastly broaden your research capabilities

Internet access greatly enhances your ability to do the research you need to uncover career opportunities, identify target companies, and prepare for interviews. It isn't only that the information available online far exceeds what you can find on a typical library shelf. More important is how much faster and easier it is to gather this information online.

Whatever the task — developing a list of target companies in a particular region or tracking down magazine articles written about specific companies — you can accomplish it far more quickly and efficiently online than you can by using traditional methods. When you're accessing a database, for example, you can bring to the screen in a matter of seconds a list of companies located in specific regions and, with a click of your mouse or a few keystrokes, capture that information to a file in your own computer, eliminating the tedium of writing down names, addresses, and phone numbers. Also, Internet resources are available 24 hours a day from the comfort of your own home.

Widen your access to job listings

The proportion of job openings that are advertised on the Internet still represents only a fraction of the total job openings available at any given time. However, the picture is rapidly changing. No longer limited to high-tech areas, the number of job postings on the Internet is growing exponentially. According to the 1997 Electronic Recruiting Index, for example, in 1996, more than 2 million available jobs were listed online, and more than 1 million resumes were uploaded by job seekers.

It's true, of course, that answering classifieds, whether you read them in a newspaper or on a computer screen, is not the most productive job search strategy. Still, online job listings have many advantages over newspaper want ads, everything else being equal. Online job listings are generally easier and quicker to sort through and, as a rule, are much more detailed than typical newspaper classified ads. You have more information to work with when the time comes to respond. Another advantage is that the larger online classified services give you an opportunity to search for jobs in parts of the country for which you may not have access to local newspapers. These jobs are also frequently available online before they appear in print, which can give you a jump on the competition.

Get career guidance and job search help

General information about job searching and managing your career is available in abundance on the Internet and through commercial online services such as America Online. Among the typical offerings are resume templates, articles about job search and career management, and forums or message boards in which job seekers can ask questions of and exchange information with job search authorities and other job hunters. Many career-related sites also host live online discussions focusing on key career issues.

The information that gets passed back and forth through these services is also available in books and articles that you can find in your library or bookstore. But having the data on the Internet makes it easy to access, and the fact that you're hearing it directly from other people (even if via a computer) can be reassuring — particularly to job seekers who are beginning to lose heart.

Communicate via e-mail with people throughout the world

Electronic mail (e-mail) messages have become the communication medium of choice for an increasing number of business professionals throughout the world, especially high-tech professionals with six-digit frequent flyer totals. In fact, many high-tech professionals are likely to read and respond to electronic messages more quickly than to conventional mail or voice mail. One explanation for this is that when people read their e-mail, they're already at their computers and can thus respond without having to do anything but type a reply and send it to the same address from which it came.

Expand your network of contacts

Taking part in online forums and chats is a way to converse with other people who have similar professional interests and, by doing so, expand your base of networking contacts. Here, again, the principal advantage is that online networking can take place during nonworking hours — an important consideration if you're currently employed.

Enhance your job prospects

One positive outgrowth of all the "Web surfing" you'll be doing during your job search is the effect it can have on your career prospects. The simple fact that you know how to conduct research on the Internet makes you a stronger candidate for many jobs. According to a recent Robert Half International survey, more than 60 percent of the human resources professionals and senior managers in major U.S. corporations now believe that knowing how to navigate the Internet makes you more marketable as a job candidate, and more than 75 percent believe that having a strong understanding of the Internet will be either somewhat or very important to your career advancement five years from now — regardless of your occupation.

The Cost of Gearing Up

You can take advantage of most online resources today with a personal computer and a modem that transfers data at 14,400 bps, and you can buy serviceable used equipment in this range for about $500.

To get the most out of online computing, though, you need something a little more state-of-the-art. The most advanced features on the Internet, for example, make extensive use of graphics, and in order to handle those graphics, you need a PC powered by at least a 486 or Pentium processor (or a Mac with a 68040 or PowerPC processor), at least 16MB of RAM, and a modem capable of transferring data at 28,800 bps or faster. Anything short of these capabilities can slow the information transfer process to a crawl.

Online fees

Online computing isn't as expensive as, say, playing polo, but it's not free, either. Service fees for Internet service providers and commercial online services average around $19.95 a month for unlimited access, with varying plans available for users who want to be billed by the hour. The average hourly fee is around $2.50. If surfing the Internet becomes a routine activity in your job search, your best bet is to opt for unlimited access.

And while you can download much of the information you access at no added charge, some subscriber-based magazine and periodical databases charge you a per-article fee (it's usually around $1.50) for every download. So if you're not careful — especially if you select multiple articles — you can easily run up hefty charges.

Your computing abilities

The one factor that hasn't been mentioned yet in this discussion of online computing is *you* — that is, whether you have the time, patience, and temperament to learn how to get around on the Internet. It's a classic good news/bad news situation.

The good news is that it takes most people far less time to learn the ins and outs of navigating the Internet than it used to. Internet service providers and commercial online services provide software that does much of the complicated setup work that you once had to do yourself. No longer do you have to concern yourself with perplexing questions about initialization strings, modem protocols, parity, data bits, stop bits, and all the rest. Most Internet software automatically configures your equipment and then, after you're set up, makes it possible for you to connect to many destinations without having to actually dial the access number and log on.

There's good news as well in that once you log onto the Internet, your Web browser employs an attractive graphical interface to present you with information that you can relate to and understand even if you didn't go to M.I.T. On-screen menus enable you to move through the various areas simply by pointing your mouse and clicking. The online help is logical and well indexed — a far cry from the way things were as recently as five or six years ago. Commercial online services such as America Online offer these same user-friendly interfaces.

But even with these enhancements, online computing still has its glitches, especially when it comes to connecting to and navigating your way through the Internet, even if you prepare yourself well by reading such guides as *The Internet For Windows For Dummies* or *The Internet For Macs For Dummies* (both published by IDG Books Worldwide, Inc.).

Things happen. Things you can't explain. The access number that your computer is automatically programmed to dial doesn't always respond the first or second time you call, because it is either busy or out of service. Sometimes even the alternate number you've entered is unresponsive, who knows why. Interference on the phone line can suddenly kick you offline, and software glitches can cause your computer to freeze, forcing you to reboot and start the process anew.

The point is this: Don't expect things to always go smoothly. If you're the sort of person who goes ballistic when the mechanical things around you don't work as well as you would like them to, you may have to take a few deep breaths during the process.

Chapter 18

The Job Seeker's Tour of the Information Superhighway

*O*kay, you just set up your new, supercharged PC or Mac, and you've got your jackrabbit of a modem hooked up and raring to go. Your favorite coffee mug is close at hand, and your favorite CD is playing in the background. All of which means you're ready to take your job search online, right?

Not quite. Getting yourself geared up on the technical side (your favorite CD included) is only half the battle in online job searching. The other half is figuring out which job search and career-related destinations on the Web are worth your while. Those destinations are the focus of this chapter. Happy travels!

Choosing an Internet Service Provider

One of the first choices you probably need to make when you decide to go online is which Internet service provider to sign on with. There's no one "best" choice for job seekers. Fortunately, it's fairly easy to discover which service provider is best for you without having to invest a lot of money.

Most offer introductory memberships that give you several hours of free hookup time (excluding normal phone charges and any premium service charges) in your trial month. That's plenty of time to get an idea of whether the Internet and the World Wide Web can help you in your search.

Considerations that may affect your decision include the following:

- **Ease of initial hook-up:** Some Internet service providers offer all the software you need in one easy package. Often, it's available on a disk or a CD-ROM. If the Internet service provider you're considering does not offer software, evaluate the time and effort it may take for you to first find and then download the software you want. Examples of this kind of software include the basic, but quite complex, connectivity software that your ISP may require, spell check programs that check your e-mail messages for mistakes, and applications that make the most of the Internet's advanced features.

  As part of your research going in, look at reviews of local service providers as well as the commercial online services to see whether they can make accessing the Internet easy and affordable.

- **Pricing structure:** Most services charge a monthly fee that entitles you to unlimited hours online. Arrangements vary, however. With some services, you have the option of paying a lower monthly fee, which gives you only a certain number of hours online.

  Another key cost consideration is the availability of local access numbers — in particular, those that can transfer information at speeds in excess of 14,400 bps. This consideration is critical because any charges you incur when you're logged on to an online service are exclusive of normal phone charges. That's not a problem if you can connect to the Internet service provider or commercial online service through a local number that charges you a flat fee per month. But if the access number you use to reach the service is long distance, you had better be sitting down when your phone bill arrives.

  All the ISPs make it fairly easy to find the nearest access number, but, alas, there's another complication: baud rate. Many local access numbers have limits to how fast they can transmit information. This means that even if you have a modem capable of transmitting data at, say, 56,000 bps, the local access number you want to use may only be equipped to handle transmissions at 14,400 bps or less. If you do not live in a major metropolitan area, a higher-speed number may be a long-distance call.

  If this is the case, you have a tricky decision to make. You have to decide whether, in the long run, it is more economical to transmit information at the faster speed when you're accessing the service through a long-distance call or whether the extra charge on the phone lines eats up the savings you get from faster transmission.

- **Technical assistance:** In general, all Internet service providers handle customer inquiries and problems in a way that doesn't make you feel like a complete basket case (although you should expect delays in getting through to technical support). As long as you're evaluating services, it may be a good idea to call their technical support departments if you're running into problems and see how quickly and courteously they help you.

Some ISPs offer "live" support, meaning that you can call a help desk and receive immediate assistance. Others prefer to help their customers online, so you have to send an e-mail or navigate your way to a chat area to ask your question; then it may take a while before someone gets back to you.

The free introductory memberships that Internet service providers and commercial online services offer aren't necessarily as free as you may think. At first, you're entitled to either unlimited or a specific number of free hours per month, but you may still be expected to pay for extended services, such as specialized databases. Best advice: Make sure that you understand exactly what the free package offers before you type in your credit card number.

Internet Service Providers: The Key Players

Most people access the Internet by using an Internet service provider. ISPs, including UUNet, Netcom Inc., AT&T WorldNet, and GTE InterNetworking Services, generally provide only Internet access — including World Wide Web, Usenet newsgroups, Telnet, and Gopher — and e-mail, which may be all you need. A commercial online service like America Online is an Internet service provider that also offers unique content in addition to e-mail and Internet access. These services have become a popular way for the general public to access and use the Internet.

To help you start your search for a service provider, here's a listing of the major services, along with their mailing addresses, toll-free phone numbers, and Internet addresses. You can obtain all the details about features and costs by telephone (this information changes frequently). When you call, you're also given information about how to set up and enroll. Generally, you have a choice. The service either sends you — at no charge — software specifically designed for new users or gives you a number that you can dial through your modem, along with sign-up instructions. If you go the latter route, expect a bumpier start because the instructions — and the adjustments that you may have to make to your modem settings — can be confusing if you've never signed up before.

America Online
8619 Westwood Center Drive
Vienna, VA 22182
800-827-6364
`www.aol.com`

The America Online Career Center, Business Indexes (including *Hoover's Company Profiles*), and online periodicals (such as *The New York Times, Business Week,* and *Dow Jones News*) may be of special interest to job seekers.

AT&T WorldNet
P.O. Box 563
Morrisville, NC 27560-8408
800-967-5363
www.att.net

In May 1997, *Smart Money* selected AT&T WorldNet as the top ISP in the areas of network reliability, customer service, and technical support. This ISP has exclusive content for users, including news services.

Concentric Network Corporation
10590 N. Tantau Avenue
Cupertino, CA 95014
800-939-4262
www.concentric.net

Earthlink Network
3100 New York Drive
Pasadena, CA 91107
800-395-8425
www.earthlink.net

Membership with Earthlink Network includes unique content and classified job listings. For Macintosh users, Earthlink is one of the better ISPs.

GTE InterNetworking Services
1411 Greenway
Irving, TX 75038
800-927-3000
www.gte.net

Netcom
2 North Second Street
Plaza A
San Jose, CA 95113
800-638-2661
www.netcom.com

MCI Internet
2495 Natomas Park Drive
Sacramento, CA 94833
800-550-0927
www.mci2000.com

Sprint Internet Passport
P.O. Box 260157
Tampa, FL 33685-0157
800-786-1400
800-747-9428
www.sprint.com/sip

UUNet
3060 Williams Drive
Fairfax, VA 22031
800-488 6383
www.us.uu.net

If you intend to enroll with any of these Internet service providers, you can save yourself a considerable amount of time (and no small measure of grief) by calling the service and asking them to send you the software that their service requires. These applications are free, automatically configure your system, and walk you through the initial sign-on process.

If you're a rookie when it comes to online computing and are accessing the Internet for the first time, take several minutes to surf around and familiarize yourself with the basic navigational techniques. Pay particular attention to the following:

✔ Setting preferences, including determining your *home page* (the page that your browser automatically opens when you log on).

✔ Noticing the difference between hyperlinks and regular text (hypertext). Hyperlinks are usually underlined and in a different color. When you click on them, your browser jumps to the location designated by that link — either somewhere on the same Web page or to another page altogether.

✔ Saving Web pages in a Bookmarks or Favorites file so that you can easily find your way back to them. (In the next section, you can find a number of sites to bookmark.)

✔ Configuring your e-mail. For example, if you want every message you send to include your name, address, and contact information, you can create a signature file, and your application automatically appends this information to the bottom of your messages.

✔ Saving important e-mail addresses in the e-mail program's address book.

Numbers game

When CIOs from 1,400 U.S. companies were given a chance to talk about the Internet in a recent RHI Consulting survey, 50 percent said that their companies have Web sites. The primary use of the sites, according to two-thirds of the CIOs, is to market their company's products and services. Providing customer service and technical support came in a distant second, followed by research and e-mail.

The Job-Related Online Resources Most Worth Exploring

Keyboards ready now: This section lists the services and areas of the Internet that are of specific interest to job hunters and people seeking career advice.

The top services on the Internet

The top ten career-related sites on the World Wide Web based on the number of people who log on to them are as follows.

Career Mosaic

How to access: www.careermosaic.com

What it offers: Several services, including a college connection directed toward students looking for entry-level openings and internship opportunities, classified listings, and the capability to search for jobs by region, job title, and salary.

Best features: Corporate "home pages" that offer a multimedia introduction to client companies. Easy to access and get around — with good, basic information about job hunting in general.

Career.com

How to access: www.career.com

What it offers: A communication link between hiring managers at high-tech companies and candidates looking for jobs.

Best features: Periodic job fairs that enable hiring managers and candidates to conduct online interviews.

Career Path

How to access: www.careerpath.com

What it offers: Nearly 500,000 new jobs each month and newspaper classified advertising updated daily. Career Path also features a searchable database of employers and a Help Wanted index.

Best features: Links to local newspapers are helpful to long-distance job seekers.

America's Job Bank

How to access: www.ajb.dni.us

What it offers: This site is the national clearinghouse for the public employment sector, offering positions with the local, state, and federal governments. Updated daily with new information about local public service positions, it features a keyword search by job title. The job descriptions vary in style and content, mostly because open positions are submitted from 1,800 offices throughout the United States.

Searches are easier if you know the government code for the public position you seek.

Classified 2000

How to access: www.classified2000.com

What it offers: A complete listing of classified advertisements — including, but not limited to, Help Wanted ads. The built-in search engine is relatively powerful and lets you type in a number of position requirements that it sorts based on your preferences.

Best features: The Cool Notify feature allows you to specify exactly the position you're looking for. Each time the site finds a match, it e-mails you.

Online Career Center

How to access: www.occ.com

What it offers: A large, loosely structured, and constantly changing mix of career- and job-related information from a wide range of sources. Includes a job search menu, employment events, career assistance, and resume upload options.

Best features: This site was one of the first online career sources.

JobTrak

How to access: www.jobtrak.com

What it offers: Geared primarily toward students and university alumni, JobTrak features thousands of listings and also offers expert job hunting advice and resume preparation tips.

Best features: JobTrak is partnered with 650 college and university career centers, MBA programs, and alumni associations and lets you submit an application directly to your local recruiting center.

E.span

How to access: www.espan.com

What it offers: Online access to thousands of job openings — the majority offered to employers as an extension of classified newspaper ads that they ran throughout the country. The site is updated daily.

Best features: This service is comprehensive and easy to use.

NationJob

How to access: www.nationjob.com

What it offers: NationJob's P.J. Scout asks you for a complete job profile, and then it searches its database once a week and sends you an e-mail with a list of positions that fit your profile. You can view and reply to interesting advertising online.

Best features: A great design, sophisticated search engine, and detailed listings.

Intellimatch

How to access: www.intellimatch.com

What it offers: This site offers matching technology to help job seekers and employers find each other. It also helps you create a resume with its PowerResume feature.

Best features: The HotJobs! database includes thousands of positions from hundreds of employers.

More Internet services

Here are a few additional multifeatured Web sites that may be helpful in your job search.

In addition to these career-related resources, staffing and recruiting firms use their Web sites to list available positions — by industry, job title, and region — and can search for your specific criteria. Many of these sites offer additional career advice and resources as well.

Yahoo/Business and Employment

How to access: www.yahoo.com/business/employment/jobs

What it offers: In one menu, Yahoo! brings together more than 100 job- and career-related online resources, including Career Mosaic, the Online Career Center, Career.com, regional and academic job banks, and career-related publications.

Best features: The capability to view and access from one Web page most of what the Internet has to offer in the way of career resources.

Careers.WSJ.com

How to access: `careers.wsj.com`

What it offers: A free service of the subscription-based *Wall Street Journal* Interactive site, Careers.WSJ.com includes a searchable jobs database, career news, information about relocation, and a full listing of career-related resources.

Best features: Content and career advice from *National Business Employment Weekly,* a great interface, and ease of use.

About Work

How to access: `www.aboutwork.com`

What it offers: Discussion groups where you can ask questions, share information, and let off steam about your job search activities. Resume help and interviews with people who are conducting or have recently completed their own job searches.

Best features: Lighthearted features about the workplace and scheduled chat sessions for people with interests similar to yours.

America Online Career Center

How to access: America Online, Keyword: Career Center

What it offers: Regularly scheduled online career counseling, live chats with other job seekers, resume help, occupational profiles, how-to articles about various aspects of the job search process, and an extensive listing of classifieds that you can search by region and occupation.

Best features: Nicely balanced variety and an attractive, easy-to-navigate interface.

Cost: Membership to America Online costs $19.95 a month for unlimited access to its services and the Internet. Alternative subscription plans are available.

CareerBuilder

How to access: `www.careerbuilder.com`

What it offers: CareerBuilder provides resources to those looking for jobs and career advancement advice. Its features include a Personal Search Agent that helps match your criteria to available positions, an online magazine called Achieve, relocation information, and select company prospect uses.

Best features: The Getting Started feature includes tips on using the site, planning your career, and developing your resume and cover letter.

The Monster Board

How to access: www.themonsterboard.com

What it offers: The MonsterBoard features career search options; an advice-oriented career center, including resume and relocation tips; and information about starting your own company. It also notifies you of career fairs, open houses, and industry events in your area.

Best features: The MonsterBoard's international employer profiles are listed both alphabetically and regionally. Profiles include in-depth information about the companies and link you directly to the firms' available positions.

Research

The following are great places to conduct research on various career- and business-related topics.

Dun & Bradstreet's Companies Online

How to access: www.CompaniesOnline.com

What it offers: Bare-bones information about organizations on the World Wide Web, including listings for more than 100,000 public and private companies, government agencies, and schools and universities. Easy-to-follow format.

Best features: Ease of use and variety of information available.

Dialog

How to access: dialog.krinfo.com

What it offers: Access to more than 450 databases offering either full-text articles or abstracts of articles from more than 50,000 publications and directories in dozens of fields. Some databases offer complete text online.

Best features: Extent of offerings and cost effectiveness relative to similar services. Features include access to nearly 40 major metropolitan dailies, including the *Chicago Tribune, USA Today,* and *The Washington Post.* Full-text access to the *Harvard Business Review* from 1976 to the present is also available.

Cost: The price varies with the database you want to search, but usually includes an hourly rate and a charge for each article downloaded. Prices are published online, on the Help page.

Hoover's Online

How to access: www.hoovers.com

What it offers: Information about more than 11,000 public and private companies worldwide. The Hoover's Company Capsules offer basic information and links to corporate Web sites. These are free.

Best features: The Hoover's Power Search lets you search by company name, stock ticker, or keyword. There's also a comprehensive custom search option that lets you search by industry, location, or annual sales.

Cost: A personal subscription to Hoover's Online costs $12.95 per month or $109.95 per year and grants you access to Hoover's Company Profiles of more than 2,700 companies, plus historical financial data for more than 8,000 companies, and Hoover's Online Library.

Lexis/Nexis

How to access: www.lexis-nexis.com

What it offers: A comprehensive source of electronic information. The Nexis half of the service offers full-text access to more than 1,000 regional, national, and international newspapers and magazines, in-depth reports on companies, and hundreds of key trade publications from dozens of industries. The Lexis half of the service deals with specialized legal research.

Best features: Exhaustive information resource.

Cost: Subscription cost varies. Lexis/Nexis also offers fee-based research for nonsubscribers, usually around $1.50 per article.

News.com

How to access: www.news.com

What it offers: News.com is the technology news service from C|Net: The Computer Network. The site is updated three times a day and features breaking stories as well as additional news on computing, business, and a feature called "Rumor Mill." News.com asks you to subscribe, but membership is free and offers access to all areas and the opportunity to personalize the page. It also sends you an e-mail with daily news updates.

Best features: A search tool lets you look for information about specific companies or topics.

EDGAR

How to access: www.sec.gov/edgarhp.htm

What it offers: EDGAR is the Electronic Data Gathering, Analysis and Retrieval system of the forms filed by companies with the U.S. Securities and Exchange Commission (SEC). This site is a good source for information about companies as it collects and indexes all SEC submissions.

Best features: If you know the name of a company, use the Quick Forms Lookup feature. If you want to search for keywords instead, search the archives.

PointCast

How to access: www.pointcast.com

What it offers: A free and personalized news feed right to your computer monitor. PointCast broadcasts current national and world news, stock quotes, sports scores, and industry updates — flashing the headlines across your screen.

Best features: Easy to use — once you download and customize PointCast, there's nothing more to do.

Company information and job listings

Internet search engines are a good place to begin your research on the companies you're interested in and also to find postings for open positions.

All these sites work similarly: Type the name of a company in the search line, hit Return/Enter or click Search, and these engines find relevant information — including the company's own Web address and articles that have been written about the firm. Or if you're looking for positions rather than for companies, try typing **Jobs in [Anywhere, USA]** to see what the search engine comes up with.

Many companies list available positions on their Web sites, so it's a good idea to find out whether a company you like has a Web site and then go there to see what you can learn about the firm and about its job openings. Which search engine you use is a matter of personal preference; they are all free of charge.

Search.com

How to access: www.search.com

What it offers: Search.com has collected many of the best features of several different search engines to help you find information. You can select the subject area you want to search and then choose the search engine you want to use. Search the Web as powered by Infoseek; search the Yellow Pages with City Surf; find stock quotes with the help of Data Broadcasting Corporation.

Best features: An all-in-one search engine.

Yahoo!

How to access: www.yahoo.com

What it offers: Yahoo! is a database of links and a subject-oriented guide for the Web and the Internet. Like the search engines, you type in what you're looking for and Yahoo! returns hyperlinks that match your request.

Best features: Because Yahoo! is a good Web directory, you can search within its subject categories. You can also limit the number of matches that the engine returns.

AltaVista

How to access: www.altavista.digital.com

What it offers: AltaVista claims that it can find any word in any document published on the Web. A downside to this is that you may not *want* to review every document. AltaVista is a powerful and comprehensive search engine with more than 30 million Web pages in its index.

Best features: The Customize AltaVista feature lets you specify how you want to see your search matches — in what format, language, and level of detail.

HotBot

How to access: www.hotbot.com

What it offers: HotBot boasts more than 50 million documents in its database, and the simple search query includes pull-down menus and buttons that enable you to refine your search criteria.

Best features: SuperSearch lets you be very specific with your query. HotBot makes intelligent guesses about what you're looking for, based on the organization of your queries, and returns the best matches first.

Infoseek

How to access: www.infoseek.com

What it offers: In addition to a standard search engine, Infoseek offers comprehensive information about companies, provided by Hoover's Online, and access to a News Center, which includes feeds from news wires and daily papers. Infoseek Investor finds stock quotes and price history information about any publicly traded firm.

Best features: The "browsable" reference collection can help you write your cover letter — it includes links to *Webster's Dictionary,* a thesaurus, and zip code directories.

Excite

How to access: www.excite.com

What it offers: Excite's 14 channels organize the Web like a newspaper or *TV Guide.* The channels of most value to job seekers are Business and Investing, Careers and Education, and News. The Excite search line appears on every page, so you can always type in a more specific query.

Best features: Excite's NewsTracker scans hundreds of online publications to bring customized news to your desktop.

Lycos

How to access: www.lycos.com

What it offers: Lycos has the capability to search 55 million Web pages and has 19 million of these fully indexed. Search the directory with keywords, and a brief description is provided for each site located. The Advanced search includes options to refine your search, specify the amount of detail in the results display, and set the number of results displayed per page.

Best features: The subject-based directory of the most popular pages from the Lycos database is called a2z.

DejaNews

How to access: www.dejanews.com

What it offers: DejaNews searches 20,000 Usenet newsgroups for references to your topics. You can also browse newsgroups of interest. Use the Power Search feature to find industry and company information quickly.

Best features: This site is comprehensive and claims to save more than 500,000 megabytes of new information daily.

Chapter 19

Traveling Smart: How to Get the Most from Your Online Efforts

. . . .

In This Chapter

▶ Getting yourself set up for e-mail

▶ Managing yourself while you're online

. . . .

As any veteran Internet traveler will tell you, online computing can be highly addictive. That's no problem if going online is your hobby and it's a priority for you to get the up-to-the-minute football scores from *USA Today*. But if you're using online resources in your job search, you have to exercise some discipline — especially if you don't have a lot of time to squander.

The point is this: You can't expect the technology — as remarkable as it is — to do all the work. You have to be able to manage the technology, which means being able to manage yourself. This chapter focuses on some of the specific things you can do online that can make your search more productive.

E-Mail: Not Just for Breakfast Anymore

E-mail (short for *electronic mail*) is that rare breed of computer term: You know what it is simply by what it's called. E-mail is mail that is sent electronically, from computer to computer, rather than through the postal service or by fax. Other than calling someone on the phone, e-mail is the fastest way to get a message to someone, and it has numerous advantages over conventional mail service, faxes, or overnight service. You don't have to worry about envelopes and stamps. You can send the same message to many people without having to duplicate it each time. And you can send a long document much faster and less expensively than you can send it by fax or by overnight service.

To send and receive e-mail, you need an Internet address and a software program that handles the mechanics of e-mail. Fortunately for you, dozens of services and organizations — including commercial online services, Internet service providers, and some phone companies — can provide the tools that you need to create and receive messages. Most e-mail software programs have similar procedures for inputting messages, storing addresses, organizing incoming mail, and so on.

How E-Mail Works

The majority of e-mail service providers adhere to an international set of transmission standards that enable you to exchange messages not only with other users of the same service but also with users of the Internet. Because of the vast, worldwide connections of the Internet, it doesn't matter whether you're a member of America Online or you have your own connection to the Internet. Likewise, it makes no difference whether you use a computer in Jersey City or Jakarta. You can use e-mail to send messages to people regardless of where in the world they live or work.

Why E-Mail Matters in a Job Search

E-mail can no longer be dismissed as a high-tech frill for job seekers, for it is rapidly becoming the communication medium of choice for millions of people — especially professionals who use computers daily. For example, if you're looking for a job with a company in the high-tech industry, not having e-mail capability can put you at a disadvantage. Many online classified ads that run on the Internet list the e-mail address of the employer or person placing the ad. In fact, many list only an e-mail address and no postal address or phone number.

Establishing an E-Mail Address

Getting your own e-mail address is a simple, painless process. You get one automatically when you sign up with an Internet service provider or commercial online service. In most cases, you're prompted through an on-screen process that takes less than a minute. A few services oblige you to use your user name as your Internet address. Others allow you to choose whatever e-mail name you want, as long as it isn't being used by someone else.

Choosing your e-mail name

If you expect to be using e-mail for work or job-search-related purposes, resist the temptation to use a gimmicky name like Avenger, GrateDead, or DreamLover. Keep it straight and businesslike. Most service providers allow you to have more than one e-mail address, so you can reserve your "colorful" e-mail address for private use and establish a more professional-sounding one for your job search activities.

Typical e-mail addresses look like this:

`PRabbit@aol.com`

`Jane_Smith@xyzcompany.com`

`president@whitehouse.gov`

Each address has two components: the user name or ID number (PRabbit, Jane_Smith, and president) and the "post office" or domain name — that is, where the person receives messages. The characters @aol.com stand for "at America Online," which means that PRabbit receives messages when he or she logs onto America Online. The letters xyzcompany.com and whitehouse.gov are typical Internet domain names.

Other Important Things You Should Know about E-Mail

Using e-mail opens up a whole new range of possibilities for communication, but you need to consider the following when using this unique tool:

✔ **Confidentiality:** In most cases, any message you send via e-mail is reasonably secure and confidential — that is, read only by the recipient — but you can never be sure. There are people who go to great lengths to intercept other people's e-mail messages. If you have something truly confidential to say, don't say it over the Internet! Another problem is that you have no control over what happens to the message once the recipient captures it to his or her own file. So if you want what you say to remain confidential, label the message as such. Doing so alerts the recipient to keep the file or a hard copy of it out of public view.

- **Privacy:** If you're using e-mail at work, be aware that your management has the right to read messages you send over the company's e-mail system, regardless of how personal or embarrassing those messages may be. Be alert to the possibility, too, that your manager — the person you described in your last e-mail message as "difficult" — may be the one who reads the message. The safest route: Don't use company e-mail in your job search if you're still employed.

- **Accuracy:** Misspelling a person's name when you're sending a fax or mailing a letter may insult the other person, but it doesn't usually affect whether the message arrives. Not so with e-mail. Computers are unforgiving when it comes to typos and misspellings. A mistake as innocent as omitting a single letter in a long address either prevents the letter from being received or sends it to someone else.

- **Urgency:** People who send messages via e-mail are usually in a hurry to get a response. So if you go to the trouble of getting an e-mail address, make sure that you're prepared to log on frequently so that you can check your incoming messages. At least once a day is considered adequate by most people, but a few times daily is better.

- **Special features:** You can do more with e-mail than send and receive short messages. You can also exchange files (such as your resume or samples of your work) and send out a single message to a large group of people. For more information about sending documents via e-mail, check out *The Internet For Windows For Dummies* or *The Internet For Macs For Dummies* (both published by IDG Books Worldwide, Inc.).

Driving Tips: How to Handle Yourself Online

By now, you should have a pretty good idea of what's available to you in the way of online job search tools. If you intend to take advantage of some of these resources, the following general pieces of advice can make you more productive and your Internet activities more enjoyable.

Make sure that you're set up properly

Nothing does more to sabotage your online search efforts (and, in the process, drive you nuts) than failing to take the time before you begin your online activities to make sure that your computer, modem, and phone line are set up properly and that you understand (and can put into practice) the log-on procedure that each service requires. By all means, take this precaution before you plunge into any session in which you're under the gun to access information. An ideal scenario is to have a friend or colleague who lives, eats, and breathes online computing help you get set up and coach you through your initial session.

Learn your way around first

As eager as you may be to cut to the chase and go directly to the area of the Internet that focuses on your field, take a few moments to familiarize yourself with the basic commands. If your computer is hooked up to a printer (and it ought to be!), go to the Help section of your browser, call up the screen that gives you basic commands, and then print it out. Having these commands on paper where you can refer to them is much easier than interrupting your search activities to figure out which command you need to issue to get yourself out of the dead end you've managed to get into.

Plan your sessions ahead of time

Decide ahead of time what, specifically, you want to accomplish in each online session. Simply logging on to a service with no clear job-hunting-related goal is not unlike going to a supermarket without a list, the difference being that in a supermarket, the aisles are clearly labeled and you can navigate your way around the entire store in a matter of minutes. The Internet, as you quickly discover, is vast, and your online activities can be extremely time-consuming if you lack a set agenda.

Establish a budget

Determine in advance how much time and money you can afford to spend each month on Internet-related job search activities, and make sure that you stay within these guidelines. Track your Internet usage, even if your Internet provider grants you unlimited access. You'll want to leave enough time for other job search activities. Remember, the Internet is just one of many tools that you should use to find the job of your dreams.

Learn how to work smart

Once you get the hang of things, you should be able to develop techniques that enhance your online productivity. Here are a few tips:

✔ Pay attention to the name that you give to each file you download. Set up a system that enables you to view the directory of downloaded files and know instantly what each directory contains.

✔ If you're working on a tight budget, choose your downloads (those you're being charged for, that is) with care. You can always print out the abstract (for which you don't generally pay a fee) and then use that information (name of article, publication, date, and so forth) as the basis of your library search.

✔ Bear in mind that if you schedule your online research activities during times of peak usage (that is, normal business hours and early evening), you may encounter delays. Opt for less busy times, such as late in the evening or on weekends — you'll have an easier time connecting with your local access number, and your search activities will progress more quickly.

✔ Disconnect from the Internet while you're not working online. This helps cut down on some of the congestion (aka traffic jams) that is currently affecting the Internet.

Internet "Netiquette"

When surfing the Net, you need to pay attention to the rules of the road. Some advice:

✔ Never say anything in an e-mail message that you wouldn't say to the recipient in person. This means never sending e-mail when you're angry or unhappy — you may regret it later.

✔ Always double-check the address to which you're sending e-mail. You don't want an unintentional audience (say, a prospective employer) to receive a message from you that was meant for someone else (say, another prospective employer).

✔ Be polite. "Please" and "thank you" are common courtesies. Remember, e-mail communication is no different from sending a personal letter. Also look for misspelled words and grammatical errors.

✔ Keep it short — the shorter the better. The person with whom you're communicating may receive hundreds of e-mail messages a day. It's best to get right to the point.

✔ Avoid typing in all capital letters. To readers, it looks as if you're SHOUTING! This advice also applies to chat sessions in which you participate.

✔ Always include a subject in your message, and make sure that this information is meaningful. If you're applying for a job opening, list the exact title of the position in the subject line of the e-mail message — for example, "Re: group marketing manager job opening." This subject immediately tells the recipient the purpose of your message.

Part VI
Answering the Call: Keys to Successful Interviewing

THE **WRONG** WAY TO TAKE CONTROL OF AN INTERVIEW

" JOHN SMITH...COLLEGE GRADUATE...SOCIAL SECURITY NUMBER 333-22-4444...BUT ENOUGH ABOUT ME, LET'S TALK ABOUT YOU."

In this part...

The interview is your chance to show a company that the skills and experience that impressed them on your resume come from a talented, enthusiastic human being who would be a great addition to any department. This parts shows you how to prepare for the interview, field those tough questions, and close the interview on a winning note. In addition, you'll find advice for negotiating the job offer.

Chapter 20

Getting Ready for Show Time

. . . .

In This Chapter

▶ Taking an inside look at the hiring process

▶ Understanding what interviewers really care about

▶ Gearing up for the interview

▶ Cramming for the questions you'll most likely be asked

. . . .

The *best* thing that someone can say to you during a job hunt is, "We'd like to hire you." Before you can hear *those* words, though, you need to hear the *second* best thing that someone can say: "We'd like to set up an interview."

Simply put, you're not going to get hired for any job worth accepting until someone sits down with you face to face, interviews you, and comes away from that interview reasonably convinced that you're the best person for the job. And although the way you handle yourself during the interview is only one of *several* factors that ultimately has a bearing on that hiring decision, the interview is without question one of the most critical factors — especially in two situations.

The first is when most of the candidates for a particular job have fairly similar credentials and backgrounds, in which case the nod often goes to the candidate who comes across as the most personable, enthusiastic, and motivated during the interview process. The second is when the key qualifications for the job have more to do with personal attributes and communication skills than they do with technical qualifications.

The way you come across during the interview would be extremely important, for example, if you were applying for a job as a host for a restaurant company. It would be less important if you were applying for a position in the financial department of that same firm, where the key qualification was the ability to operate the company's financial software program.

First, a Heart-to-Heart Chat about "Selling Yourself"

The core message about interviewing is that you have to do a good job of selling yourself. Through your appearance, demeanor, and the way you answer questions, you have to convince the interviewer that you possess the skills and personal attributes necessary to be successful in the job.

Some people, of course, are better at selling themselves than others. And more than simply being able to sell themselves, some people have the chameleonlike ability to create almost any impression they want during a job interview. They can go into large, bureaucratic companies and pass themselves off as the ultimate bureaucrat — someone who knows his or her place in the system and doesn't like to rock the boat. And two hours later, they can walk into a different office and convince the interviewer that they're the ultimate entrepreneur — someone who thrives in a nonbureaucratic, seat-of-your-pants environment.

With a little practice and experience, you can learn to create whatever impression you want to create during a job interview. The question, though, is how far you really want to take this skill.

True, the better your ability to tailor your approach to what an interviewer might be looking for in a candidate, the more offers you're likely to get. But in some situations, you may well *not* be the ideal candidate — not because anything is wrong with *you* but simply because the fit between you and the job or company just isn't there. The job for which you're being interviewed may require someone who is good at — and *enjoys* — handling deadline pressures, for example, and you may not particularly enjoy handling deadline pressures. The company you're interviewing with may be highly bureaucratic, whereas you may be much more entrepreneurial by nature. So even though you may be able to look and act the part of the "ideal" candidate, there's a good chance that even if you're hired for the job, you're not going to be happy there.

In other words, as important as it is to "sell yourself," it's always better to sell the true *you,* and not simply a role you're able to play during the interview. That's why it pays to take the time early on in your job search to set appropriate job targets and choose your target companies carefully (see Chapters 3 and 4) so that when you *are* asked to come in for an interview, you're reasonably sure that you are well suited for this job and company. That way, you won't be tempted to give answers that don't represent your genuine views.

What Interviewers Care About

A job interview, at root, is nothing more than a conversation — a chance for you and someone else (or maybe two or three someone elses) to exchange information. And because the main topic of this conversation is *you* — who you are, what you've done, what you're good at, and what you want — job interviews should actually be a lot of fun. After all, how many other opportunities do you get to talk about yourself at length, knowing that the other person is paying careful attention to everything you say?

The problem is that a job interview isn't a *typical* conversation. Both you and the interviewer have an agenda that goes beyond what you actually say to one another. Your objective, of course, is to sell yourself — to do everything you possibly can to make the most favorable impression (assuming, that is, that you want the job). The interviewer's objective, in the meantime, is to try to get answers to three basic questions:

- ✓ Can you do the job?
- ✓ Will you fit into the company or department in which you'll be working?
- ✓ Will you be a reliable, motivated employee (based on what the company can afford to pay you)?

Here's a closer look at these basic questions and how interviewers generally go about getting the answers to each one.

Your ability to perform the job

Except for those situations in which you are given some sort of a skills test (one that measures your proficiency in a particular software package, for example), you rarely get an opportunity during a typical interview to demonstrate your ability to perform the specific tasks or meet the responsibilities that the job entails. A job interview, in other words, is not quite the same thing as an acting audition or a tryout for a baseball team. As an actor or athlete, you get an opportunity during an audition or tryout to *directly* demonstrate your skills. You act out a scene, sing a song, or throw a few high, hard ones. In a job interview, you mainly *talk* about what you've done and can do.

Practically speaking, the only way for interviewers to determine whether you possess the basic skills to perform most jobs is through inference — *intelligent guesswork*. They look at what you've said about yourself in your resume and other correspondence — what you have actually done and accomplished in the past and what specific skills you possess. And they ask questions whose answers will bring into clearer light the information you wrote on your resume. They then try to tie their impressions, coupled with the information contained in your resume, to what they see as the key requirements of the job they're seeking to fill.

It is for this reason that a good interviewer won't let you get away with vagueness and generalities in your answers. Good interviewers will probe. They want specifics — concrete information that they can use to verify the impression you create. If your resume says that you saved your company $25,000 on a particular project, a good interviewer will want to know what, specifically, you did to produce savings. Did you simply fire someone, or did you introduce some innovative productivity measures? If you make a point in your resume and in your answers of stressing that you're highly organized or detail oriented, a good interviewer will look for some illustration of how those skills made a difference in specific projects or tasks.

It's easy to get defensive when someone is prodding you to be more specific in your answers, but you should welcome the opportunity to elaborate on your answers. If you've prepared well for the interview, you should be able to document with specific examples every assertion you make concerning your qualifications and skills. Those examples are the heart and soul of your case. And if you don't get a chance to present them, you lose one of the few opportunities you have to make yourself stand out from the other candidates.

The "fit"

The fact that you possess the skills and background needed to perform a particular job doesn't always mean that you'll be taken seriously as a candidate — not if the interviewer has concerns about you as a person and your ability to adapt easily to the company's culture. Nearly every organization — even the smallest of businesses — has its own style and atmosphere. Some companies have highly conservative, traditional views on how employees should dress, behave on the job, and even decorate their offices. Other companies are more entrepreneurial and freewheeling; they don't really care how you dress or behave (within reason), as long as you do your job and don't make life miserable for your coworkers. Some companies prize conformity. Others encourage individuality and diversity.

How well you are likely to fit in with a company is almost always a subjective evaluation. And the standards vary from one situation to the next. The fact that you're wearing an Armani suit may favorably impress an interviewer who works for a company that places a high premium on image and appearances, but it can work against you in companies where most people come to work in jeans. Being assertive and aggressive will score you points at a company whose walls are decorated with murals of sharks and other predatory creatures, but it will work against you at one in which every painting on the wall is by Norman Rockwell.

Your motivation

Regardless of how qualified you may be for a job and how well you fit the company mold, most interviewers will be reluctant to hire you if they're not reasonably convinced that you are genuinely interested and enthusiastic about this particular job, company, and industry. Companies want to be sure that if they do hire you, you're not going to decide two weeks after you're hired that you really want to work for the forestry department or join the circus.

You show motivation in two ways during an interview: through your general demeanor (how upbeat and enthusiastic you are) and through your ability to demonstrate that you know a great deal about the job, company, and industry. At the very least, you should be prepared to talk about any important trends or issues that might be affecting that industry.

Before you go into an interview, take an hour or two (either at the library or on-line) to look through recent business publications or industry journals to get a sense of what's going on. Pay attention to major mergers that have taken place and new technological developments that are likely to have an impact in the years to come.

The Basics of Interview Preparation

Being prepared for an interview means three things:

- ✔ Having a basic understanding of yourself: your values, skills, interests, job targets, and what, specifically, you hope to accomplish in the interview.
- ✔ Understanding and being prepared for the fundamental interpersonal dynamics of the interview process: that is, being able to handle the give-and-take of the question-and-answer routine.
- ✔ Being reasonably knowledgeable — *before* you go into the interview — about the job and what it requires, the company, the industry, and, whenever possible, the person conducting the interview.

These three elements of preparation are interrelated. The clearer you are about your own values and job targets, for example, and the more you know about the company, the more comfortable you're likely to be when you're answering questions. You won't have to fake it. You'll speak from the heart. If, on the other hand, you lack basic interviewing skills — if you're not an attentive listener or are not especially articulate in your answers — you're not going to be able to capitalize on the preparation you've done.

The following sections take a closer look at each aspect of preparation.

Clarify your objectives

Interviewers usually have one objective: to come away from the interview with some idea of whether you are — or aren't — the right person for the job they are trying to fill. You, on the other hand, could have one of two objectives, depending on your situation:

> ✔ You're definitely interested in the job and want to convince the interviewer that you have what it takes to do the job well.

> ✔ You're not really sure whether you're interested in this particular job or company, but you'd like to find out more about both.

There's nothing wrong with the second objective — just as long as you have a clear sense of what you want to accomplish. Generally speaking, though, you run a risk when you go into a job interview and are not convinced that you definitely want this job. In these situations, you may well decide during the interview that, yes, you really are interested in this job. However, you probably haven't prepared sufficiently for the interview.

As a general rule, you should do your best to determine *before* you actually go on an interview whether the job or company is right for you. And when you are definitely interested in a job opportunity, make sure that you do your homework.

Hone your basic interviewing skills

You can improve your ability to handle yourself confidently and smoothly in job interviews in two ways. One is trial by fire: Go on as many interviews as possible, make mistakes, and learn from them, applying those "lessons" in subsequent interviews. The problem with this strategy — apart from the fact that it's a painful way to learn — is that you can damage your business reputation if you make enough poor impressions in the early stage of the learning process.

You can also improve your interviewing skills without having to take too many hard knocks and put your reputation in harm's way — through practice. Here's how:

Practice listening

One of the most important, and underrated, interviewing skills is the ability to listen — to pay attention to, understand, and thoroughly absorb what the other person is saying without misinterpreting, jumping to conclusions, or allowing emotional responses to cloud the objectivity of your responses.

Few people are genuinely skilled at listening. That's because most people underestimate the effort and concentration that being a truly active, effective listener requires. People assume that because they can *hear* what somebody else is saying, they're listening. But effective listening involves much more. It's being sensitive to the more subtle elements of communication — tone, inflection, and so on — that themselves communicate a message. Listed here are some of the common listening pitfalls that can undermine your ability to make a favorable impression. See how many of them apply to you:

- ✔ Beginning to frame your response to a statement before the person talking has completed the statement

- ✔ Jumping in to fill in the words when someone pauses in the middle of a sentence

- ✔ Failing to ask for clarification when you're not sure of what the person has said or asked

- ✔ Failing to pay sufficient attention to the tone and emotional nuances that underlie what is said or asked

- ✔ Focusing so much on what *you* want to say that you lose track of what the other person is saying

As it happens, listening is one of the easiest skills to develop. That's because you have so many opportunities in a typical day to practice it. Start small. The next time someone calls you on the phone, for example, resist the temptation to sort through papers or watch something on television at the same time you're conducting the conversation. Focus — *really* focus — on what the other person is saying. Get interested.

And when you're with people on a one-to-one basis, focus *all* your attention on what they're saying. Do your best to block out — difficult as it sometimes is — extraneous noise. Make frequent eye contact, and give frequent feedback by nodding your head or acknowledging agreement with a word or two ("I understand," "I see what you mean," and so on).

A good way to develop your active listening skills is to periodically test your powers of recall, and an excellent tool for this purpose is a VCR or tape recorder. Here's what to do: Videotape your favorite show, newscast, or even infomercial — anything that has a good deal of dialogue. Set aside 20 minutes or so. Replay a section of the show and, without taking notes, focus all your attention on what is being said. Turn off the tape and write down as verbatim as possible what each person said. Then replay the tape to verify how closely you were able to recreate the conversation. After you can recall conversations of short duration, gradually increase the duration of the segment you listen to.

The *real* test is to put your listening skills to effective use during the interview itself, and that's not always easy when you're trying to make a good impression. The biggest pitfall to avoid: focusing so much on the information you want to get across that you don't listen carefully enough to the questions you're being asked. Ask for clarification so that you know exactly what the interviewer is trying to find out by asking any specific question.

Practice your responses

Most interviewers ask pretty much the same questions (for a list of the most commonly asked questions, head to the end of this chapter). So there is no excuse for not being prepared to answer the vast majority of the questions you're likely to be asked.

Don't take this advice *too* literally, though. Being prepared to answer common interview questions doesn't mean that you've memorized rote answers to dozens of them. Not at all. It simply means that you know what questions you can expect and are aware of the key points you want to get across when answering each question.

You can practice your responses to common interview questions in any number of ways, such as when you're alone and in front of a mirror (as Winston Churchill used to do when he was developing his public speaking abilities); when you're driving in your car; or even when you're taking a shower.

One of the best methods is to tape-record practice sessions and then critique your responses. Pay attention to the pauses and hedges that creep into your answers (phrases like "um," "y'know," "like," and "I mean"). Try to eliminate as many of these pauses and hedges as possible, but without rushing. Listen to your inflection. Is your voice flat and monotonous? See if you can add a little more enthusiasm, but don't force it or do anything that feels unnatural.

Train yourself to pause for a second or two *before* you answer a question instead of thinking about what you want to say as you speak. The more you nail down the answer ahead of time, the easier it should be to give your answer in a sustained, articulate manner. Keep at it. And don't get discouraged. Although speech patterns are habitual, you can break old habits and establish new ones with practice.

Videotape a session with your friends

If you own or can get a hold of a videotape recorder, recruit a friend or family member and do what successful politicians and performers do to improve the way they present themselves on talk shows. Videotaping yourself is the optimal choice for interview preparation.

Make the session as real-world as you can. If possible, do it in an office type of environment. Have the person interviewing you sit across from you with a list of questions. And answer the questions as though you were in an actual interview, as opposed to saying, "Well, what I would say in that situation is . . ." You may feel self-conscious at first. After a while, though, you'll forget about the camera.

When you're reviewing the tape, pay attention to — and try to improve — the following:

- ✔ **Posture:** Are you sitting up straight with your shoulders back, or are you slouching?

- ✔ **Eye contact:** Are you making frequent eye contact with your interviewer, or are your eyes looking just about everywhere else?

- ✔ **The pacing of your answers:** Are you talking at a comfortable pace — slowly enough to be understood and get your points across but not so slowly that the listener starts to doze off?

- ✔ **Emphasis and tone:** Do you sound authoritative and believable? If not, why?

- ✔ **Distracting mannerisms:** Do you notice any mannerisms — foot tapping, overusing your hands, or running your hands through your hair, for example — that might prove distracting to an interviewer?

Again, don't get discouraged if you don't like what you see on-screen. You're not Oprah Winfrey or Phil Donahue, and no one expects you to be. Focus on specific aspects of your performance, and work on one aspect at a time. Give yourself time and keep at it. Even the slightest improvements will make a big difference when you're actually interviewing.

Preparing for Specific Interviews

One of the tried-and-true axioms of job searching is that you can never know *too* much about the company or person interviewing you. The more you know about the company, the more topics of substance you will be able to discuss and the easier it will be to find common ground with the interviewer and give answers that enhance your credibility as a candidate.

Here, in brief, is what you should try to find out about any company that asks you to come in for an interview:

- What business or businesses is it in?

- What products or services does it sell?

- Who are its chief competitors, and how successful is it in comparison to the competition?

- Who are the key executives, and how long have they been with the company?

- What, if any, specific problem or problems is the company now facing, and what, if any, problems has the company recently overcome?

- What are the company's values? (Does the firm place a high value on ethics, for example?)

- What is the work atmosphere like in the company: intense or laid back?

- What is happening in the industry right now that may have an impact on the way the company does business in the future?

- What major events have taken place in the industry or company in the past two or three months?

If you're interviewing with a major corporation, you should be able to get most of this information through the resources described in detail in Chapters 10 and 18. Typical sources are directories, databases, annual reports, 10-Ks, and articles that appear in business and trade journals.

With smaller companies, you may not be able to access this information as easily, which means you may have to do some additional digging. Some suggestions include the following:

- When you're first informed that you're being interviewed, ask the company to send you its descriptive literature.

- Talk to your network of contacts to see whether anyone has worked for the company or is familiar with its operations.

- Try to talk to people who either sell to or buy from the company.

- Ask your reference librarian to help you find articles and other information that might give you some background on the company.

When you're doing your research, do more than simply gather facts; look for some indication of how the company envisions itself. Try to access in-house publications and pay attention to articles written by top management. If the company is public and you have its annual report, read the president's message and try to get a sense of the company mission. Then take a second look at your own skills, background, and career aspirations and try to make a direct connection to that mission or vision. In short, try to get a feel for where the company wants to go and what you can do to help it get there.

Gearing Up for Interview Questions

From what some books have to say about the interviewing process, you would think that as an interviewee, you have an unlimited ability to tailor your answers to each situation — and that your success in the interview depends on how effectively you exploit that ability.

That's not really the case, however. Yes, you can certainly modify your answers to the demands of each situation, but there inevitably comes a point at which the elasticity of your answers reaches its limits. There's a limit, in other words, to how much of a spin you can put on your answers. You might recall that Ed Norton, Ralph Cramden's sidekick in the Jackie Gleason series *The Honeymooners,* sometimes described his occupation as "subterranean engineer." (What he actually did for a living was work in a sewer.)

This doesn't mean that you should give up on any job that doesn't mirror your specific work experience. Your challenge in these situations is not to stretch the truth of your answers, but rather to persuade the person interviewing you that your background and skills do indeed qualify you for the position. If you've done your homework, you should have a pretty good idea of which *skills* are required to handle a job. You should be prepared to show how the skills you demonstrated in your previous jobs apply to the job at hand.

You will spend the bulk of your time during a job interview answering questions — that's a given. Those questions will fall into one of three broad categories: *closed, open,* and *leading.* The following sections give a brief description of each type and offer suggestions for approaching them.

Closed questions

Closed questions require either a yes or no answer or a one-word answer. Examples include the following:

- ✔ "Where did you go to school?"
- ✔ "How long did you work for the XYZ Corporation?"
- ✔ "How many employees did you manage?"
- ✔ "Have you ever had to fire anyone?"

Experienced interviewers will generally ask closed questions for one of two reasons: to verify information in your resume or set the stage for more probing down the line. The key to answering such questions is to be direct and concise. If you think that the answer doesn't quite speak for itself, it's okay to qualify or elaborate upon it, but avoid overexplaining. Answer the question and then let the interviewer make the next move.

Open questions

Open questions require more than a one- or two-word answer. Examples include the following:

- ✓ "Tell me about your last job."
- ✓ "What was it like working for the XYZ Corporation?"
- ✓ "What is it about our company that interests you?"

Open questions give you an opportunity to elaborate on answers you give to closed questions — that is, to frame your responses in a way that is relevant to the job you're seeking. The main pitfall to open questions is that they are sometimes too broad to answer concisely. So there's nothing wrong — *if* you do it politely — with asking the interviewer to narrow down the question somewhat. If an interviewer asks you to describe your last job, for example, you might counter with, "Is there any specific aspect of the job you would like to hear about first?"

Leading questions

Leading questions can be a minefield if you don't see them coming or are unable to recognize them. Consider this example:

"Wow, you worked for the XYZ Corporation in the early 1990s. That must have been a difficult place to work."

Chances are that any interviewer who asks this question is trying to bait you a little — trying to get you to show a side of yourself that you may be attempting to conceal. The main thing to do with leading questions is to stay focused and not allow yourself to be drawn into responses that will not help your cause. Saying negative things about former employers could make you sound bitter — or worse, like someone who blames others for your own shortcomings. The best approach is to underplay the answer, as in, "It was difficult, but it had its positives, too."

Interview Questions You'll Hear Over and Over

The following questions represent a cross-section of those that are typically asked during job interviews. Notice that no attempt has been made to tell you *how specifically* to answer each question. The reason? No two interview situations are the same, and the answer that works well for one candidate may not work well at all for another. Instead of a specific response, each of the following questions is followed by a brief description of what the interviewer might be looking for in your answer, and each question points out one or two pitfalls you should be aware of when you're responding.

Tell me a little about yourself.

This question is frequently the first question an interviewer asks simply because many interviewers consider it to be a good ice-breaker. A good way to handle the response is to ask the interviewer to narrow the scope of the question, as in, "I assume you would like me to give you a sense of what I'm looking for. Is that right?" Also, it's usually better to begin your answer with what is *currently* going on in your career and then work your way backward.

Pitfall to avoid: A rambling documentary filled with information of no relevance to the job at hand. In other words, don't start your answer with, "Well, I was born in . . ."

Why did you leave your last job?

This question may seem more frightening than it actually is, so don't overreact or get defensive. The fact that leaving your last job wasn't *your* idea won't disqualify you from consideration — not in today's environment and not if you can offer a good explanation. Keep in mind that the answer to this question is relevant only insofar as it relates to your ability to do the job for which you are now being interviewed.

Pitfall to avoid: Framing too defensive an answer or saying that you were let go because they didn't "appreciate" you in your last job. (Remember, it's never a good idea to show bitterness toward former employers, regardless of how tempting it may be.)

How much do you know about our company?

For your sake, you'd better be able to answer, "Quite a bit." Don't worry, the interviewer will not view the fact that you've taken the time to research the company and gather information as a sign of how desperate you are — far from it. Your response to this question gives you a chance to demonstrate motivation. The opportunity here — and it's an important one — is to show that you've done more than simply gather a few facts but have taken an analytical look at the problems the company is facing.

Pitfall to avoid: Knowing little or nothing about the company.

Tell me about your last job.

You should be prepared to talk knowledgeably and enthusiastically about your last job. Most interviewers will look for two things in this answer. The first is a direct connection between what you did in your last position and what you'll be called upon to do in the position under discussion. The second is your motivation. Employers want candidates who get *involved* with their work.

When answering this question, emphasize — without forcing — those elements in your last job that are relevant to the requirements of the job for which you're interviewing. That connection breaks down into the following categories:

- Broad parameters of the job
- The title of the person you reported to
- The number of people who reported to you
- How what you did related to the company's business
- Specific contributions you made

Pitfall to avoid: Being too general in your answers — that is, failing to go beyond the most superficial aspects of the job, such as how well you enjoyed it, how nice the people were, and how much fun using the company's health club was.

What are your strengths?

Many candidates mistakenly answer this question by mentioning strengths that don't necessarily have a bearing on the job at hand or the company's current situation. If, for example, you know that the company is going through a good deal of turmoil at the moment, and one of your strengths is your ability to work under pressure, mention that strength right off the bat, even though you might feel that your organizational skills rank just as high.

Pitfall to avoid: Underselling strengths that you clearly possess but may be reluctant to talk about because you're afraid of coming across as boastful. There's nothing wrong with tooting your own horn, as long as you have a legitimate reason for doing so.

What are your weaknesses?

You should be candid, but brief — don't knock yourself out of the running by detailing weaknesses that clearly relate to the job. (Then again, if the qualities you're weak in are essential to the job, you may want to give a second thought to whether the job is right for you.)

Pitfalls to avoid: Not being able to cite *any* weakness or beating up on yourself too much.

Where do you hope to be five years from now?

You don't need to have a clearly thought out, detailed answer to this question — not in today's business environment. Indeed, having too set an answer to this question could hurt you in smaller companies, suggesting that you're not flexible and won't be able to roll with the punches. Even if you gave a detailed answer, it might not ring true. (How many people do you know who can tell you exactly where they intend to be five years from today?) The safest answer is one that represents a logical future step in the career path you'll be heading down if you're hired for this particular position.

Pitfall to avoid: A canned answer that lacks believability.

What is it about our company that appeals to you?

Interviewers asking this question are usually fishing for two pieces of information: whether you have done your homework on the company, and why (other than the fact that you need a job) you've focused your job search on this company. You can focus on either the company or the specific job in your answer. It's usually a good idea to qualify your answers with phrases such, as "From what I've heard (or seen) . . ."

Pitfalls to avoid: Answering in too contrived a manner; using lightweight words like "fun."

What do you think you can bring to this company?

This question is simply another version of "Why should we hire you?" Your ability to answer it successfully depends largely on how informed you are about the company's needs.

Pitfalls to avoid: Having *too* much to say; giving an answer when you haven't really thought about the contributions you can make.

Knowing what you know about this job and our company, would you make changes if you were offered this position?

The motivation that frequently lies behind this question is to determine how familiar you are with the company and whether you're likely to rock the boat. The more you know about the company and the job (see Chapters 10, 17, 18, and 19 for more information about research), the better off you are. However, since you are an outsider, it is often risky to suggest changes — and it could backfire as an insult to the interviewer. Your best bet is to hedge a bit and to speak in more general terms about what your objectives would be.

Pitfalls to avoid: Offering ideas that you're not sure about; indirectly criticizing the firm.

Describe a typical day in your last job.

This question has become a favorite of savvy interviewers because it helps to verify (or work against) the information you spell out in your resume. One reason interviewers use this question is to tell whether you're able to set priorities — that is, to distinguish between the important and the less important.

Pitfall to avoid: Dwelling too much on the minutiae of your job, rather than the big picture.

Why should I hire you?

This question is sometimes asked early in the interview — sometimes for surprise or shock value. Interviewers who ask it figure that if you can't answer the question in a fairly convincing or compelling way, you're obviously not the right candidate. The thing to avoid when you're answering are cliches, such as, "Because I'm the best person for the job," or "Because you won't regret it." A better approach is something along the lines of, "From what I know about the job and your company and what I know I can do, I think I can make a contribution." Just make sure that you can back up that assertion with some specific examples — better still, examples that relate to the skills needed for the job itself.

Pitfall to avoid: Jumping into an answer before you clearly think it out.

Tell me about your previous bosses.

Interviewers who ask this question are usually looking for some indication of how well you're likely to get along with the person who will be supervising you in the new job, assuming that you're hired. You may be asked to describe your best and worst bosses. The best tactic here is to give as thoughtful and diplomatic an answer as possible, focusing mainly on their managerial styles.

Pitfall to avoid: Overstatement. Think twice, in other words, before you describe the person you worked for as "saintly," "brilliant," or, worse, as a "jerk" or "slave driver." Avoid getting mired in a long treatise on how unfair or difficult a supervisor was.

Do you consider yourself a team player?

Of course you do. You pretty much have to be in today's business environment. Be prepared, though, to clarify the answer if the interviewer asks you to define your idea of a "team player."

Pitfall to avoid: Hedging the answer with phrases such as, "It depends on the situation."

What's the biggest problem you faced in your last job and how did you solve it?

The purpose of this double-edged question is usually twofold: one, to give your interviewer some insight into what you consider a "challenging" or difficult situation. Two, to shed some light on how you like to handle challenge: whether you step back and do a lot of thinking before tackling a problem or like to grab the bull by the horns. This is one of the more important questions you may be asked to answer, so try to have one or two stories that show you off in the best light. Be specific in your recollection of the situation, but don't overplay your hand.

Pitfall to avoid: Citing problems that have no bearing on the problems you're likely to face in the job at hand or that show an inability to get along with others.

I'm going to give you a hypothetical situation, and I'd like to know how you would handle it.

It's tough to finesse a question like this — particularly since you have no idea ahead of time what the hypothetical situation is going to be. Be sure to give yourself some time to think before you answer. It's always easier to start with general reactions and then gradually get more specific.

Pitfall to avoid: Winging it. If you're not sure of how you would handle a particular situation, admit it, but at least explain what your general thought process would be.

If I were to call your former boss, what would he or she be likely to say about your strengths and weaknesses?

This is one of those minefield-type questions whose answer could blow up in your face if it isn't in sync with the answer the interviewer gets from your former boss. (For information on handing references, see Chapter 22.) So you better play it safe. Give an honest answer, bearing in mind that most people, when they're asked to give a reference, rarely give you as much praise as you think you deserve or as much criticism as you're afraid they might unload.

Pitfalls to avoid: Not being able to provide any answer at all; overemphasizing the negative.

What did you like best about your previous job?

The answer to this question can work against you if the tasks you cite as having liked best in your last job differ from those that the job for which you're being interviewed entails. If you're reasonably sure that this is not the case (here, again, you can see the value of preparation), be as open and honest as you can.

Pitfall to avoid: Not being able to name *anything* in your last job that you liked.

What did you like least about your previous job?

The only real danger lurking behind this question is the possibility that everything you *didn't* like in your last job is included in the job description for the job at hand, in which case you probably shouldn't be interviewing for the job at all.

Pitfall to avoid: Citing as negatives principal features of the job under discussion.

How satisfied are you with how far you've advanced in your career?

The real question being asked here is, "How hungry or ambitious are you?" You won't get yourself into too much trouble by telling the interviewer that you're proud of what you've been able to accomplish but that you still feel as though you have much to prove.

Pitfall to avoid: Worrying more than you have to about the specifics or the length of the answer. Keep it simple.

Based on what I see in this resume, you seem to be overqualified for this position. What do you think?

In many cases, the main concern of an interviewer who brings up the issue of being "overqualified" is that you're taking this job as a stop-gap measure and that as soon as something better comes along, you'll be out the door. Sometimes, too, the interviewer simply feels uncomfortable hiring you for a job that is clearly "beneath" you.

The best way to respond to this question is to acknowledge that, yes, you may be overqualified, but that this fact works to the company's advantage. Your ability to override the concerns embedded in this question depends on your ability to give the interviewer reasonable assurance that you're going to make this job a priority. Among the reasons that could carry some persuasive weight are the following:

- ✔ You have decided to make a career change and recognize that you can't aim as high as you normally might.

- ✔ The jobs for which you *are* qualified are in short supply in this particular region, and you have decided that you don't want to move.

- ✔ You have a personal interest in the job at hand that has little to do with your qualifications (that is, it's something you've always wanted to do but never had the opportunity to do before).

Pitfall to avoid: Arguing the point — insisting that you aren't overqualified when you clearly are; suggesting that you are "curious" or intimating that you are halfhearted in your pursuit.

What do you like to do in your spare time?

Technically speaking, what you do in your spare time is none of the interviewer's business, but many interviewers ask the question anyway simply to gain some added insight into you as an individual. If you're being interviewed for a position in sales, for example, the interviewer would be happy to hear that you like competitive sports.

Pitfall to avoid: Mentioning so many hobbies and pastimes that your interviewer begins to wonder how you find time to work.

What kind of a salary do you require?

This question only comes up when salary hasn't been previously mentioned or when you haven't specified your requirements. Views differ on how best to answer it. Some job search experts consider it a major negotiating error to reveal your salary demands *before* you have a chance to find out more about the job and, in particular, what the employer is willing to pay. But here's a classic illustration of a generalization that simply does not apply across the board. Yes, it's generally better to postpone discussions about salary until you're well into the interview, but if the interviewer insists, don't be too coy or evasive.

A sound strategy to take when answering this question is to establish your bare-bones salary needs, emphasizing, however, that you would hope to be paid the market value for your work. (For more information about discussing salaries, see Chapter 24.)

Pitfalls to avoid: Getting bogged down in a salary discussion before you have a chance to talk about what you can offer; telling the interviewer that salary "doesn't matter."

If we were to hire you, when could you start?

This is music to most candidates' ears since it means that you have passed a series of interview hurdles. Here, the interviewer is not only asking a logistical, practical question; he or she may be looking for insight into how ethical you are in terms of the notice that you would give your employer or, if you're currently unemployed, how serious you are about getting back to work.

Pitfalls to avoid: Sounding like you're not too eager to start soon; saying that you'll give your current employer less than two weeks' notice (unless there are special circumstances); or saying that you've been toying with the idea of joining a new bike club that will be taking a series of weekday trips for two months.

Chapter 21

Winning Ways: How to Handle Yourself during the Interview

*I*f the world were a perfect place, here is what would happen each time you went on a job interview:

First of all, you would wake up on the morning of the interview feeling as though there were no mountain in the world too steep to climb. You'd hear the *Rocky* theme in the background, even though your radio wasn't turned on.

Second, everything you did in preparation for the interview — getting dressed, getting your things together, driving or walking or taking a train or bus to the interview site — would go according to plan, with no unpleasant surprises. You would arrive at the interview site looking as if you just stepped out of a *Wall Street Journal* ad — smooth, professional, a future CEO, to be sure. And once inside the building itself, you would be greeted not as a job applicant but rather like visiting royalty — with everyone going out of the way to make you feel comfortable.

After the interview itself got underway, you and the interviewer would hit it off instantly — like two childhood friends who meet after a long separation. You would be asked a number of questions, of course, but you would be well prepared to answer and you would know from the way your interviewer nodded and beamed and took notes that your answers produced exactly the impact you wanted them to produce, depicting you as the exact sort of person the company needed. At interview's end, the interviewer would stand up and, without necessarily coming out and telling you directly, let you know that, without question, you were the number one candidate.

Curtain closes. Unfortunately, you don't always wake up on the morning of an interview feeling as though you could slay every dragon that would dare cross your path. In the real world, the button on your shirt or blouse sometimes pops off as you're getting dressed in the morning, or the state highway department decides that the morning of your interview would be a great time to commence demolition of the highway.

Then, too, the interview itself rarely goes exactly the way you would prefer it to go. Sometimes the interviewer seems so distracted that you wonder if he or she is even listening to you. Other times, you find yourself being peppered with questions delivered in such a hostile tone that you feel as if you're being grilled at a police station. And at the end of interview, all too often — you're not really sure of how well you did.

Which scenario is likely to unfold the next time you go on a job interview? You never know, but if you heed the advice offered in this chapter, you'll be better prepared to combat the unexpected.

Making Sure That You Look Your Best

Few aspects of job interviewing are more important to the impression you create than your appearance: how well you're groomed and how appropriately you're dressed.

If you feel that appearance is a superficial factor on which to base a hiring decision, put yourself in the shoes of the interviewer. The person interviewing you, remember, has never met you and knows you only by the information printed on your resume and, if you've spoken on the phone, by the sound of your voice. Your appearance, therefore, becomes the first *directly observable* factor in the impression you make. If you fail that initial test, you're fighting an uphill battle from that point on.

Comic relief: Weird things that candidates have actually done on interviews

When executives in an independent survey commissioned by Accountemps® were asked to name the most unusual thing they had ever witnessed during a job interview, the answers revealed more than a few bizarre situations. Here's a look at some of the more — well, unusual.

- The candidate who said, "If you hire me, I'll teach you how to ballroom dance at no charge," and then proceeded to stand up and demonstrate.

- The candidate whose excuse for arriving late was, "I accidentally locked my clothes in my closet."

- The candidate who, after being asked a difficult question, asked, "Do you mind if I go outside to meditate for a moment?"

Which is not to mention the candidate who

- Shortly after sitting down, whipped out a display of cosmetics and started making a sales pitch

- Brought his five children and a cat to the interview

- Asked to borrow the fax machine to send out personal letters

- Arrived with a snake around her neck and explained that she took her pet everywhere

- When asked a question about loyalty, showed a tattoo of his girlfriend's name

*Accountemps® is a registered trademark of Robert Half International Inc.

What is "appropriate dress," anyway?

This question would have been a lot easier to answer 10 or 15 years ago. Today, many companies — particularly in the U.S. — have liberalized their dress codes. Then, too, what's "appropriate" in one profession, industry, or region of the country may be inappropriate in another industry or region. If you're applying for a job at an investment banking firm in Boston in the middle of winter, you're obviously going to wear something different from what you would wear if you were applying for a job as a construction worker in Nevada in the middle of the summer. And if you're applying for a job as a reporter at a high-fashion magazine, the interviewer will undoubtedly pay more attention to your clothing than would be the case if you were applying for a job as a computer programmer at a university.

Generally speaking, "appropriate" dress in the working world still means getting reasonably dressed up — even today. It means making sure that nothing about your appearance — whether it's your choice of clothing, the jewelry you wear, your hairstyle, or even your choice of perfume — falls outside what most people in a particular profession or industry would consider the norm. Your goal when you go on a job interview is not to make a fashion statement or draw attention to yourself. Your goal is to blend in — to look the part of the job you hope to fill.

Even when your interview is scheduled to take place on an office "casual day," you should still plan to dress in a professional manner. The only exception — and it won't happen very often — is when the interviewer tells you specifically not to dress up.

Making the safest choices

The safest interview wardrobe choices for most office-style jobs are pretty much the same as they've always been. The classic "uniform" for men is a dark, conservative business suit (preferably wool or a wool blend), a white or light blue long-sleeved shirt (always long-sleeved, even in summer), and a subtle-patterned, well-coordinated silk tie. The "uniform" for women is a suit or dress that, whatever the color or pattern, is fashionable, tasteful, and businesslike — nothing flashy, showy, or too high-fashion.

If you are at all uncertain about what "appropriate" business attire looks like, take a look at how business people on television dress. If you're still not sure, go to a reputable clothing store and put yourself in the hands of one of the more experienced salespersons. Another suggestion: If you have time, go to the office building of the company interviewing you and take note of how the people who come and go are dressed.

You should be prepared to spend more money than normal for interview clothing. The extra money gets you quality fabrics — wool or wool blends as opposed to synthetics, such as polyester or rayon — a good fit, and durability. Better clothing also holds its shape and color even after repeated dry cleanings. Think of the money you spend on your interview outfit(s) as a direct investment in your future. That said, the main criterion is whether you look neat and professional — you shouldn't have to drain your bank account to achieve this. Make sure that you're neatly groomed and your clothes are pressed.

Don't overdo it by spending so much money on your apparel and accessories that you look inappropriate for the job.

Additional thoughts on your appearance

Now that you have an idea of the basic guidelines of dressing for success when you go on a job interview, here's a brief look at some of the smaller but no less important aspects of appearance that can contribute — or detract — from the impression you make.

✔ Go easy on the jewelry.

✔ If you're taking a briefcase with you (which is probably a good idea), spend a little more money to buy one that's made of leather, not vinyl.

✔ Don't wear any button that endorses a political candidate or cause.

✔ If you're a smoker or heavy coffee drinker, bring breath mints (but don't have them in your mouth when you go into the interview).

✔ If you're a man, pay attention not only to clothing but also to your footwear. Avoid "outdoorsy" shoes — the kind with thick rubber soles — and wear socks that are mid-calf high and coordinate with the color of your trousers. Never wear white socks.

Controlling the Pre-Interview Jitters

It's only natural that you should feel a little nervous on the day of a job interview. The fact is, you *need* a higher than normal amount of adrenaline pumping through your system on the day you're interviewed if you hope to do your best. The trick is to keep the adrenaline — and your nerves — under reasonable control.

Everyone has his or her own way of keeping the demons of stress and anxiety at bay. What works for other people may not work for you. But here are some techniques that have worked not only for job hunters but for those trying to stay under control in pressure situations.

Be prepared

The more diligently you prepare for each interview, the more confidence you'll have on the big day. If you can say to yourself before you go into an interview that you've done as much (within reason) as you can to do your best at the interview, you'll take some pressure off yourself. The key to preparation is to do more than simply assemble a hodgepodge of facts about a company. Absorb the information so that you have a clear idea of what the company does and how you fit into the picture.

Organize yourself ahead of time

Always take 15 minutes or so several days before an interview to decide what you're going to wear and make sure that everything is cleaned and pressed. Listen to the weather forecast. If there's a chance of rain, make sure that you know where your umbrella is. If you're driving to the interview site, check to make sure that you have enough gas in your tank. Double-check your briefcase to make sure that you have extra resumes, a pad of paper, a pen, and suitable reading material in case you have to cool your heels in the reception area. Finally, make sure that you have *detailed* instructions for signing in. Find out who you should call if, for some reason, you run into a problem.

Get a good night's sleep

Try, anyway. Watch what you eat and drink on the evening before the big day, and if you have any plans that evening, make sure that you get home at a reasonable hour.

Stick to your routine

On the day of your interview, try your best to follow your usual routine. It's usually a good idea to wake up at your normal time (or a few minutes earlier). Avoid any foods or beverages that you don't normally eat or drink. And if you're a coffee drinker, this is not the day to skip your morning caffeine fix.

Pay attention to your breathing

From the moment you get up in the morning on interview day to the moment you arrive at the interview, pay attention to your breathing. When you're nervous, your breathing becomes more shallow, which only adds to the anxiety you're feeling. As soon as you sense that your breathing is becoming more rapid than normal, make a conscious attempt to take deeper, slower breaths.

INSIDE SCOOP

Mind your Ps and Qs

The impression you make on the interviewer's administrative assistant has more influence on the hiring decision than you may think. According to a recent OfficeTeam® survey, *60 percent* of executives from the nation's largest companies consider their administrative assistants' opinions of candidates an "important" part of the selection process.

*OfficeTeam® is a trademark of Robert Half International Inc.

Give yourself more than enough time to arrive on time

Find out exactly how to get to the interview site. If you've never been there before (and assuming that it's not outrageously far from where you live), take a trial drive to the location a day or two beforehand to pace yourself — ideally at the same time you expect to be on the road as you head for your interview. Even then, give yourself additional time in case you run into extra traffic. And while you're at it, make sure that the car is clean and that the interior doesn't look like the back room of a junk shop. You never know who you're going to bump into in the parking lot — maybe the person interviewing you.

Slow yourself down

Make a conscious effort when you wake up on the day of your interview to slow the pace of everything you do. It won't get you behind (you're probably behaving more hyper than normal, anyway) and the fact that you're slowing yourself down physically often sends a message to your brain that helps you relax. And remember to smile.

BLOOPERS

What *not* to say if you arrive late

Some ideas about what *not* to say if, for some reason, you arrive late for a job interview, based on the answers given in an Accountemps® survey in which executives were asked to name the most unusual excuse they'd ever received from an employee who showed up late for a meeting:

✔ "The ceiling fell in on me because of a plumbing problem."

✔ "I was so intent on making this meeting that I dropped my money into the sewer and it took a long time for me to get it back."

✔ "My cat had a litter of kittens on top of the report I wanted to bring to the meeting."

✔ "The bartender wouldn't let me leave."

✔ "I was talking to the President of the United States on the phone."

✔ "Security stopped me because they thought I was on a 'wanted' poster."

✔ "I got stuck in the men's room — someone took the handle off the door."

✔ "Someone turned off my alarm clock."

*Accountemps® is a trademark of Robert Half International Inc.

Arrival Advice: What to Do When You Get There

Your interview officially starts as soon as you arrive at the interview destination — well before you begin to talk to the interviewer. From that moment on, it's show and tell, and you need to be on your toes. More than a few job candidates have knocked themselves out of the running, not because they didn't do well during the interview itself but because they acted inappropriately while they were waiting in the reception area.

The larger and more organized the company, the more likely it is that you will have to sign in at a reception desk, be announced, and then be directed to or escorted to a waiting area. In some instances, you'll be sent to the human resources department, which is usually set up for interviews. In other instances, you'll be sent directly to the department offering the job.

In smaller companies, everything is much more informal. The person greeting you may, in fact, be the person who will interview you and make the hiring decision. You may find yourself waiting a long time if a business crisis just occurred.

Whatever the circumstances may be, pay attention to the following basics of what you may want to think of as *arrival etiquette* — the way you conduct yourself before the interview even begins.

Don't do the following:

- ✔ Bring someone with you. If someone has driven you, ask your chauffeur to wait outside.
- ✔ Smoke, eat, or chew gum.
- ✔ Wear sunglasses indoors.
- ✔ Bring a shopping bag or gym bag to the interview.
- ✔ Apply makeup or look at yourself in a compact mirror. If you want to check your appearance, do it in the restroom.
- ✔ Brush off a receptionist who tries to strike up a conversation with you.
- ✔ Pester a receptionist who *hasn't* struck up a conversation with you.
- ✔ Ask to use the phone.
- ✔ Hum, whistle, or rustle papers.
- ✔ Play a Walkman or portable stereo.
- ✔ Read any book or magazine whose subject matter is likely to raise an eyebrow.

Do:

- ✔ Read through company literature, such as an annual report.

- ✔ Go over in your mind the three or four key points you want to get across in the interview.

- ✔ Look over your notes.

- ✔ Be patient if the interviewer is running late.

- ✔ Be pleasant to all receptionists and administrative personnel. If someone tries to strike up a conversation, participate!

- ✔ Smile.

Getting Off to a Good Start with Your Interviewer

Everything you've heard about the importance of first impressions in job interviews is true. Virtually every survey, study, or experiment on the topic confirms the same general finding: The first impression you make on the interviewer has a lasting effect on the opinions and conclusions that the interviewer draws throughout the remainder of the interview. Psychologists call it the *halo effect* — a tendency to reconcile judgments with initial impressions. If you make a highly favorable first impression, the interviewer will be inclined to view your subsequent behavior in a positive light. If you get off to a bad start, the opposite is likely to occur. You can often rebound from a bad first impression (just as you can quickly lose the advantage of a good first impression if you falter badly during the interview), but why put yourself under the pressure?

A good part of the impression you create depends on how you're dressed — a subject covered in earlier sections of this chapter. Other factors that should concern you when you first meet your interviewer are how you carry yourself into the room and handle the greeting.

If you're lucky, the interviewer will make things easy for you. He or she either will come out to welcome you in the reception area and initiate the greeting or will make the initial overture when you walk into the office, shaking your hand and indicating where the interview is going to take place.

You can't always count on the fact that your interviewer will be adept at social graces. If you're kept waiting in the reception area while the interviewer is on the phone or huddled with a staff member, don't let it faze you. What you're encountering isn't necessarily rudeness; it's busy people.

Handling the handshake

Don't tie yourself into knots worrying about how to handle the handshake. The rule of thumb is to let the interviewer take the lead — that is, not to extend your hand unless the interviewer extends his or her hand first. The handshake should be firm, but not a hand-crusher — unless you're applying for a spot on the Worldwide Wrestling tour.

There's one exception to the rule of letting the interviewer take the lead. If, for whatever reason, the interviewer is standing when you walk into the room but doesn't initiate the greeting, take the lead yourself. Walk over, introduce yourself ("Hi, my name is May Phillips. It's nice to meet you."), and extend your hand.

Breaking the ice

The most awkward time for both you and the interviewer is the first couple of moments. Experienced interviewers are sensitive to this and in most cases will try to put you at ease with small talk. A typical question might be, "You didn't have any trouble getting here, did you?" or "Was there much traffic?"

Go along with the game. Small talk isn't a waste of time. It serves an important function, giving you and your interviewer an opportunity to break the ice. In the meantime, you have an opportunity to settle in and calm yourself. If it's possible — and natural — you can bring up your own topics, but don't overdo it and don't prattle. If something genuine captures your interest, such as an unusual painting, piece of sculpture, or view — something really obvious — respond to it. If the office is unusually attractive (and it looks as if the person has put his or her own mark on it), say so — but only if it's an honest opinion. You're doing your best to make a good impression, but be yourself.

Executing Your Interview Strategy

You should always go into a job interview with a clear sense of what you hope to accomplish. This advice may sound obvious, but it's not as obvious as it seems.

The problem lies with the nature of the interviewing process. From the employer's perspective, interviews fall into different categories based on what the employer hopes to accomplish. The three main categories are often referred to as follows:

- Screening interviews
- Selection interviews (employment decisions)
- Confirmation interviews

Here's a closer look at each type of interview and what you should focus on in each situation.

The screening interview

The purpose of a screening interview is to narrow down a relatively large number of likely candidates to a smaller list of top possibilities. In large companies, these preliminary interviews are generally handled by the human resources department. In some smaller companies, the screening interview may be conducted by an assistant of the final decision-maker. In most cases, however, the person responsible for the hiring decision will handle this initial meeting.

Regardless of who's doing the interviewing, your strategy in a screening interview should be to concentrate on one objective above all: to stay in the running and move ahead to the next phase of the process. Don't think about getting the offer yet — one step at a time!

The main thing that people who conduct screening interviews care about is how closely your skills and qualifications match the criteria that have been developed for the job at hand. Other key hiring criteria — how well you fit into the company and your motivation — are obviously important but not paramount at this stage of the interview process. So as long as you don't come across as someone who *clearly* won't fit, you don't have to worry as much about these two aspects of your interview performance as you do in later interviews.

The important things to focus on during a screening interview are the following:

- ✔ Being able to cite specific examples that verify the information in your resume

- ✔ Being able to articulate a clear, concise, and convincing reason for why you are interested in this particular job

- ✔ Being able to defend any obvious weaknesses in your resume (the fact that you've got to the screening interview to begin with probably means that you don't have any apparent weaknesses to defend)

- ✔ Responding to questions in an open, direct way that communicates to your interviewer that you have nothing to hide

- ✔ Gathering information about the position that can give you a clearer idea of the job, the company, the culture, and the person who will make the final hiring decision

Impressive numbers

When executives in an independent survey commissioned by Robert Half International were asked to name the one quality, apart from ability and willingness to do the job, that impressed them the most about a candidate during a job interview, here is how the numbers came out:

Verbal skills	38%
Enthusiasm	24%
Honesty/integrity	7%
Past experience/accomplishments	7%
Poise/self-confidence	4%
Sense of humor	2%
Directness/eye contact	2%
Preparedness	2%
Professionalism	2%
Etiquette/manners	2%

Even though the person interviewing you during a screening interview may be a mid-level employee with little influence on the hiring decision and no in-depth knowledge of the position, be on your best behavior. Don't say or do anything that shows disrespect or impatience. Remember, before you can proceed to the next stage of the interviewing process, you have to get by the screener.

The selection interview

In a selection interview, you can safely assume that your basic qualifications are no longer a primary issue in the hiring decision. If you weren't qualified for the position, you wouldn't be talking to the decision-maker. Your strategy, therefore, should be to focus on what you can bring to the company *in addition to* those basic skills and qualifications. What you want to sell more than anything else in a selection interview is *value*.

The confirmation interview

In most but not all cases, confirmation interviews are rubber-stamp affairs. The person responsible for the hiring decision has decided that you are the candidate of choice but, as a matter of courtesy, is introducing you to his or her boss before finally making the offer.

Bear in mind that you don't have to *sell* yourself too hard during a confirmation interview. You simply have to be on your best behavior and not do anything that would cause anyone to raise an eyebrow. Stay circumspect, and keep your opinions to yourself.

The Art of Effective Answering

Chapter 21 looks at some of the most commonly asked job interview questions and reviews what interviewers might be looking for in those questions. The following guidelines apply to the general demeanor you would be wise to adopt, regardless of the answers you give. Remember, savvy interviewers pay attention to more than your responses. They pay as much attention to the confidence, commitment, and sincerity that those answers embody.

Remember why you're there

Your goal during a job interview is to sell yourself, pure and simple. The fact that you're talking about yourself and your accomplishments is nothing to apologize for or conceal. You have to show some restraint, of course, and you don't want to come across as a boastful know-it-all. Most candidates, however, err in the opposite direction; they *undersell* themselves.

Remember to emphasize your accomplishments without, however, going overboard. According to an executive RHI survey, one of every three candidates is too reluctant to tout his or her accomplishments during an interview.

Take your time

Regardless of how prepared you are to answer a question that you've been asked, don't be in too much of a hurry to rattle the answer off as though you were an auctioneer. Doing so may reinforce the suspicion that the response you're giving is the answer you think the interviewer wants to hear.

Be wary of interview "games"

Some books and articles that deal with job interviews offer you detailed advice for "reading" your interviewer and then offer some techniques ostensibly designed to help you gain better rapport with the interviewer. They advise you to mirror your interviewer as much as possible — that is, to match your body position, gestures, and vocal pace to those of your interviewer. They also give you advice for tailoring your answers so that your wording strikes a responsive chord, based on the interviewer's social or personality style.

These concepts may contain some validity, but many hiring managers are familiar with these techniques. Should they suspect that you're using these methods to manipulate their responses, your credibility goes out the window.

Don't wing it

If you're not really sure of an answer to a question, say so. You're much better off admitting that you don't know the answer to a question than you are giving an answer that *proves* you don't know. *Never* say that you know someone you never met, and never say that you understand a term you don't understand.

Keep your answers concise and direct

Limit the information you give in your answers to the question that was asked. You can elaborate, of course, but don't ramble. Give the interviewer the opportunity to probe.

Back up your assertions with real-world examples

When you're asked a question designed to shed some light on how you might handle certain aspects of the job, try to frame your answers in terms of your actual experience rather than on your opinions. Instead of saying, "It's important for a manager to find out about problems *before* they become serious," describe a situation in which you acted in a manner that illustrates that principle.

Watch your interviewer's responses

Be alert to signs that what you're saying to the interviewer isn't conveying the impression you want to convey. Interviewers usually demonstrate that they're losing interest in the interview by doing any of the following:

- Asking you a question before you finish answering the preceding question
- Taking surreptitious looks at their watches
- Letting their eyes wander

Body Language: How Not to Send the Wrong Message

Body language is the term used to describe the messages you communicate (either consciously or unconsciously) through nonverbal cues: your posture, gestures, facial expressions, and eye movements.

Some interviewers place a great deal of stock in body language as an accurate reflection of the intent and motivation behind what you're saying. Others don't. The problem is that you have no way of knowing whether the interviewer is going to be paying attention to your body language.

Unless you're very skilled at it, it's a mistake for you to focus *consciously* on your body language, the pitfall being that your movements may seem contrived. A better approach is to be aware of specific gestures and motions that can send a message that you don't want to send. Consider the following examples:

- ✔ **Crossing your arms** is a sign that you're resisting or protecting yourself.

- ✔ **Avoiding eye contact** signals that you're embarrassed or may not be telling the truth.

- ✔ **Persistent, hurried nodding** is a sign that you're impatient. (Nodding as a natural response, however, signals agreement.)

- ✔ **Tense facial expressions** can be a sign that you're nervous or simply tightly wound. Your mouth is the key. Try to sense when your facial muscles are getting tense, and do your best to relax them.

What to Do When It's Your Turn to Ask Questions

In most interviews, you will be invited at some point to ask questions about the position, the company, or anything else that may be on your mind. These questions, apart from giving you additional clarification about the job or the company, are also a test of sorts. Asking questions that the interviewer considers inappropriate is as bad as giving inappropriate answers.

What not to ask

The mistake that some candidates make when they're given the opportunity to ask questions is that they focus too much on the trees and not enough on the forest. This is not the time to ask about how much vacation time you'll be entitled to if you're hired or how many molars you're entitled to get repaired under the company's dental plan. It's not the time to talk about where and how large your office is going to be or whether the company will help finance your MBA.

The problem with these questions is not that they're unreasonable to ask. It's a matter of timing. Questions of this nature are best dealt with after it's clear that the company is seriously considering hiring you and you are in the offer or negotiation phase of the process, which is covered in Chapter 24.

BLOOPERS

Interviewing Don'ts

Some ways to make sure that you *don't* get the offer, based on what some candidates have actually *done* on job interviews, according to an independent survey commissioned by Accountemps®:

✔ If you're asked to take your time answering, write down the answer to each question before you respond.

✔ Interrupt the interview to place or receive cellular phone calls.

✔ Ask the interviewer to switch chairs so that you can sit in the interviewer's chair and he or she can sit in yours.

*Accountemps® is a trademark of Robert Half International Inc.

Focus on success

When the opportunity arises, the best questions to ask relate to big-picture issues — where the company hopes to be in a few years and how the job you are applying for fits into that plan. It's important, too, that you're genuinely seeking answers and not simply asking for the sake of appearing interested and intelligent. The best time to formulate your questions is during your pre-interview research. The more you find out about the company *and* the job, the easier it will be for you to come up with questions that are substantive and relevant.

Here are some examples of the topics you might want to address in the questions you ask (keeping in mind that your interest in the answers must be genuine):

✔ The interviewer's own history with the company — how long he or she has been with the company and the various jobs (if applicable) the interviewer has held there

✔ The type of person who is likely to be successful in the company

✔ What mix of skills and attributes are needed to be successful in the job under consideration

✔ The specific kinds of contributions you can make immediately that would have a measurable impact on the company or department

✔ Industry outlook — what the competitive challenges in the industry are likely to be over the next several years

✔ The company's long-range plans — the kind of company it wants to be in five years, plans for proprietary expansion, and so on

Chapter 22

Staying in Control: When Bad Things Happen to Good Interviewees

Regardless of how many you've gone on or how diligently you prepare, no interview goes exactly according to plan. Interviews don't always start when they're supposed to start. The person who interviews you isn't always prepared ("Let's see now. Your resume was here *somewhere*.") And in rare situations, the interviewer makes you feel as though you've been accused of the crime of the century.

It's hard to know what to do in these situations. True, you could always excuse yourself and leave, but walking away from a job interview isn't easy, regardless of *how* you're being treated. Not when you really need the job, and not when it's taken you weeks to set up the interview. Then, too, there's always the possibility that some of the unexpected and unwelcome things that occasionally happen during an interview are simply a calculated part of the interviewer's game plan — designed to test how well you deal with pressure.

So what do you do? How do you handle those difficult situations that crop up every once in a while in job interviews? This chapter gives you insights into this tricky and often troubling issue. And while it may not cover *every* eventuality that can knock you off your stride in an interview, it will alert you to the most common situations and give you some ideas about how to respond in a way that strikes a balance between keeping you in the running for the job and protecting your dignity and self-respect.

Dealing with Difficult Interviewers

The one thing that varies most from one job interview to the next is the interviewer — more specifically, the personality, skill, and interviewing style of the person (or persons) who conducts the interview.

Ideally, interviewers should be able to do their jobs — that is, make a reasonably accurate assessment of your qualifications and your suitability for the position — without making you feel as though you're on the witness stand. But most *skillful* interviewers — those who are adept at making accurate assessments — are not necessarily Mr. Sensitive or Ms. Congeniality. And the interviewers who are pleasant and comfortable to be with aren't necessarily good at interviewing. They don't ask the most intelligent questions or probe for relevant details, and, consequently, they don't make it easy for you to differentiate yourself from other candidates.

No matter what type of interviewer you encounter, it's essential to bear in mind your fundamental objective: to tie your qualifications and background to the requirements of the job and, at the same time, show interest, motivation, and poise. Still, you need to be prepared to make adjustments. So here's a brief look at some of the less-than-ideal interviewer types, as well as advice for adjusting to each type.

The bumbler

Bumblers have virtually no idea of how to conduct an effective job interview. They know that they need to hire someone, but they haven't gotten around to formulating any specific hiring criteria. So instead of asking probing questions and tying your answers to the requirements of the job, they tend to base their impressions on factors that have almost nothing to do with what it takes to do the job.

Bumblers work to the advantage of candidates who look the part and know how to assume control of the interview. They work to the *dis*advantage of candidates whose strengths lie beneath the surface and who are uncomfortable about taking initiative. Bumblers, in other words, are often easy to impress, but *you* have to do the work; you can't expect *them* to come to the conclusions you want on their own.

When you're dealing with a bumbler, stay in command of your own story and keep hammering away at your strengths. Bumblers need to be led: Don't drop the leash.

The chatterbox

Chatterboxes like to talk. And talk. And talk. They talk about themselves, the company, their kids, their vitamin regimen, their pets, their hobbies, and, if you're fortunate, the specifics of the job. They talk so much, in fact, and so incessantly that if you're not careful you never get a chance to present your case.

Not that it's a bad thing when an interviewer likes to talk. Generally speaking, the more you can get an interviewer to talk, the easier it becomes for you to get a clear fix on what the interviewer is looking for. Chatterboxes, however, take a good thing to a bad extreme.

The *worst* approach you can take with a chatterbox is to talk so much yourself that you prevent the chatterbox from doing what he or she likes to do the best: talk. The *best* thing to do is to pick your spots: to dart in and out of the interviewer's conversation, making short (but self-serving) comments that play off whatever topic the chatterbox is chattering about. Even more important, perhaps, is the quality of the questions *you* ask. If you ask the right questions of chatterbox interviewers (see Chapter 21 for more information), you'll get the chatterbox to talk about things that work in your favor.

The poker face

Poker face interviewers can make your skin crawl. They sit there, sphinxlike, as you talk about yourself and your qualifications. They don't nod. They don't smile. Nothing seems to faze or impress them. You could tell them that you're a candidate for the Nobel Peace Prize, and the best you would get would be a tepid "Very good."

The main pitfall to avoid when you're being interviewed by a poker face is trying too hard to evoke a response. Turning up the heat on your own enthusiasm or energy isn't likely to make a difference with truly stoic interviewers. If anything, you're better off toning down your approach somewhat (but not all the way). Above all, don't read too much into the fact that you don't seem to be making an impression on the interviewer. You're probably making your case; it's simply not registering on the interviewer's face.

The gamesperson

Gamespeople view the job interview as a game of cat and mouse or chess. The principal challenge of this game — from their perspective — is finding ways to trip you up. Sometimes their methods are subtle and harmless. But occasionally, interviewers who are fond of playing games can be disquieting and mean-spirited.

Among the tactics sometimes used by this thankfully rare breed of interviewer are the following:

- Ignoring you when you walk in to see whether you initiate the greeting — a "test," presumably, of how assertive you are

- Inviting you to sit down in a seat that subjects you to the direct glare of sunlight to see whether you'll sit there and be inconvenienced or take command and ask if you can sit somewhere else

- Arranging things so that the seat you occupy is either extremely uncomfortable or so deep and plush that you're literally buried in it

- Acting in the beginning of the interview like your close friend and confidant, but only because they want you to lower your guard and reveal aspects about yourself that you wouldn't normally disclose

- Actively (and sometimes rudely) challenging your answers just to see how you react when your views are challenged

The biggest problem you face when you're forced to deal with these types of situations is figuring out the interviewer's motivation. If you're being *tested,* you need to determine which response would best serve your interests. Or if the interviewer is simply rude or abusive, you need to ask yourself if you want to work for this person (or for a company that would give a person like this a position of authority).

It's not an easy call. You certainly don't want to overreact in a stressful situation. Then again, you don't want to subject yourself to unwarranted abuse. The best advice is to keep your cool and remain professional but set boundaries. And when those boundaries are violated — when the tactics get out of hand or become abusive — let the interviewer know how you feel. Tell the person quietly and firmly that you're not sure what's going on but that it is making you feel uncomfortable and that you would prefer, if possible, to focus on the job and whether you're the best candidate.

The late interviewer

It's unreasonable to expect every interview you go on to start exactly on time, but if the interviewer is running 20 or 30 minutes late *and you haven't been given an apology or any explanation,* try (if at all possible) to reschedule the interview. The fact that the interviewer is already running late suggests that he or she is under pressure and, for that reason, might not be able to give you a full measure of attention.

Be careful to conceal whatever impatience you may be feeling. What you should convey when you make this suggestion is that you understand that unexpected things frequently happen in business and that you would be happy to return when things are less hectic.

Groupthink: When You're Interviewed by More Than One Person

In certain companies, the decision to hire or not hire you will be made not by one person but by two or more. And it is likely in these situations that you will be interviewed by more than one person at a time.

The fact that you are being evaluated by more than one person is an important piece of information in and of itself. It tells you that the company places a fairly high value on teamwork. It tells you that you should do your best to come across during the interview as a team player.

Group interviews can be intimidating. Instead of having to tailor your responses to *one* particular style of interviewer, you have to adjust to two or more styles — styles that may not necessarily be compatible with one another. One of your interviewers may prefer short, cut-to-the-chase answers. Another may prod you to elaborate. One interviewer may be as patient as your Uncle Ned. Another may be as edgy and cantankerous as your cousin Paul — the one who raises Dobermans. One may play good cop while the other plays bad cop.

A bigger problem is that group interviews make it difficult for you to assume control. Keeping the conversation focused on your strengths isn't as easy in group interviews as it is in one-on-one interviews. Occasionally, too, you'll get mixed messages. It may become clear to you, simply by the way the various individuals in the room are responding, that not everyone in the room shares the same feelings about what qualifications count the most in the job.

That's the downside. The upside to group interviews is that they give you an opportunity to demonstrate skills and attributes that you wouldn't necessarily get a chance to demonstrate in a one-on-one situation. The fact that you can successfully handle group dynamics may turn out to be the very quality that gets you hired.

Here are some guidelines to keep in mind:

- ✔ **Respond to each member of the group on an individual basis.**

  Don't make the common mistake of viewing the group of people interviewing you as a single audience with a single agenda. View each member of the group as an individual with his or own agenda and values. Pay attention to their names when you're first introduced. Refer to each person by name whenever possible.

- ✔ **Don't ignore anyone.**

  The people who do the most talking and ask the most questions in a group interview are not necessarily the people who will have the most say in the decision. So try to get a sense early on of which person in the group is the senior decision maker, and make sure that you don't disregard this person, even if he or she doesn't ask a single question. Pay attention to eye contact. Regardless of who asks the question, try to make direct eye contact with each member of the group as you're giving your answer.

- ✔ **Stick to your game plan.**

  It may not be easy to do, but try your best to keep the *group* aspect of the interview from interfering with your own strategy. The number of people notwithstanding, your objective in an interview remains the same: to relate your background and qualifications directly to the requirements of the job and, at the same time, to show interest, enthusiasm, and poise.

  Don't allow yourself to be rushed into giving hasty answers. If you're not sure of a question, ask for clarification. If you're not sure of the answer, admit it. The ground rules, in other words, don't change. They simply take a slightly more complicated dimension. You need to adjust, but not by as much as you may be inclined to think.

When the Interview Takes Place during a Meal

Whenever a job interview is conducted during a meal — or even over coffee or drinks — your ability to handle social graces could become a factor in the impression you convey.

Keep these tips in mind:

- ✔ Pay scrupulous attention to your table manners.
- ✔ Don't order alcohol, even if your host or hostess does. And if your host or hostess orders a bottle of wine for the table, indulge only moderately.

✔ Don't order the most expensive item on the menu.

✔ Don't order items that are messy or difficult to eat (lobster, for example).

✔ Don't allow the informal atmosphere to affect the professionalism of your discussion or behavior.

Recognizing Questions That Are Illegal

Federal law sets limits on the kinds of questions that interviewers are permitted to ask. Questions asked of you that relate to the following areas are considered off-limits:

✔ Religion

✔ Age

✔ Ethnic origins

✔ Race

✔ Marital status

If you are being interviewed at a large company by someone in human resources or personnel, the chances that you will be asked questions *directly* relating to any of these areas are remote. Seasoned interviewers understand the discrimination laws and go to great lengths to avoid asking questions that relate to these prohibited areas. That's why you shouldn't be surprised — assuming that, say, you're in the seventh month of a pregnancy — that the interviewer makes no mention of the impending event.

Testing 1,2,3: What You Should Know about Pre-Employment Tests

The likelihood that you'll be asked to take some sort of a test as part of the interview process is greater today than ever before. The reason: Companies of all sizes and in almost every industry are increasingly using different types of tests (aptitude, personality, handwriting analysis, honesty, and so forth) to offer feedback that isn't confined to the impressions they gather during interviews.

Whether the tests you may be expected to take during a job interview are a valid indicator of your ability to handle a particular job is a sensitive and controversial issue among human resources professionals.

You don't perform well on tests, you say? You tighten up and break into hives? Relax. In most situations, your test results are only one of the factors that will determine whether you'll be hired. You don't have to ace the test to stay in the running. Usually, you simply have to fall within some fairly broad norms. Experienced interviewers know that not everyone who gets good grades in school does well in the workplace, and they also know that your basic aptitude is only one of many factors that they need to consider.

At the very least, find out which kinds of tests you may be asked to take, what the tests are designed to measure, and what, if anything, you can do to ensure that how you perform on these tests won't sink your chances. The following sections summarize the different types of tests.

Aptitude tests

Aptitude tests are designed to measure how adept you are at certain physical tasks (hand-eye coordination, for example) or how well you handle certain mental tasks, such as problem solving or mathematical calculations. The theory behind these tests is obvious: If you lack specific skills or faculties that are thought to be necessary to perform certain types of jobs, you're never going to excel at those jobs and would thus represent a hiring risk.

Unfortunately, you can't do much to mask weaknesses that an aptitude test might uncover. Just bear in mind that you have plenty of margin for error. Remember, too, that if you clearly *don't* have the aptitude to handle a particular job, it's not a job that you're going to do well, anyway.

Intelligence tests

Intelligence tests are designed to test your ability to think and problem-solve and usually take the same general form as the IQ and SAT-type tests that high school and college students take. If you've done well on these tests in the past, you don't have to worry about them; you won't run into many surprises.

If, on the other hand, you've never done well on these types of tests, you may want to buy a book that gives you advice on improving your scores. (Check out IDG Books Worldwide's line of test-prep books, which includes *The SAT I For Dummies* and *The GRE For Dummies*.) Another suggestion: Get hold of an SAT or similar software package that gives you the opportunity to take practice runs of the kinds of tests you may be asked to take.

BIG MISTAKE!!!

> # Four of the worst things you could possibly do during a job interview
>
> 1. Refer to the older man interviewing you as "pops."
>
> 2. Tell an off-color joke.
>
> 3. Refer to your former boss as a "chauvinist pig."
>
> 4. Comment on how young the interviewer seems for his or her position.

Honesty tests and psychological tests

Honesty tests are a relatively new tool in hiring and have become increasingly common now that lie detector tests (with certain exceptions) have been declared illegal in most states.

With the typical honesty test, you're given a series of statements and asked to indicate the extent to which you agree or disagree. The statements generally measure your attitudes toward situations and issues that directly or indirectly relate to honesty and integrity.

Psychological tests (sometimes referred to as personality tests) are designed to measure certain traits and inclinations that are thought to underlie a successful performance in certain types of jobs. Again, there is much debate among human resources professionals as to whether many of these tests are valid indicators of a candidate's ability to succeed at a job.

Drug testing

Depending on the kind of job you're applying for and the company offering the job, you may be asked at some point in the interview process to take a drug test as a condition of employment. You have the right, of course, to refuse to take the test, but refusal isn't likely to enhance your chances of being employed. If you're concerned about privacy issues, you can always ask to have the testing done through your personal physician.

If you're asked — and agree — to take a drug test, make sure that you give a detailed account of all the medications (asthma medications, in particular) that you're currently taking to ensure that the results don't depict you as something you're not. Be careful of your diet as well. Certain foods — poppy seeds, for example — and medications can sometimes produce false positives. Consult your doctor for more information.

Chapter 23

End Game: Closing the Interview on a Winning Note

*L*ike a good movie, the closing moments of an interview can be just as important as the opening moments — and sometimes just as tricky to handle. If you've made a good showing up to this point, you want to be sure that you end the interview on a graceful, positive note, reinforcing the solid first impression you made earlier in the interview. This chapter shows you how to do it.

Reading between the Lines

How you handle yourself at the end of an interview depends mainly on two factors: one, how convinced you are that, yes, this is the job you want; and two, how you feel the interview has gone.

The second factor is obviously the more troublesome. Even if the interviewer seems interested and attentive, how can you really tell whether your efforts to sell yourself have met with success?

Look for these clues:

✔ The interview goes much longer than it was originally scheduled (not, however, because in the middle of the interview the interviewer has to take her Yorkshire terrier to the vet).

✔ Questions toward the end of the interview begin to focus on practical issues: when you would be able to start, how much money you're looking for, and what sort of limousine you would like to have drive you to work each day (just kidding about that last one).

✔ You're asked to submit a list of references or to provide some additional information, such as a sample of your work.

If, based on these observations, you're reasonably convinced that you are indeed a serious candidate for the job, you can probably get away with being a little more assertive than you might otherwise be. There's nothing wrong with coming out and telling the interviewer that you're very interested in the job.

Do not (repeat, do not!) fall victim to the myth that by showing enthusiasm for the job or the company, you weaken your chances of being hired. Playing it cool may work in poker, but it doesn't work in job hunting.

If you feel that the interview went well but the interviewer seems undecided, an assertive approach may be called for. Here are two techniques worth considering:

✔ **Make an offer to start on a trial basis.**

Offering to come to work on a trial basis before you have been officially offered the job may sound risky, but if you're currently unemployed and have done a good job at the interview, the gambit can pay off. What you should do, basically, is come right out and say that, from the way the interview has gone, there seems to be a good fit between what the company is looking for and what you can offer. You then suggest that the best thing may be for you to start out on a trial basis — to come in for a week or so to show what you can do.

The interviewer may not take you up on your offer or may ask for some time to think about it. Either way, don't press. Keep in mind, too, that if your offer is rejected, it doesn't mean that you're out of the running or that you failed miserably at the interview. It simply means that the interviewer doesn't want to commit just yet. Meanwhile, you haven't lost anything by being assertive.

✔ **Suggest a deadline.**

This strategy can be a little risky as well, but the risk is sometimes worth it. You ask the interviewer when he or she thinks there may be a final decision. If you phrase the request diplomatically ("I'd love to get the final word from you by July 8. Is that possible?"), it won't sound like an ultimatum. You don't have to give a reason for wanting to hear by a certain date, and you can always retreat from that deadline. What you're trying to do here is to plant the seed that the interviewer may not be able to take you for granted.

Knowing What Not to Do

Things you should *never* do (or at least think long and hard about before doing) at the close of an interview include the following:

- ✔ **Bluff:** Telling an interviewer that you need to hear about this job pretty soon because you have another offer is a tired, obvious ploy that most interviewers will not believe even if it's true. If you truly don't have other offers, don't use this tactic — it often backfires.

- ✔ **Ask for an interview critique:** Asking the interviewer to comment on how well you performed during the interview accomplishes very little other than to put the interviewer in an awkward position. Interviewers are not career counselors. You should be critiquing your own interviews.

- ✔ **Pressure the interviewer into making a decision:** If an interviewer hasn't described the next steps or shows reluctance to accede to one of your requests, don't press the issue. Doing so won't get you anywhere and can undermine everything you worked to achieve during the interview.

- ✔ **Ask the interviewer for names of other people you might contact:** The reason you shouldn't ask a person who has just interviewed you to supply you with other contact names should be obvious, but there *is* one exception. If, at some point in the interview, it becomes clear to both you and the interviewer that you are clearly not the right person for the job, it's sometimes a good idea to change gears — to acknowledge to the interviewer that you're clearly not a good match for the position. *At that point,* ask nicely if the interviewer has some ideas or names for you. Many interviewers will be so relieved that you've spared them the tedium of asking questions of a candidate who clearly isn't qualified that they'll go out of their way to help you.

Writing the Follow-Up Letter

Regardless of how well or how poorly you think that you handled yourself during the interview, and regardless of how you and the interviewer left things standing (who was supposed to get in touch with whom and so forth), you should always send a short thank you note. Ideally, you should send it by mail, but e-mail and faxes are better than no letter at all. Just do it soon, and make sure that the letter accomplishes three things:

- ✔ Expresses your gratitude
- ✔ Reinforces your interest in the job
- ✔ Recaps the two or three strongest points working in your favor

The letter needn't be long — three or four paragraphs at the most. The letter on the following page illustrates what a good follow-up letter should do. Note the following qualities:

✔ Paragraph 1 shows gratitude and makes a specific reference to the job.

✔ Paragraph 2 reiterates interest in the position and stresses key points working in the candidate's favor.

✔ Paragraph 3 stresses the "fit."

✔ Paragraph 4 restates gratitude and closes on a positive note.

Managing Your References

Whatever you do, don't get tripped up by mismanaging the references aspect of your job search. Reference checks, by all rights, should be a formality — the icing on the cake. To lose out on a job because your references don't check out is like running the first 25 miles of a marathon in record time and spraining your ankle on the last turn.

Here are four simple guidelines about references that are well worth paying attention to if you're not already following them. The advice may seem obvious, but it's important enough to mention:

✔ **Ask first.**

Never use anyone's name as a reference unless you have asked the person for permission.

✔ **Stack the deck.**

Never use anyone's name as a reference unless you're *certain* that what that person is going to say about you will be positive.

✔ **Keep them in the loop.**

As soon as you give the names of your references to anyone who is thinking of hiring you, get in touch with your references and let them know that they can expect a call.

✔ **Have them go to bat for you.**

If you're fortunate enough to have a reference who has a personal connection to a company that is thinking about hiring you, ask the person to make a call. Make sure, though, that the call comes to the *interviewer* and not the interviewer's superior. Going over the interviewer's head to gain a favorable hiring decision is an almost certain recipe for losing out on the job.

June 19, 1995

Mr. Duke Carson
Director of Marketing
Animal World
1232 Lake Drive
Orlando, FL 84034

Dear Mr. Carson:

I am writing, first of all, to thank you for taking time with me yesterday to talk about the opening you now have for a chief landscape designer at Animal World.

As I mentioned to you at the end of the interview, I'm very much interested in the position, and I know that the five years I have spent in the gardening and landscape design business, coupled with my specialization in creating animal shapes, would enable me to make an immediate contribution to your team.

I also believe, based on what I was able to observe during my visit to Animal World, that I could readily adapt to the working style of the company. I eagerly look forward to the challenge.

Once again, I thank you for your time and your interest and look forward to hearing from you shortly.

Sincerely,

Arthur Clipper

If the list of references you supply to your interviewer doesn't include the name of *recent* employers, you're likely to raise a few red flags, and the interviewer may attempt to get in touch with them, anyway. If you're worried that a former employer might not go to bat for you, you have two options. One is to explain to the company to which you've applied why your former employer might not have great things to say about you. The second is to call the employer and let him or her know that a reference check might be in the works and that you would appreciate letting bygones be bygones. Keep in mind that in today's litigious society, many companies do little more than give the proverbial "rank, file, and serial number" when receiving these calls, and they may just confirm start and end dates, position, and salary.

Knowing What to Do When the Phone Doesn't Ring

First of all, don't jump to unhappy conclusions. The company may still be interviewing other candidates, and you may still be in the running. A few weeks may seem like an eternity to you, but it isn't an excessive amount of time for a company to take when there is a key position to fill.

If, on the other hand, you were told that you would hear from the company within a week or so and at least two weeks have passed, there's nothing wrong with making a follow-up phone call as long as you're psychologically prepared to hear bad news. Try to get directly in touch with the person who interviewed you, and go out of your way to be pleasant, professional, and concise. Reintroduce yourself, remind the person when you interviewed, and ask, very simply, whether the company has made a hiring decision yet. If the best you can do is to talk to the person's assistant or to voice-mail, leave the same message.

Play it straight. Don't talk about the "fabulous" offer you've just received from the company's chief competitor. Don't talk about the pressure you're feeling. And make it clear that all you're looking for is some indication of whether the job has been filled and whether you're still in the running — nothing more, nothing less.

If, on the other hand, something has happened in the interim that would strengthen your appeal as a candidate — you've just received an award, published a paper, and so forth — it doesn't hurt to mention it. And don't forget, it never hurts to keep saying, "I'm really interested in this job, and I know that I could do it well."

Learning from the Experience

Even if you don't end up with an offer, the interview process can still be valuable — as long as you're willing to objectively analyze how you handled yourself and can learn from your mistakes. Here are some questions that you should ask yourself after the interview:

- Did I look my best?
- Did I do a good enough job of preparing, learning as much as I could about the company, the position, and anything else relating to the job?
- Did I arrange things ahead of time so that I arrived at the interviewer's office in plenty of time and in a relaxed state of mind?
- Did I observe proper business etiquette from the moment I arrived until the moment I left?
- Did I carry myself with poise and confidence when I first walked into the interviewer's office?
- When I was given the opportunity, did I present an overview of myself in a focused, concise manner?
- Was I an active, focused listener throughout the interview?
- Was I able to answer questions in a calm, confident manner?
- Did I show enthusiasm and interest in the job?
- Did I tie my skills and accomplishments to the requirements of the job?
- Did I handle distractions or interruptions without any fuss?
- Did I close the interview on an upbeat, positive note?

Take a balanced approach to these questions. Be objective, but don't be too hard on yourself. And instead of dwelling on the things you did "wrong," determine what you need to do the next time around to avoid the same pitfall. Always look ahead — and keep your head up.

THE *WRONG* WAY TO PLAY UP TO YOUR INTERVIEWER'S OUTSIDE PERSONAL INTERESTS...

Chapter 24

Nailing Down the Offer

● ●

In This Chapter

▶ Responding to the offer when it first comes in

▶ Deciding how much you want (or need) the job

▶ Bridging the gap when the offer falls short of what you want

▶ Negotiating more effectively

● ●

*T*he first thing to do when a job offer comes through is to give yourself a well-deserved pat on the back. Don't worry for now about specifics — whether the offer needs to be sweetened before you'll accept it. The fact that you've been offered the job means that someone has chosen you over all the other candidates. You've achieved a victory, and victory doesn't come your way every day in a job search. Savor it!

But hold off on the champagne — for a while, at least. Just because you have achieved the ultimate prize of a job search — a job offer — doesn't mean that you can hang up your job search spikes or pack your resume away in moth-balls. It simply means that your search has entered a new and critical phase. Now is not the time to get careless or arrogant.

First Response: What to Do When the Offer Comes In

In some situations, you may be offered a job at the end of the interview and may even be asked to show up for work the next day. This occurrence is rare, however, and usually reserved for entry-level positions. Most people do not get hired on the spot.

You do not usually have much time in these situations to make up your mind. If you don't accept right away, the employer could well decide to offer the job to someone else. You have to trust your instincts. If the job appeals to you and is the best thing out there on the horizon, you should probably accept the offer. If, once you're hired, things don't pan out, you can always look for something else.

Typically, though, you'll have more than a moment or two to decide whether you want the job you're being offered. What generally happens, assuming that everything goes according to script, is that you receive a call — correction, *the* call — a few days to several weeks after your interview, during which you're informed that you are the person the company wants to hire. At this point, the three most likely scenarios are as follows:

- ✔ You're invited to come back to the company so that you can ask some final questions and nail down the details of the offer.

- ✔ You're invited to take a little bit of time — two or three days — to think about the offer, talk it over with your spouse or others, and then let the company know whether you want the job and when you can begin.

- ✔ You're pressured to give an answer by the end of the day, or by the next morning at the latest.

The third scenario is much more common when the offer comes from a small, entrepreneurial-style company, where people pride themselves on making important decisions quickly. The fact that you require a lot of time to make up your mind could work against you.

It is at this point in the job search that you begin to be rewarded or penalized for how systematically and intelligently you conduct your job search to this point. If you do a good job of formulating realistic job targets (as described in Chapter 4) at the beginning of your job search and if you focus your efforts on companies and situations that are consistent with those targets, you can be reasonably sure that just about *any* offer you receive will be well worth accepting.

It's a safe bet, in other words, that you'll like the job you're being offered and that it represents an intelligent career move. That's the fundamental purpose of setting targets: to make sure that any job you're eventually offered is one that you'll probably be eager to accept — assuming, of course, that you can work out the financial arrangements and other details.

If, on the other hand, you aren't particularly diligent about formulating job targets and if you haven't been disciplined in uncovering and pursuing job leads, the job offers you get may require a good deal of thought and soul searching. You have to focus on issues that go beyond the financial aspects of the job. You have to look at the job itself, determine if it represents a good career move for you, and take a good, hard look at the company.

Regardless of how prepared you are to make a decision and how excited you are at the prospect of taking this particular job, the tone of your response to the job offer should always be one of great interest and enthusiasm. Why? One reason is simple courtesy: The person offering you a job has presumably thought long and hard about the hiring decision and may have gone out on a limb for you. A little gratitude is definitely in order here.

The second reason is more practical. If your response to a job offer is one of those "Gee, it sounds interesting, but . . ." responses, you could create some doubt in the mind of the person who made the hiring decision. He or she may start to wonder if you were the right person for the job after all — particularly since you now appear to be on the fence. If you're not careful, the person doing the hiring could experience "buyer's remorse" when you do decide that you want the job. He or she may begin to second-guess the original decision.

So the guideline here is simple: You can always ask for a little time to come back with a final decision about an offer, but make sure that you communicate to the person who makes the offer that you're grateful, flattered, and *very interested* in the position. Expressing these views doesn't cost you anything, but failing to express them could come back to haunt you. Don't risk it.

Knowing When to Say No

That's easy. You turn down any job offer that (a) doesn't appeal to you and (b) you are under no real pressure to accept, thanks to the fact that you already have a job, have a better job offer, or are in good enough financial shape that you don't have to take whatever is being offered.

It's rarely that simple, of course. It's not unusual for certain aspects of an offer — the money, for example — to appeal to you while other aspects — say, the 90-minute commute — may *not* appeal to you.

And *pressure* is a relative term. Everyone has different stress thresholds. It all comes down to you and how you're holding up in your own situation.

All of which is another way of emphasizing the fact that no one can tell you *not* to accept an offer: It's too big a decision for anyone else to make. The main thing, however, is not to sell yourself short. By accepting an offer that *clearly* isn't right for you, you may be settling for far less than you deserve and may have otherwise gotten if you hadn't accepted this particular offer. It's your call. Make it carefully.

Assessing a Job Offer

Most books about job hunting devote at least one chapter — sometimes more — to the process generally referred to as "assessing the offer." Much of the how-to-assess-a-job-offer advice you find, however, is based on assumptions that may not apply to your particular situation.

One assumption is that you have the luxury of being able to walk away from the offer if it doesn't meet most or all of your requirements.

You may indeed have such an option. It's possible, for example, that you already have a job that is not making your life thoroughly miserable. It's also possible that you have a large cash reserve, you've been able to find temporary or part-time work, or you've just won the lottery — you are not under severe financial and psychological pressure to accept an offer that isn't appealing to you. If this is the case, bravo! You're in the "catbird seat." You can afford to be objective and analytical. You have the ultimate leverage: You can always walk away from the offer.

Then again, you may not have this luxury, in which case you need to view much of the advice you find in job hunting books — as solid as that advice may be — in the proper perspective. Yes, it would be nice if you could say to the person who has made you the offer, "I might very well be interested in this job if you could do a little better on the stock options and maybe throw in a country club membership. By the way, how big is the limousine that will pick me up at my home each morning?" Chances are, you're not in a position to make such demands.

A second assumption underlying much of the advice that some books dispense is that most companies are in a position to offer good candidates as much as they were offering, say, ten years ago. Yes, companies still want the offers that they make to strong candidates to be as attractive as possible, but the "perks" now take different forms. In lieu of company cars, for example, companies are offering things such as sign-on bonuses and flexible hours.

This little bit of reality isn't meant to discourage you from assessing each offer carefully and doing your best to negotiate better terms. Just make sure that you handle this phase of your search with a clear sense of how things *are* in the job market and not how things *used* to be. Mind you, you still have options (and more than you might think), but it's no longer business as usual.

Sizing up the company

✔ Is the company in solid financial shape?

To answer this question, you may have to do some research, using sources such as *Value-Line* or *Moody's Investors* to gain insight into the company's recent financial performance. With smaller, private companies, you may have to do some snooping or base your assessment on what you learned when you were being interviewed.

✔ Are the company's values (as far as you can tell) consistent with your own values?

✔ Is the company going through any turmoil (legal or ethical problems, for example) that could jeopardize its future (and yours)?

Determining how "good" the offer is

Assuming for the moment that you have the luxury of deciding on a job offer on the merits of the offer itself (as opposed to how badly you need a job), the best thing to do is to break the offer into three different components:

✔ The job itself

✔ Career implications

✔ The salary, benefits, and perks

Here's a closer look at each of these elements and the questions you should be asking yourself as you assess the offer.

The job itself

✔ Do the actual tasks to be performed daily appeal to you?

✔ Are you likely to find this job (and industry, if applicable) challenging after you've been in it for a few months or a year from now?

✔ Is the level of responsibility consistent with what you want and need in order to do the job effectively? (In other words, is the job doable as it's now structured?)

✔ Are the working conditions reasonably pleasant and conducive to quality work?

> ✔ Do you think that you'll enjoy working with your boss and coworkers?
>
> ✔ Will taking this job oblige you to make any major changes in your lifestyle (more travel, longer hours, a longer commute, and so forth) that could have an impact on the quality of your life?

Career implications

> ✔ How does this job fit into your overall career plan? Are you moving forward, backward, or standing in place with respect to your career goals?
>
> ✔ How interested are you in the company's business or industry?
>
> ✔ What are the career prospects in this industry or business likely to be in five years?

The salary, benefits, and perks

> ✔ Is the compensation package (including what you're likely to earn in bonuses or commissions) high enough to cover your basic monthly expenses?
>
> ✔ Is the compensation package competitive with what other companies in this field are paying for similar work?
>
> ✔ How does the package compare to the income you're currently earning or were earning in your last job?
>
> ✔ Does the benefits package give you adequate health coverage, based on your current needs? What percentage of the benefits package (if any) will you be expected to pay for in the event that you're hired?
>
> ✔ How generous and attractive are the perks (assuming that the company is offering perks such as company car, tuition reimbursement, vacation, and so on)?

Comparing perks

If you're fortunate enough to be in a position to compare the merits of two or more offers and want to look at how the various benefits packages stack up against one another, here is a list of some of the more common components of the typical corporate benefits/perk package.

Just bear this in mind: Large corporations, as a rule, are systematically cutting back their benefits packages. At smaller companies, too, "standard" benefits, such as medical coverage, may be bare bones, and there may be greater latitude in the variable or flexible (that is, bonus) portion of the compensation package because the environment is generally less structured.

✔ Hiring or sign-on bonuses

✔ Medical benefits (including dental and vision care)

✔ Pension plans

✔ Performance bonuses

✔ 401(k) plans

✔ Stock options

✔ Life insurance

✔ Disability insurance

✔ Company-paid car or gas allowance

✔ Company-paid subscriptions or association memberships

✔ Tuition reimbursement (how much and under what conditions)

✔ In-house training programs

✔ Child care assistance on-site or at nearby centers

✔ Employee assistance programs (for example, smoking cessation, weight and exercise programs, and counseling)

✔ Expense accounts

Miscellaneous benefits

Operating on the theory that it never hurts to ask, you might be able to get your new company to pay for (at least partially) some other items, depending on their policies and depending on how badly they want you:

✔ Financial assistance for child care or elder care, such as for a day-care center or a home assistant for a disabled family member

✔ Extra vacation time or personal days (in lieu of a higher starting salary)

✔ Flexible hours

✔ The opportunity to do some of your work at home (or *telecommute*)

Getting More Out of the Offer

After you think about the issues in the last section, you should be in a reasonably good position to decide whether accepting this offer is in your best interest. In all likelihood, you may find that some aspects of the offer appeal to you whereas other aspects don't.

So now you have a *new* problem to solve: Can you — and should you — go back to the company and try to negotiate a better offer?

The short answer to this question is yes. Trying to get as much as you possibly can out of a job offer is nothing to be embarrassed about; you would be foolish *not* to try to get the best offer possible. And it is undeniably true that the best time to negotiate a better offer, in most instances, is *before* you actually begin the job. Presumably, you have some leverage. The company, after all, has chosen *you*; seeing to it that you're a happy camper when you start is to its advantage.

This section gives you a summary of the various components of an offer that can sometimes be negotiable, along with an idea of how to get the offer sweetened.

Starting salary

Your starting salary, interestingly enough, is among the most negotiable components of the offer. Companies usually have a general range in mind when hiring for a specific position and are usually prepared to go to the top end of the range for a truly outstanding candidate. The challenge is to demonstrate that your accomplishments and background entitle you to the high end of the range. Some factors you can use to buttress your case for a higher starting salary include the following:

- ✔ The market value of your position is considerably higher than what the company is offering.

- ✔ The starting salary is significantly less than what you were earning in your previous job (not as strong a point as market value, but still worth mentioning).

- ✔ The company expects you to pay a major portion of the costs of the benefits package.

 A good way to break a deadlock over salary is to agree to a salary below what you would like but with the following contingency: that if your performance achieves a certain level in a specified amount of time — say three to six months — you'll be rewarded with a raise or bonus that takes you to the salary level you seek.

Negotiating don'ts

When executives in an independent national study commissioned by Accountemps® were asked to recall the most "unusual reasons" they'd ever heard from employees seeking raises or promotions, they gave the following responses, each of which is a good example of an answer *not* to give when you're trying to persuade an employer who has just made you an offer to give you more money:

"I just bought a new boat and it's waiting to be picked up."

"Hey, I'm broke."

"I need more money to support both my wife and my girlfriend."

"I need a maid."

"I just bought a horse."

"I've just enrolled all my kids in private polo lessons."

"My mom says I should get more money."

*Accountemps® is a trademark of Robert Half International Inc.

Hiring bonuses

Hiring or sign-on bonuses have become increasingly common, but usually only for highly sought-after professionals at the middle to upper range. A typical bonus might be anywhere from a few hundred dollars to a certain percentage of your yearly salary. It's usually paid to you in a lump sum with your first paycheck.

Health benefits

Although you don't have as much room to negotiate a different benefits package, you may have choices *within* the package. With small companies, you often have some flexibility — especially when it comes to how long you have to work for the company before the benefits take effect and how big a percentage of the monthly fee you are required to pay.

If you or someone in your family suffers from a serious disease or condition that is covered by your present program, make sure that the program your new employer offers doesn't exclude you or your family from the same coverage.

Relocation expenses

If accepting an offer obliges you to uproot yourself and your family, you're obviously going to incur some substantial relocation expenses. The question of who pays what expenses is negotiable. Here, again, the larger the company, the more standardized the policy is likely to be. Consider the following specifics:

- ✔ Travel and lodging costs for house-hunting trips for you and your family
- ✔ Moving costs
- ✔ Temporary housing costs
- ✔ Assuming the mortgage for the home you currently own
- ✔ An allowance for getting settled
- ✔ A higher cost-of-living subsidy
- ✔ A higher mortgage cost allowance
- ✔ A bridge loan if you're unable to sell your house
- ✔ Outplacement and other assistance for a spouse who has to quit his or her job

Obviously, you want the company to pay as many of these expenses as possible. So when you begin to negotiate this issue, make sure that you have estimates in hand, and try to document each estimate with paperwork (an estimate from a moving company, for example).

Severance provisions

Talking about severance payments before you're even hired may seem no different from discussing alimony payments on your wedding night. But severance arrangements can be important if, by accepting a new offer, you're leaving a fairly secure position. Don't be afraid to discuss this issue, all the more if you're relocating in order to take the job. Take some time to figure out how much money you would need to live at your present level for six months and use that number as the starting point of your negotiations.

Negotiating More Effectively

The principles that underlie effective job offer negotiations are no different from the principles that underlie all other negotiations, with two important exceptions:

✔ **Leverage:** In typical job offer negotiations, the employer usually holds the upper hand. Just how much of an upper hand the employer holds will vary from one situation to the next, with the key factor boiling down to who stands to lose the most if you decide to turn down the offer. Remember, though, you're dealing with perceptions. You may well think that the company will be all the poorer if it lets you slip out of its hands, but the person you're negotiating with may not necessarily feel the same way.

✔ **Relationship:** Unlike a negotiation you might have with a store owner or a person whose car you're trying to buy, the person you're bargaining with is probably someone (your future boss, most likely) whom you're going to be dealing with long after the negotiation is over. Playing hardball, in other words, may help in the short-term but could put strains on a relationship that is obviously important.

Keep these exceptions in mind when you review the following guidelines to successful negotiating.

Know what you want

Before you begin discussing your offer, make sure that you're certain about two things. The first is your ideal objective — what you want to come away with after the negotiations. The second is what you are willing to *accept*. Don't be afraid to aim high, and remember that you're unlikely to get what you don't ask for. At the same time, though, make sure that your expectations are reasonable, based on the situation and on whether the person with whom you are negotiating has the authority to give you what you want.

Have a realistic sense of your leverage

Your leverage in any negotiation is measured by how important it is to the person or company that you come to work there. How *important* you are to the company, however, isn't necessarily a function of how good you are at your job. If there are candidates in the wings whose skill and track records are comparable to yours, your importance diminishes, and so does your leverage. If the skills you offer are in short supply, though, your perceived value grows, and your leverage climbs with it.

Do your homework

The greatest weapon in any negotiation is *information,* which enables you to justify the things you want. At the very least, you should be conversant with industry norms in any aspect of a job offer that you intend to negotiate. If possible (it is sometimes tough to do), find out as much as you can about the norms that prevail in the company itself — what people in positions comparable to the position for which you're applying earn and what special perks or arrangements other employees have negotiated, for example.

You're more likely to get this sort of information from a former employee than from a current employee. Finally, it also doesn't hurt to find out how long and hard the company has worked to find a candidate to fill the job. The more eager the company is to fill the job, the stronger your negotiating position.

Think win/win

Negotiations in which one (or both) of the parties is intent upon "winning" at the other person's expense invariably create an adversarial atmosphere that rarely works to anyone's advantage. Try to go into the negotiation envisioning you and the other person not as adversaries but as two people on the same side working toward the same general goal.

Think needs and wants, not positions

The surest way to create an impasse in any negotiation is to lock yourself into a position ("I won't accept the job unless the initials *VP* are in my title") that has symbolic rather than real significance. Focus on your actual needs and wants — your salary, responsibilities, role in the chain of command, and so on — and think twice before issuing ultimatums. No matter how far apart you and the other party may be, keep the door open.

Be flexible

If you try to come away with *everything* you want in a negotiation, you could very well come away with nothing. Figure out before you begin to negotiate which issues or items are most important to you and be prepared to give in on those items or issues that aren't paramount.

End things on a graceful note

Regardless of how the negotiation turns out, be gracious. You don't want to walk away from a job offer negotiation with a bad taste in your mouth, and you certainly don't want the person with whom you've negotiated the offer (who, in all likelihood, will be your boss) walking away with a negative impression of you.

Get it in writing

While it's not always possible (it often depends on the company's policy), try to get a letter of employment that details the specifics of the offer — in particular, the job's fundamental responsibilities and tasks, the basic salary offered, and whatever special arrangements (allowance for moving costs, flex hours, and so forth) you may have worked out during your negotiation.

Part VII
The Part of Tens

"...I'M ALSO WHAT YOU MIGHT CALL A *PEOPLE PERSON*"

In this part...

This part includes information about a variety of topics in a list of tens format: how to start your new job on a good note, how to keep your spirits up during your search, and more.

Chapter 25

Ten Ways to Get Started on the Right Foot in Your New Job

. . . .

In This Chapter
▶ Understanding what your new responsibilities are
▶ Fitting in at your new company
▶ Keeping your job search network going

. . . .

Recharge your batteries

If it's at all possible (and if it won't put you in jeopardy of losing your job before you even start), try to take a break of at least one week between the day you accept a job offer and the day you actually begin your new job. Use that week to relax, decompress, and clear your head. Try to begin your new job with your mental and physical batteries fully charged.

Accept the new order

Don't expect the things in your new job to be the way they were in your old job, particularly if your new job is with a company that's much smaller than the companies you're accustomed to working for. And even if your new job is with a larger company, keep in mind that the corporate world is more competitive these days. If your job is typical of most new jobs today, you're going to be expected to accomplish more with less support than you may be used to. Embrace the challenge.

Identify the superstars

Make it a priority to figure out who the winners at the company are. These are the people with outstanding track records — the top salespeople, the creative geniuses, the dynamic managers. They're easy to spot because their accomplishments are well known. Observe these company superstars and emulate their approaches to the job.

Clarify expectations

As soon as possible after you officially begin your new job, plan to get together with your new boss and make sure that the two of you are on the same wavelength with respect to your basic mission and objectives. Before the meeting, take time to write down your understanding of your key responsibilities, and have that sheet with you when you go to the meeting. The questions you should have answered early on include the following:

- ✔ What is the overall mission of the company, and how do my department and job fit into that mission?
- ✔ What immediate priorities and challenges need to be addressed?
- ✔ On what basis will my job performance be evaluated?

Study the culture

You should spend a good portion of your first week or two on the job observing the unwritten rules that govern behavior in your new company. Plan to arrive on your first day of work at least a half-hour before you're officially scheduled to start and take note of how many people are already at their desks. Stay a half-hour later that night and do the same thing.

Pay attention, too, to how people in the company prefer to communicate: through written memos, face to face, by voice mail or e-mail, and so forth. Observe the dress code. See when people go to lunch (and how long they take), and follow suit. And regardless of how you're accustomed to working, adapt your style to the company's.

Don't upset any apple carts

Not at first, anyway. It's okay to hit the ground running in your new job, but wait until you establish yourself and earn some credibility before you begin pushing hard for changes. You have time. Nobody expects you to accomplish miracles overnight. And if you try too hard in the beginning, you run the risk not only of falling on your face but also of alienating people whose support may be critical to your success.

Be discreet about your salary

Never tell anyone who has no business knowing how much you're being paid. And never ask anyone else the same question. It's unprofessional and will invariably come back to haunt you.

Get yourself up to speed technically

If your job obliges you to work with equipment (computers or software packages, for example) with which you're not yet proficient, be prepared to spend extra time on your own (unless it's appropriate to do so on the job) to master the required skills.

Thank the people who helped you get the job

After you've been on the job for at least a few weeks, set aside 15 minutes a day and write or type short notes to everyone you approached for help during your job search, regardless of whether they went to bat for you or not. Let them know about your new job and thank them for their support. This simple act will be appreciated and remembered.

Keep your guard up

Without getting too paranoid, keep yourself mentally prepared for the possibility that the job may not work out. Stay in touch with recruiters. Maintain your networking activities. Keep current. Be visible. And be alert to signs that your company is in trouble or that your job may be in jeopardy.

Chapter 26
Ten Ways to Keep Up Your Morale

· ·

· ·

Get into better physical condition

Getting into a regular exercise routine — whether it's walking, jogging, swimming, or whatever — may not have a *direct* effect on your job search fortunes, but it will help you indirectly, and in a variety of ways. You'll look better. You'll sleep better. You'll radiate more energy. You'll project a more positive image during interviews. There's increasing evidence, too, that being in good physical shape helps to minimize the psychological impact of stress.

Become an expert

As long as you do it as a sideline and not in a way that interferes with your job search, start to study something in depth — something that interests you and that you can get passionate about. It could be anything: the Civil War, Renaissance art, or opera, for example. The point is to gain knowledge and insights that go beyond the superficial.

Becoming an expert not only bolsters your confidence but also keeps your mind active. It makes you a more interesting person in general and gives you a broader perspective beyond your job search. Who knows, the time may come when the person interviewing you happens to be interested in the very subject in which you've become an expert.

Do volunteer work

There is no more effective way to take your mind off your own problems than to do something constructive for people whose problems are far worse than yours. Opportunities to make a difference in the lives of people in need are almost infinite. Work them into your schedule.

As an added bonus, the people you meet throughout the course of your volunteer work could become a key part of your personal network.

Join a support group

Job and career support groups have become not only far more numerous in recent years but also far more varied and sophisticated. And what will surprise you about these groups is not how *depressed* everyone is but how eager people are to help one another. Even if you feel that *you* don't need the help, you might be able to help others, which is good for them and good for you.

Listen to self-help tapes

You may not believe everything you hear on audio tapes that are designed to bolster your self-esteem and confidence, but a steady diet of these tapes can be an effective antidote to the negative messages you may be sending yourself. Most bookstores carry a large line of audio tapes (most of them audio versions of popular books), and the tapes are roughly the same price as the books. You can also check out audio tapes from most libraries.

Don't get into a rut

A routine is a good thing to get into when you're looking for a job, but only if the routine is producing results. If the routine isn't getting you anywhere, change it. The changes don't have to be dramatic. Change libraries. Get up an hour earlier every day. Listen to a different radio station.

Give yourself time off

Doing so is not always easy, but give yourself permission to designate at least one day — Sunday, for example — on which you give yourself a mental vacation. On that day, don't talk or even think about anything related to your job search.

Hang out with people who make you feel good

And don't burden these people with your problems. Otherwise, they may not be too eager to hang out with you.

Read biographies of successful people

What you'll notice over and over about these individuals is how often they "failed" and how much rejection they experienced before they achieved success. For example, read David McCullough's biography of Harry Truman or any biography of Abraham Lincoln.

Keep a journal

Buy a notebook (or use your computer) and get into the habit of putting your thoughts down on paper for 10 to 15 minutes a day. A journal is not a diary; it's not an hour-by-hour accounting of what you did, where you went, and who you talked to. It's simply a mirror for your ideas and feelings, and it can be a catalyst for new ideas or approaches.

You don't have to worry about how interesting or compelling your ideas are. Write from the heart. Whatever you're feeling, write it down. You'll be surprised at how useful or at least calming this exercise can be.

Chapter 27

Ten Bold Interviewing Tactics to Make You Stand Out from the Crowd

In This Chapter

▶ Wowing the interviewer with your poise and preparation

▶ Ending the interview with *you* in control

The safest strategy to follow whenever you're being interviewed for a job is to play it conservatively and to be careful not to do anything that might create concern in the mind of the person making the hiring decision. But if that strategy, sound as it is, isn't getting the results you want, here are ten steps to take that your competition won't be taking. Just bear in mind that none of these tactics will work if you try to implement them in a forced, unnatural way.

Take your time when you enter

Make a conscious effort when you first walk into the interviewer's office not to rush things. Pause at the door to make sure that the interviewer is ready for you *before* you walk in. Take a few seconds to look around and acclimate yourself when you enter the office. After you and the interviewer greet one another and shake hands, take your time when settling yourself into the chair. By taking things a little slower, you appear more poised and professional.

Ask the first question

It's usually the interviewer's place to ask the first question during a job interview, but there's no law forbidding *you* to take the initiative. A simple question such as, "What's been the reaction to your new ad campaign?" establishes right from the start that you know something about the company, and it can get the interviewer to reveal needs and concerns that you can capitalize on later in the interview.

Don't be afraid to be yourself

Assuming for the moment that you have no blatant personality flaws that would knock you out of contention for most jobs, don't be afraid to let the "real you" shine through in interviews. If there's an offbeat side to your personality (and if that side of you doesn't suggest that you're an out-and-out "kook"), don't suppress it entirely. Most interviewers like to come away from an interview with at least a general sense of who you really are. Ironically, you often do yourself more harm than good when you go out of your way to play the part of the "ideal candidate."

Go easy on the "charm"

As important as it is to establish rapport with the person interviewing you, don't overdo a good thing. Your main task in a job interview is to draw a connection between what you have to offer in the way of skills and attributes and what the job requires. If you focus on that issue in an honest, enthusiastic way, the rapport will usually develop on its own. If you focus *too much* on winning the interviewer over, however, you begin to arouse suspicion. Your credibility suffers.

Show candor

While it is *not* generally a good idea to volunteer any information that could call into question your ability to perform the job for which you are being interviewed, try not to respond too defensively to questions whose answers might bring to light certain "weaknesses" (with respect to the job at hand) in your background. The challenge here is to be aware, ahead of time, of those weaknesses so that you can admit to them but at the same time point to strengths that offset those weaknesses.

Don't over-answer

Keep your answers to interview questions as focused and brief as possible, and don't feel obliged to fill any silence that follows your answer with additional information. Let the silence work in your favor, giving the interviewer time to absorb what you've said. Pay attention to visual cues — nodding of the head, for example.

Make your case in writing

Even though you can assume that your interviewer has seen your resume, there's nothing stopping you — after you've done some research on the job and the company — from preparing a short list that spells out the specific skills and attributes that you bring to this particular opportunity. The big advantage of handing the interviewer that list at the beginning of the interview: If, by some chance, the interviewer hasn't prepared a list of questions, that list will most likely serve as the focal point of the interview.

Make an offer

If things go well in an interview and you're sure that you want the job, make the interviewer an offer. Offer to *do* something — solve a problem, write a research report, spend two or three days on the job for no pay — that will demonstrate to the interviewer that you have what it takes to do the job. You may get turned down, but the fact that you make the offer should favorably impress most interviewers.

Invite yourself back

The typical interview ends with the interviewer thanking you and telling you that they'll be getting in touch with you later, after the company has a chance to interview other applicants. Before the interviewer can give you that message, let him or her know that you would like to come back and talk more about the job. Here, again, the worst thing that can happen is that the interviewer will politely turn you down.

Leave behind a relevant keepsake

Prepare ahead of time something you can leave behind (apart from your resume) that can enhance your chances of being hired. It could be a report that you did for your previous company (make sure, though, that you're not violating any confidentiality agreements) or even a research paper that you did at school that is relevant to the position for which you're interviewing.

Chapter 28

The Ten Most Valuable Resources in Your Job Search

*H*ere's a brief look at ten valuable resources that are there for you as a job hunter — provided that you know how to take advantage of them and are willing to do so.

You

Don't underestimate the judgment, insight, and power that *you* bring to your job search. Take the time in the beginning to do a thorough inventory of those skills and attributes that make you a strong candidate for the jobs you're seeking. Think back to every job you've ever had and each project you've undertaken, and zero in on the contributions you made and the strengths and attributes that enabled you to make those contributions.

And trust yourself. As open as you are to advice from other people, remember that *you're* in command. Don't relinquish that responsibility. Keep your strengths in mind at all times, and make sure that you lead with those strengths when talking to people who might be able to help you find the job that's right for you. Remember, too, that you're a work in progress: You can always do and learn more to become a more competitive candidate.

Your family

Your family is there for you. Let them be a source of support. Keep them in the loop, but do your best — and it's not always easy to do — to keep the pressures you may be feeling from becoming the dominant theme in your home atmosphere. A key suggestion: Set aside at least one weekend day on which you and your family take a mental vacation from your job search. Devote that day exclusively to recreation and relaxation.

Your friends

Rely on your friends not only for moral support but also for concrete help in your search. Enlist them as part of your job search "team," making sure that they know what you're looking for. Call upon them for information and names of people who could be potential sources of job leads. They have friends and contacts, too, who could supply you with leads or help you to convert a lead into an interview. Bear in mind that the majority of people who get hired first hear about the job through word of mouth.

Your business contacts

Virtually everyone you have ever worked with or worked for, and everyone who has worked with or for you, is a potential source of information that could be valuable in your job search. Don't hesitate to get in touch with them, let them know what you're looking for, and ask them to keep their eyes and ears open. The very worst that can happen when you seek this kind of help — and it doesn't happen that often — is that the people you approach won't do anything. In short, you have absolutely nothing to lose.

Your local library

Much of the background information that you need to carry out each phase of your job search productively and systematically is available in the reference section of your local library. To get the most from these resources, introduce yourself to the people who work in the reference section and spell out what you're looking for. If the library has an audio section, look for self-help and other business-related tapes that you can play in your car as you do routine errands.

Your local college or university

Even if you didn't attend your local college or university, you can still (in most cases) tap many of the career- and job-related resources that most universities offer their students. Use the course catalogues to determine which skills are being emphasized in programs being taken by the students pursuing jobs in your field, and be on the lookout for ways to remain competitive. Take advantage of lectures, seminars, and other programs that might give you some new ideas about the kinds of jobs you want to pursue.

Your alma mater

If you haven't already done so, become a member of your college's alumni association (assuming that it has one). Attend meetings to expand your network. Use the association's newsletter or magazine to learn more about your former classmates and identify those who may be in a position to help you. Look into the possibility of adding your resume to the university's resume database service (if it has one). If you think that it might help, make use of the school's access to the Internet.

Your local job support group

Nearly every community today has at least one (and in most cases many more than one) organization, usually a community or church group, that offers job support groups. Keep in mind that the basic function of these groups goes beyond giving you simple moral support.

Your radio or television

The number of radio and television programs that are broadcast in your area and might be useful to you in your job search is probably greater than you think. Check your local cable service to find out which channels offer home-study courses. Call your local radio station to find out when it broadcasts programs that focus on local businesses and business leaders (you're most likely to hear these programs on Sunday mornings). Check the program listings for National Public Radio, whose nightly show, *Marketplace,* can be a great source of ideas and possible leads on job openings.

Your computer

The ability to use a computer for day-to-day administrative and research tasks may be the single most important skill you can bring to a job search. If you do not yet own a computer, give serious thought to buying one (you can pick up a highly serviceable used computer for around $500). Look for inexpensive courses that teach you the basics, or buy computer books (IDG Books Worldwide has *...For Dummies* books on a wide range of computer-related subjects) and be your own instructor.

You don't have to be a techie to get the most from computers. Think of the money and time you spend as an investment in your future. *Not* knowing how to use a computer could put you at a competitive disadvantage for many of the jobs you will be pursuing.

Chapter 29

Ten Questions Frequently Asked by Job Hunters

. . . .

In This Chapter

▶ Determining whether you're really on track

▶ Getting your foot in the door

▶ Winning the interview game

. . . .

How can you tell whether your job targets are realistic?

The only way you can tell for certain is to go through the basic steps of your job search and see how far you get. If you find yourself running into a brick wall early on — that is, you have absolutely no luck uncovering job leads through networking, the classifieds, or recruiters — it's a safe bet that your personal goals are out of sync with the realities of the marketplace, in which case you may have to scale down or rethink your targets.

What's the best way to approach a company that you would like to work for but that hasn't advertised any job openings?

The *best* way is almost always to try to network your way into the company — that is, to find someone you know who knows someone else in the company and can arrange an introduction. The person you're introduced to, incidentally, doesn't necessarily have to be in the department you ultimately want to work in. All you're looking for is a name that you can use to make the connection to the right person.

After you get a name, the best thing to do is to write a concise note that spells out what you think you can offer and to follow up that note with a phone call. To increase your chances of gaining a meeting with the person you're trying to reach, don't ask about a job. Instead, ask if you can come in and get some information about the best way to get launched in the field.

Is there anything you can do to make your resume stand out from the rest?

Apart from making sure that your resume looks neat and professional, there isn't much you can do *cosmetically* to differentiate it from everyone else's. Using unusual typefaces or a color other than white makes your resume *look* different, but it could also knock you out of the running if the company uses any sort of resume scanning device. Other devices — including a scanned-in photograph of yourself — might get someone to pay attention who wouldn't otherwise do so, but they may also turn people off.

Sometimes the method of delivering can draw more attention, such as through overnight mail or fax. These approaches are only worth considering if you know you have the credentials, but the competition is stiff.

The most important thing is to spell out as early as possible in your resume the specific accomplishments or skills that qualify you for the position you're pursuing.

What's the most common mistake that job hunters make when writing their resumes?

The most common mistake, by far, is filling up the resume with a laundry list of functions and responsibilities that you've held in your past jobs as opposed to the specific accomplishments that made a difference in the companies you've worked for. You can never assume, simply because you had a particular responsibility or performed a particular task, that the person reading your resume will automatically think that you can make a contribution to his or her company.

A second common mistake is not being specific enough when it comes to the skills you possess. Mentioning your "computer skills" is no longer enough, for example. Companies — and the resume-scanning software now being used — are interested in the specific programs with which you're familiar.

What's the best way to build your network of contacts?

There is no "best" way. What's important is to get the most out of *every* source: family, friends, business associates, former classmates, association affiliations, and so on. You have to be visible and put yourself in situations — volunteer work or temporary assignments, for example — in which you have an opportunity to meet new people.

Most important, when you get that opportunity, you have to make the most of it. Introduce yourself, let the person know what you're looking for, and ask if you may call him or her at a later date for help. You'll be amazed at how easy it is to get help from people when you're sincere and considerate of their time.

What are the pros and cons of taking on temporary jobs while looking for full-time work?

Mostly pros — especially these days, when more and more of the temporary jobs and assignments available are being offered to middle- and upper-level professionals. Temporary assignments not only give you a way to ease the financial pressure of being out of a job, but they also give you a chance to network, develop new skills, and convert the temporary assignment into a full-time position. The only downside is that you have to be prepared to handle most of your job search activities after working hours.

What is the single most important piece of advice you can offer someone who's about to go into a job interview?

Always put yourself in the shoes of the person conducting the interview. Keep in mind that person's agenda: to determine whether you have the skills, personal attributes, and motivation to be successful in the job at hand. What you are ultimately "selling" during a job interview are those elements of your background, skills, and personality that can make a significant contribution to the company interviewing you.

How truthful should you be when answering interview questions?

As truthful as possible — without going out of your way to volunteer information that could work against you. A lot depends, too, on what type of question you're being asked. It is one thing to make an overstatement when offering an opinion on your ability to handle a particular kind of assignment, as in, "I think I could handle that problem very well." But misrepresenting specific facts about your background that can be verified is another thing altogether. Even small misrepresentations can cost you dearly, casting doubt on everything else you've said during the interview and on your resume.

What's the best way to respond if you feel that the interviewer is treating you unfairly or disrespectfully?

First, try to determine if the interviewer's behavior is deliberately designed to put you under pressure — a test of sorts to see how you'll respond to pressure if you're hired. This doesn't happen too often, but it could well happen when the ability to keep your cool under pressure is a key qualification for the job. But if you're dealing with a person who is being genuinely nasty, it doesn't pay to make a scene — unless the abuse becomes blatant, which rarely happens. Keep your cool. Stay poised and professional. And thank your lucky stars that you won't have to deal with that person ever again after the interview is over.

How do you overcome the "We think you're overqualified" objection?

When someone says to you, "We think you're overqualified," he or she is concerned about, in most instances, whether you're truly interested in this job, whether you will be motivated to do your best, and whether you will be satisfied with a salary that is probably lower than that to which you're accustomed. Rather than argue whether or not you are overqualified, address the concerns. Give the person a reason to believe that you are enthusiastic about the job, that you are motivated, and that the salary drop is not going to be an issue. Stress the fact that the firm is getting added value by hiring you.

Appendix

Resources

● ●

*J*ob seekers today have access to an enormous wealth of information resources — and in virtually every medium you can name: books, tapes, videos, online, CD-ROM, and so forth. This appendix describes a variety of job search and career planning information that warrants special attention. For more information about doing research by using conventional methods and on-line, see Chapters 10 and 18.

Career Planning and Job Targeting

Occupational Outlook Handbook
U.S. Government Printing Office
Superintendent of Documents
P.O. Box 371954
Pittsburgh, PA 15250-7954
202-512-1800

Price: $23.00 soft cover. Also available on CD-ROM.

Offers detailed descriptions of 250 occupations that account for 104 million jobs — 95 percent of the jobs in the U.S. Each listing is divided into sections covering every aspect of the job, including the nature of the work itself, working conditions, employment opportunities, and basic qualities that employers in each occupation generally look for in candidates. The information is, by necessity, somewhat general and not always 100 percent up to date, but no publication covers the American workplace more comprehensively or more authoritatively. An on-line database version — *Career Profiles Database* — is available on America Online.

Dun's Career Guide
Dun & Bradstreet
3 Sylvan Way
Parsippany, NJ 07054
800-526-0651

Price: $495 for a one-year subscription.

Staffing Sources and Temporary Employment

National Association of Temporary and Staffing Services (NATSS)
119 South Saint Asaph Street
Alexandria, VA 22314
703-549-6287

Publishes a yearly directory of temporary help and staffing member firms organized according to specialty and region. Also offers information about temporary employment and group health care plans.

Discovering Careers and Jobs
Gale Research, Inc.
835 Penobscot Building
Detroit, MI 48226
800-877-4253

Price: $495 CD-ROM (stand-alone); $700 CD-ROM (2–8 users).

Provides access to requirements and outlook for 250 careers and 1,200 job titles. Includes information about salary and licensing issues. Also gives contact information for more than 30,000 companies.

National Association of Personnel Services
3133 Mt. Vernon Ave
Alexandria, VA 22305
703-684-0180

Publishes an annual directory of 1,200 member companies by specialty and geographic region.

Price: $20.95

Uncovering Job Leads

Executive Employment Guide
American Management Association
1601 Broadway
New York, NY 10019
212-586-8100

Price: $25 for nonmembers of the American Management Association, and free for members.

Extensive listing of search firms, career counselors, and employment agencies. Listing information includes job specialties.

Directory of Executive Recruiters
Kennedy Information
Kennedy Place
Route 12 South
Fitzwilliam, NH 03447
603-585-2200

Price: $44.95.

Lists more than 5,000 search firms, giving names, addresses, areas of specialty, and salary ranges normally covered. Available in bookstores.

Gale Directory of Publications & Broadcast Media
Gale Research, Inc.
835 Penobscot Building
Detroit, MI 48226
800-877-4253

Price: $460 for the print edition.

Good source for local newspapers and trade publications. For details, see Chapter 10.

Hoover's Handbook of American Business
Hoover's Inc.
1033 La Posada Drive, #250
Austin TX 78752
512-374-4500

Price: $84.95 hard cover.

For details, see Chapter 10.

Non Profits and Education Job Finder
Daniel Lauber
Planning/Communications
7215 Oak Avenue
River Forest, IL 60305
888-366-5200

Price: $16.95 plus $4.00 postage and handling.

More than 2,222 listings of job lead sources for nonprofit positions. Listings are organized according to fields (education, environment, health care, and so on) and also on a state-by-state basis.

National Business Employment Weekly
P.O. Box 300
Princeton, NJ 08543
800-JOB-HUNT

The only national publication geared expressly to job seekers. Not only is it a good source of classified ads (it combines all the classified ads published in regional editions of *The Wall Street Journal,* mainly for professional and managerial positions), it's also filled with timely and useful information about job searching in general. Available at most newsstands. For more information, see Chapter 10.

Professional's Job Finder
Daniel Lauber, Planning/Communications
7215 Oak Avenue
River Forest, IL 60305
888-366-5200

Price: $18.95 plus $5.00 shipping and handling.

More than 3,000 listings of job lead sources, including directories, classified sources, salary surveys, and trade publications. The information is organized according to fields and industries and on a state-by-state basis as well.

Electronic Job Hunting

Electronic Resume Revolution. Joyce Lain Kennedy and Thomas J. Morrow. John Wiley & Sons, Inc.: New York, 1995.

Electronic Job Search Revolution. Joyce Lain Kennedy and Thomas J. Morrow. John Wiley & Sons, Inc.: New York, 1995.

The On-Line Job Search Companion. James C. Gonyea. McGraw Hill: New York, 1995.

Resume-Writing Software

Each of these software products is designed to guide you through the process of preparing your resume. Typical features in most include automatic formatting, questions to answer as you work through each section, a word bank, templates for various types of resumes and cover letters, a spell checker, and mail merge. Special features in some programs include a contact management system and general job hunting advice.

Easy Working Instant Resume
Softkey International Inc.
1 Athenaeum
Cambridge, MA 02142
617-494-1200

Compatibility: DOS.

Price: $19.95.

Special feature: On-line job hunting guide.

The Perfect Resume
Davidson & Associates, Inc.
P.O. Box 2961
Torrance, CA 90509
800-545-7677

Compatibility: Windows. Available on 3$^{1}/_{2}$ inch disk or CD-ROM.

Price: $49.75 ($38.95 average price in most retail stores).

Special feature: On-line advice from author Tom Jackson (author of *The Perfect Resume*).

PFS Resume and Job Search Pro
Softkey International Inc.
1 Athenaeum
Cambridge, MA 02142
617-494-1200

Compatibility: DOS and Windows.

Price: DOS $49.95; Windows $59.95.

Special feature: Database function for managing contacts, and a special database that lists information about 6,000 companies.

ResumeMaker with Career Planning
Individual Software Inc.
5870 Stoneridge Drive #1
Pleasanton, CA 94588-9900
510-734-6767

Compatibility: DOS, Macintosh, and Windows.

Price: $29.95 for Macintosh version; $19.95 for Windows and DOS versions.

Special feature: A "target company manager" program — combination address book, activity tracker, and scheduler.

ResumeMaker Deluxe (CD-ROM)
Individual Software Inc.
5870 Stoneridge Drive #1
Pleasanton, CA 94588-9900
510-734-6767

Compatibility: Windows only.

Price: $39.95

Special feature: Videotaped interviews that give you advice on what to do and what not to do when confronted with different types of questions.

WinWay Resume
WinWay Corporation
5431 Auburn Boulevard, Suite 398
Sacramento, CA 95841-2801
800-494-6929

Compatibility: Windows (also available on CD-ROM).

Price: $69.95

Special feature: Interviews with industry experts on such topics as effective interviewing and salary negotiation techniques.

You're Hired
DataTech Software
6360 Flank Drive #300
Harrisburg, PA 17112
800-556-7526

Compatibility: Windows

Price: $49.95 suggested retail price; $29.95 average price in most retail stores.

Special feature: A library of occupation-specific phrases and sentences that can serve as the basis for phrases and sentences you use in your own resume. (***Note:*** As of publication time, DataTech was nailing down the final arrangements for a resume listing service to be run in conjunction with The Microsoft Network.)

Miscellaneous

Quick & Easy Federal Jobs Kit
DataTech Software
6360 Flank Drive #300
Harrisburg, PA 17112
800-556-7526

Compatibility: Windows.

Price: $49.95.

Guides you through the often confusing process of applying for a job with the federal government, helping you manage some of the specific forms and declarations that are part and parcel of the federal job application process. The newest version is consistent with the changes in application procedures instituted in January 1995.

Note: Keep in mind that many trade associations have programs geared to job seekers in their respective fields, such as job databases and job listings in association newsletters.

Index

• F •

facial expressions, in job interviews, 293
facsimile machines, 22–23. *See also* faxing
family, as support, 341–342
faxing
    equipment for, 22–23
    of follow-up letters after job interviews, 307
    to follow up on targeted mailings, 199
    of notes to contacts, 173
    of resumes, 105, 346
fax-modems, 22–23
feedback, on resume, 122
fees. *See also* expenses
    of career counselors, 40, 41
    for cellular phones, 23
    for downloading, 232
    of recruiters, 202, 209
    for resume databases, 93, 95, 96
fiends, as support, 342
files
    downloading, 254
    exchanging with e-mail, 252
financial issues. *See also* benefits/perks;
    expenses; fees; financial stability; salaries
    temporary work to ease pressure during job
      search, 212
financial stability
    assessing job offer and, 317
    of target companies, 194
first impressions
    appearance and, 280
    on gatekeepers, 284
    on job interviewer, 287–288
first person pronoun, avoiding in resumes, 78
fit with company, assessment of, in job inter-
    views, 258, 260
flexibility, for negotiating job offers, 324
fluff, in resumes, 62
follow up
    after job interviews, 307–308, 310
    of networking meetings, 175
    of targeted mailings, 198–200
fonts, for resume, 101–102
foods
    before drug testing, 303
    during mealtime job interviews, 301

footwear, for job interviews, 283
formats, for resumes, 99–100, 107–120
former employers
    interview questions about, 273
    as job references, 310
Franklin Gothic typeface, 101, 102
functional resumes, 70–72, 92
functional verbs, in resumes, 87
Futura typeface, 101

• G •

*Gale Directory of Publications and Broadcast
    Media,* 148, 152, 183, 351
games, during job interviews, 291,
    297–298
Garamond typeface, 101
gatekeepers
    establishing relationship with, 174, 199
    impression made on, 284
gestures, in job interviews, 292–293
goals, interview questions about, 271
goal setting, 27
    balance in, 33–34
    job targets and. *See* job targets
    for library research, 142
Gothic typefaces, 101
graciousness. *See also* thank-you notes
    after job offer negotiation, 325
grammar checkers, for proofreading
    resumes, 122
grammatical errors, in resumes, 61, 62, 122
graphic devices, in resumes, 99, 100,
    104–105
gratitude, for job offers, expressing, 315
The GRE For Dummies, 302
grooming, for job interviews, 280
guarantees, by recruiters, 209
guidance. *See* career counselors; career
    planning services

• H •

halitosis, for job interviews, 283
halo effect, 287
handshakes, before job interviews, 288
headhunters. *See* recruiters
heading, in resumes, 82–83, 103–104
headlines, of want ads, 184

• K •

Notes

Notes

Notes

Notes

Notes

Notes

Notes

Notes

Discover Dummies Online!

The Dummies Web Site is your fun and friendly online resource for the latest information about ...*For Dummies*® books and your favorite topics. The Web site is the place to communicate with us, exchange ideas with other ...*For Dummies* readers, chat with authors, and have fun!

Ten Fun and Useful Things You Can Do at www.dummies.com

1. Win free ...*For Dummies* books and more!
2. Register your book and be entered in a prize drawing.
3. Meet your favorite authors through the IDG Books Author Chat Series.
4. Exchange helpful information with other ...*For Dummies* readers.
5. Discover other great ...*For Dummies* books you must have!
6. Purchase Dummieswear™ exclusively from our Web site.
7. Buy ...*For Dummies* books online.
8. Talk to us. Make comments, ask questions, get answers!
9. Download free software.
10. Find additional useful resources from authors.

Link directly to these ten fun and useful things at
http://www.dummies.com/10useful

For other technology titles from IDG Books Worldwide, go to
www.idgbooks.com

Not on the Web yet? It's easy to get started with *Dummies 101*®: *The Internet For Windows*® *95* or *The Internet For Dummies*,® 4th Edition, at local retailers everywhere.

Find other ...*For Dummies* books on these topics:
Business • Career • Databases • Food & Beverage • Games • Gardening • Graphics
Hardware • Health & Fitness • Internet and the World Wide Web • Networking
Office Suites • Operating Systems • Personal Finance • Pets • Programming • Recreation
Sports • Spreadsheets • Teacher Resources • Test Prep • Word Processing

IDG BOOKS WORLDWIDE BOOK REGISTRATION

Register This Book and Win!

We want to hear from you!

Visit **http://my2cents.dummies.com** to register this book and tell us how you liked it!

- ✔ Get entered in our monthly prize giveaway.

- ✔ Give us feedback about this book — tell us what you like best, what you like least, or maybe what you'd like to ask the author and us to change!

- ✔ Let us know any other *...For Dummies* topics that interest you.

Your feedback helps us determine what books to publish, tells us what coverage to add as we revise our books, and lets us know whether we're meeting your needs as a *...For Dummies* reader. You're our most valuable resource, and what you have to say is important to us!

Not on the Web yet? It's easy to get started with *Dummies 101®: The Internet For Windows® 95* or *The Internet For Dummies,® 4*th Edition, at local retailers everywhere.

Or let us know what you think by sending us a letter at the following address:

...For Dummies Book Registration
Dummies Press
7260 Shadeland Station, Suite 100
Indianapolis, IN 46256
Fax 317-596-5498

BUSINESS AND **GENERAL REFERENCE BOOK SERIES FROM IDG**

COMPUTER BOOK SERIES FROM IDG